Joe,
"Congratulations" on
your exam results.
We wish you a very
happy time in Durham,
Much love
Grannie & Grandad.

16th August 2012

DURHAM

Fact, Fable and a Procession of Princes

For Lynn

First published in Great Britain in 2011 by The Derby Books Publishing Company Limited, 3 The Parker Centre, Derby, DE21 4SZ.

ISBN 978-1-85983-984-3
Printed and bound by Melita Press, Malta.

DURHAM

Fact, Fable and a Procession of Princes

Martin Dufferwiel

Contents

Acknowledgements

First and foremost, I would like to thank my family for their help, support and patience during the preparation of this book. Also for the miles they have been dragged, not always against their will, through fields and woods, across open moorland and along lonely coastline, in search of the: 'appropriate' photographs for the book's illustrations. Especially one particular occasion, unforgettable in its own way, when in search of W.H. Auden's Lead Mining landscape above Rookhope; biting wind, driving rain, a sheep on a lead and what seemed like an infestation of rabbits all seemed to add to the surreal atmosphere of the day.

I would particularly like to thank the staff of Clayport Reference Library in Durham City for their courteous, knowledgeable and never failing help and advice.

All photographs taken of the interior of Durham Cathedral are reproduced by kind permission of the Chapter of Durham and my special thanks go to Miss Anne Heywood, Visitors' Co-ordinator, for her valued assistance.

Author's Note

In writing this book, I have tried, as I tried with my last book about Durham, to produce a work about the history and legends of the City and County, which is written by a non-historian, for the benefit of other non-historians.

There is nothing here for the academic; indeed some of the subjects included may already be well known to the general reader. For those subjects perhaps not familiar, I have attempted simply to produce, in four thousand words or thereabouts, no more than an outline sketch of each; leaving much more for the interested reader to discover elsewhere, if desired. Above all, I hoped that the finished product would be both informative and entertaining. It is for the reader to decide whether or not I have succeeded.

The works of the 18th and 19th-century chroniclers, listed at the back of the book as Standard References, are collectively something of a treasure and they should not be thought of just as obscure old volumes, lying unread, except by obsessive authors, in some unvisited corner of the library. They are freely available today for the enjoyment of all those who have an interest in the history, lore and legend of County Durham. And if, in reading this book, interest in those subjects is either ignited or rediscovered, then I cannot advise the reader too strongly to browse at leisure through those works listed. For in their own way they encapsulate the heritage of our County; and, as it is with all history, so it is with these old volumes; as the historian Michael Wood said: 'You only have to look and the stories leap out'.

We are fortunate also to have the Treasures of St Cuthbert, in Durham Cathedral, where can be seen, not just the precious possessions of the Saint himself, or the many more conventional: 'Treasures' of silver and gold; but also items which link us physically with some of the events and characters described in this book. For there can be seen, among other survivors from Durham's long centuries, items grand and ceremonial; humble and everyday. From the decorated silver Crosier Head of the roguish Bishop Rannulf Flambard, to a pair of leather sandals belonging to William of St Carilef, the founder of the Cathedral; from precious Bibles left to the Durham Monks by Hugh of Le Puiset, nephew of the King of England, to the: 'Sword that Slew the Dragon'. And of course, the Episcopal Seal of Thomas Hatfield, with the image, first used in the 14th century and still familiar to us today, as the motif of the mounted warrior ecclesiastic; The Prince Bishop of Durham.

Finally, for the possible further interest of readers; a cumulative index has also been included at the back of this book, setting out all subjects so far covered, both in this volume and in my previous work: *Durham: Over a Thousand Years of History and Legend.*

Martin Dufferwiel

'Time's hour glides on, ages in moments fly'

The Venerable Bede

Part One

Chapter 1

At the End of the World

*'Early in 1940, the Durham City Sand and Gravel
Company Ltd cut a test pit, with a view to extending
their existing quarry, and happened to strike some masonry'*
– Archeologia Aeliana, 1944

The masonry in question was found about a mile from Durham City centre, at the place we know as Old Durham, and it led archaeologists to uncover the remains of a Roman Bath House. Nothing unusual there, the reader may think, given the extent of Roman culture and building in Britain. However, the archaeologists were excited. The very existence of a Bath House indicated to them that there must be, somewhere in the vicinity, a Villa, an extended Roman farmstead, yet to be discovered. Again, readers may think, nothing really unusual, as Roman Villas have been excavated across much of England. The significance of this find, however, was that if indeed the Bath House had been part of a Villa complex, then the Villa involved, a mile from the centre of Durham City, must have been the most northerly Roman Villa in the entire Roman Empire.

In 55 and 54BC, Julius Caesar took the first tentative Roman steps on to British soil, but withdrew, according to the Roman historian Tacitus: 'revealing, rather than bequeathing Britain to Rome'. Almost a hundred years later, the Emperor Claudius ordered a full scale invasion. In May AD43, 40,000 men under the command of Senator of Rome and General of the Army, Aulus Plautius, landed in Kent. It was much like later invasions, a gradual expansion and consolidation of military control, followed by civilian settlement. In the early years, Imperial control spread steadily across southern and midland England, with the Romans using their time honoured method of: 'carrot and stick'; accept Roman authority and embrace a Roman way of life with all its benefits; or face the Legions. In the distant north, however, things were different and an understanding, an: 'accord' was eventually reached with the native Brigantes, who controlled an area of land stretching from the Humber to the Tyne. So the north was no settled Roman Province of civic stability and civilian expansion. The area of the country between York and the northern frontier was essentially a militarised zone, with the Roman Road now known as Dere Street ensuring the supply of men, weapons and materials, via the County Durham forts of Piercebridge, Binchester, Lanchester and Ebchester, to the front line in the north.

Durham City itself was not a Roman centre, though numerous scattered artifacts have been found around the City and on the Peninsula. The 18th century Durham Antiquarian, John Cade was the first to mention Roman Coins dug up at Old Durham. Later, in 1852, it was reported in the journal of the Newcastle Archaeological Institute that: 'A fine gold

Nero was found by a woman hoeing turnips on Gilligate Moor'. However the accepted wisdom had been, that this was an unlikely part of the country for the development of secure, Roman, Villa based life. Roman Villas were essentially extended and expensive farm complexes; the Roman equivalent of a fine Country House, the grander the Villa, the more important, and wealthy, its Roman owner. The latest technology, sumptuous luxury and rich decoration would all normally be enjoyed. Hypocausts to provide underfloor heating, mosaic floors, highly decorated walls and expensive tableware to advertise the owner's wealth, social position and of course, good taste.

It was John Cade who first referred to Old Durham as a possibly significant Roman site. William Hutchinson, also writing in the late 18th century, described: 'some deep trenches and high earth fences, but so irregular that it is not possible to derive any distinct picture from the remains'. The other noted Durham Historian, Robert Surtees, later agreed that Cade had predicted the site of what was then thought to be a Roman Fort: 'with great appearance of probability', as, 'vestiges of trenches and earthen ramparts may still be traced'. However, although Cade was right about the site, its actual function had been far different to what he had predicted. It stood on raised ground above the River Wear; a mile south-east of Durham City, between Old Durham Farm and Shincliffe Bridge, and it was located in an area of land which had been worked extensively for gravel extraction.

It was a man walking his dog who first noticed the site, exposed by the Durham City Sand and Gravel Company Ltd, and he was immediately interested in what he saw. He quickly sought more expert advice and the site was examined on 9 April 1940, when half a Roman roof tile was found embedded in the remains of a wall. It was not until August 1941, that it was inspected again, with investigations revealing the red cement lining of a Roman Bath. Excavations now began in earnest: 'though much hampered and inevitably delayed by the preoccupation in war work for all concerned' and work continued until the Spring of 1943, when the time, and the help was available.

Numerous small items were found, pieces of expensive Samian Pottery, probably from Gaul and dating to the time of Emperor Hadrian. Lots of wall plaster, still showing elaborate decoration of curving stems and broad leaves in green on a cream background, and still more, decorated with red stripes. The remains were found of two different types of Hypercaust system, one for the heating of a: 'Calderium', a room for hot damp heat, and another for a: 'Sudatorium' a room for hot dry heat. The building was clearly a Roman Bath House, but it was relatively small, too small, it was thought, to be military. It was undoubtedly domestic. As part of Villa complexes, Bath Houses were detached from the main ranges of buildings. As this was a domestic Bath House, it followed that a major Roman building or series of buildings would have stood nearby. A careful search was carried out and a series of test pits were dug. Nothing more was found. The Roman Villa at Durham, the most northerly in the Roman Empire, had been destroyed and had vanished under 1,700 years of ploughing and disturbance.

The Bath House itself, according to the finds, had been in use from the second to the fourth century AD and whatever had caused its eventual demise, whether sudden or gradual, fire had played its part. The experts agreed it was typical of those attached to domestic Roman Farmsteads or Villas, and was the first such to be identified in County Durham. Previously, the most northerly had been discovered at Middleham in Yorkshire and it had been assumed that settled Roman civilian life had not advanced so far north into the militarised zone. It had been fully functional before the fourth century AD, the:

Old Durham Gardens, close by the site of the Roman Bath House and lost Villa.

'Golden Age' of the Roman Villa and its agriculture had flourished under the eye of the Legions who protected it and who provided it with a market. However, if it had not been for the sharp eyes and expert curiosity of a man walking his dog, the Bath House, as well as the knowledge of its adjoining Villa, would have been lost to the extraction of the Durham City Sand and Gravel Company Ltd and Yorkshire would still lay claim to the site of the most northerly Roman Villa in the Roman Empire.

Being essentially a military zone, today's County Durham was criss-crossed with Roman Roads. Some are well known today, some have been suggested but not found, and some no doubt, remain to be discovered. But the network was one of military necessity rather than civilian convenience. Dere Street, the major Roman Road through the County, was not known by this name to the Romans. The name was written down by the monk and historian Simeon of Durham, who, writing in the late 11th century, called it: 'Deor' Street, thought to be derived from the name given to the road through the Anglo-Saxon Kingdom of Diera. It tracked north, through the lands of the Brigantes and along its length a series of Forts were constructed.

From York the road ran north and crossed the River Tees at Piercebridge, where a large town grew up. It was only later in the occupation that a fort was built here, the reverse of the usual trend of a town growing up around an existing fort. The forts themselves were built by highly trained and skilled Legionaries; however, they would be garrisoned mainly by auxiliary troops drawn from all over the Empire and eventually, from the native British tribes themselves. Indeed, the County Durham of the time must have been a very cosmopolitan place, with men of many different nationalities carrying out military service for the Roman Empire. We know this mainly through monument inscriptions left by those very men.

Ebchester, the Roman, Vindomora, was the most northerly Roman Fort in today's County Durham. It is known through its inscriptions that the fort was at least partly built by the Fifth Cohort of an unknown Legion, under the command of their Centurion, Martialis. It was later garrisoned for a time by the Fourth Cohort of Breucorians, a 500 strong infantry regiment, natives of modern day Bosnia. Hutchinson described a portion of the Dere Street road, which he examined just south of Ebchester fort: 'It is formed in three distinct parts, with four ditches: a centre road, probably for carriages and cavalry, 42 feet wide with a narrow road on each side, for foot passengers, 12 feet wide'.

It is thought that the Roman name for Lanchester; Longovicium, may translate to mean: 'Ship Street', or: 'Ship Settlement'. This could imply that its residents had some connection with the Roman British Fleet, or that they had been involved in a famous victory against a sea-borne attack, Lanchester becoming therefore: 'The place of the ship fighters'. Built by the Twentieth Legion, Valeria Victrix, it was garrisoned in the late second and early third century by the First Cohort of the Vardulli, a thousand strong, part mounted regiment from northern Spain. Other units, from the Bourgogne region of modern day France and from Portugal, were also, over time, stationed at Lanchester.

Binchester, the Roman; Vinovium, was built high on a plateau overlooking the River Wear, meandering 120ft below. This Fort must have been a formidable sight to friend and foe alike, for its natural defensive position was further strengthened by a defensive ditch, surrounding stone walls over 16ft high.

Work on a fort at Binchester began less than 80 years after the death of Christ and was underway at the same time, between AD70 and AD80, as the construction of the great Coliseum in Rome. First as an earthwork with a wooden stockade, the construction of Binchester was carried out, possibly by the Legion of Quintus Petillius Cerialis; the ill fated Ninth Legion. The legendary: 'Lost' Legion; two thousand of its men had been killed in Boudicca's uprising and its name and honours would later all but disappear from the written record. The Legion, as the chroniclers have recorded: 'whose own fate remains uncertain'. The purpose of their fort at Vinovium was to act both as a supply station to support the advancing Roman frontier, and as a military stronghold, helping to

The Hypercaust at Binchester Roman Fort.

The small excavated part of the massive Binchester site.

control the volatile lands of the Brigantes. Covering almost 18 acres, it would have been the largest in northern Britain. Indeed, it may have been that the site of the Roman Fort of Vinovium had already long been a power centre for the northern Iron Age tribes. Claudius Ptolemy, a Greek speaking Roman citizen of second century Egypt, was the author of a number of scientific works. His: 'Geography', is an account of the geographical knowledge of the Greco-Roman world; a compilation of what was then known about the geography of the Roman Empire. In it Ptolemy tells us that Vinovium had been one of the nine cities of the Brigantes, the: 'Exalted Ones'; a powerful confederation of northern tribes who took their name from the Celtic goddess, Brigantia.

In the early days of the Conquest, the Brigantes had been allied with Rome, providing a: 'Buffer Zone' between the Roman south and the Picts in the north. An arrangement which would be echoed over a thousand years later in the relationship between the Kings of England in the south and the Prince Bishops of Durham, in the north. However internal trouble began in AD51, when the Brigantian queen, Cartimandua, very pro-Roman, handed over to them the leading British resistance fighter of the time; Caractacus. Her position was further weakened in AD60, when she refused to support the revolt of Boudicca and when she subsequently ousted her consort, the Brigantian king Venutius and took his armour bearer, Vellocatus, as her new husband; a civil war broke out. The situation became very unstable. Rome had to act. The Legions marched north from York.

The: 'pacification' of the Brigantes was begun by the Governor of Britain, Petillius Cerialis. Tacitus tells us: 'and Petillius Cerialis at once induced terror, attacking the civitas of the Brigantes...there were many battles, and sometimes they were not without bloodshed'. What was begun by Cerialis was continued by his eventual successor, Julius Agricola, the other possible builder of the first fort at Binchester, and within a few years, the pacification of the rebelling Brigantes and the consolidation of their territory into

Roman Britain were completed. In his writings, the poet Juvenal tells of a Roman father urging his son to win glory, by: 'Destroying the forts of the Brigantes', at the end of the world, where the screams of the barbarians were carried on the wild northern winds. Eventually the north of England came fully under Roman control and County Durham as we know it today became part of a Roman Empire that would stretch from the wilds of Northumbria to the sands of North Africa; from the mountains of Wales to Jerusalem's walls.

After AD84, the Romans established their frontier on a line running between Carlisle in the west and Corbridge in the east. Almost 40 years later, the Emperor Hadrian decided to consolidate the boundary of the Roman Empire along this line. Hadrian did not fit the accepted mould for a Roman Emperor. Coming from a provincial Spanish family, he chose to carry out prolonged tours of the provinces. Never really popular with the Roman aristocracy as he halted the endless expansion of the Empire and created the first permanent physical barriers to it, part of a huge frontier system right around the Roman world. In Germany he established the: 'Limes Romanus', a defensive grid system of frontier roads, fortified with defensive ditches and wooden palisades. In Britain he fortified his northern frontier. From the Tyne in the east to the Solway in the west: 'To separate the Romans from the Barbarians', the Roman Wall, as we know it today, came into existence and it would be manned by men from across the Empire.

In the mid second century, men of the Sixth Legion, Victrix, who had arrived in Britain with Hadrian, rebuilt Binchester in stone and reduced its size to about 11 acres. The fort would become an important supply depot for Hadrian's Wall, and though occasionally altered, would remain in continuous use until the end of the Roman Empire. Around AD350, a Bath House was built, originally for the use of the Commanding Officer, his family and personal guests only and an unusual memorial to its foundation has been left. The accidental signature of a child, the imprint of whose sandaled foot has been preserved in the mortar, then still wet, as the Bath House floor was being laid down.

For most of its existence Binchester would be garrisoned by cavalry units and up to a thousand troops would be based within its walls. Inscriptions have been found made by Frisians from Holland, and by the Ala Vetonum, a celebrated, 500 strong cavalry regiment, recruited from north western Spain, around Salamanca. And for almost 300 years they set up their altars and worshipped their gods; including, appropriately for military men, Fortuna, the Goddess of Fortune: 'To virtuous Fortuna, Marcus Valerius Fulvianus, Prefect of Cavalry, willingly, gladly and deservedly fulfilled his vow'.

Support Services were as critically important to the Roman Army as they are to any modern army. Foremost among them were the Medical Officers, usually under the command of a Greek, as the Greeks were noted for their medical knowledge and skills. Greek doctors were also stationed at Binchester, and homage was paid there to Aesculapius, the God of Medicine. Around the fort a Vicus grew up. Existing initially as a settlement to support the needs of the troops and the military machine, it would, over time, grow into a fully functioning, 30 acre, civilian, commercial centre. It would be home to a racial and cultural melting pot of Romanised Britons; troops from modern day Spain and Holland; from North Africa and the Middle East; medics from Greece; resident craftsmen and wandering merchants from across the Roman Empire. All protected by the fort itself and all catered for in the hustle and bustle of the markets, inns and other attractions of the Vicus.

But, as we know, the Roman Empire eventually declined and dwindled. Rome was threatened. In AD410 the Emperor Honorius told the people of Britain that they no longer had a connection to the Empire and they must look to defend themselves. So it was that the last two Legions marched away, Britain was finally abandoned and on 24 August that same year, Alaric, King of the Visigoths, sacked Rome itself. As for Binchester, Roman Vinovium continued to be used by the local population and some kind of Roman way of life probably continued for decades. Around 40 years later, the Romanised British aristocracy renewed their appeal to their former masters. How could they now defend themselves against growing attacks by invaders. Their appeal became known as: 'The Groans of the Britons'; they entreated: 'To Aetius, thrice Consul, come the groans of the Britons…the Barbarians drive us into the sea, the sea drives us back to the Barbarians. We are either slain or drowned'. But the: 'Groans' remained unanswered. The Anglo-Saxon Chronicle records: 'AD 443 – In this year, the Britons sent to Rome and implored aid against the Picts, but they had none because they were warring against Attila, the King of the Huns. And then they sent to the Angles, and implored the same of the Princes of the Angle race'.

So it was, the legend tells, that in the year AD449, three ships carrying Saxon mercenaries landed in Kent. Their leaders were two brothers, Hengist and Horsa: 'The Stallion' and: 'The Horse'. According to tradition, they were invited by the despotic ruler, Lord Vortigern to help him fight incursions by rival tribes. But Vortigern neglected to pay them; a big mistake. They took land in lieu of payment and after a time of settlement, their slow advance began. A new England was about to be born. The Romanised British were eventually overwhelmed as more and more Anglo-Saxons came; the invaders beholding: 'the nothingness of the Britons and the goodness of the land', and, as the writer Nennius tells us: 'They brought over Kings from Germany that they might reign over them in Britain, right down to the time in which Ida reigned'.

So it was that almost a hundred years later, by the middle of the sixth century, Ida the Angle, the: 'Flamebearer', came with his 50: 'keels', and established himself at the old British fortress of: 'Din Guyardi', the coastal stronghold that would eventually become Bamburgh Castle. This was the dawning of Anglo-Saxon, Bernicia, from which would later develop the Kingdom of Northumbria. By AD550 the fort buildings at Binchester had been demolished and Anglo-Saxons were burying their dead in the ruins of Roman Vinovium. A hundred years later, the same stones laid down by the men of the Sixth Legion, were being used to build Escomb Church, a mile away across the River Wear.

Over the coming centuries, Binchester would almost, but not quite, disappear from history. When, in 1183, the Prince Bishop of Durham, Hugh of Le Puiset, commissioned the: 'Boldon Buke', his very own: 'Durham Domesday', the record shows that: 'Binchester renders 5s of cornage, and one cow in milk, and one cattleman, and four scaholders of malt'. John Leland was a Sub-Librarian in one of Henry VIII's Royal Libraries. In 1533 he had written poems, celebrating the forthcoming coronation of Anne Boleyn, which were later read out at the Coronation Ceremony. Possibly as a reward, Leland received a Royal Commission: 'To make a search after England's antiquities, and peruse the libraries of the Cathedrals, Abbies, Priories, Colleges etc. and also places wherein records, writings and secrets of Antiquity were reposed' His: 'Itinerary' is a record of his travels. Leland went insane and his work existed only in note form at his death, but his notes record his visit to Binchester: 'It stoodith on the brow of the hill and there I saw, as I roode on the south side,

Escomb Anglo-Saxon Church: 'A work of austere dignity' – Stenton.

a little fosse, and indicia of old buildings. In the ploughed fieldes hard by thys village hath and be found Romaine coynes, and many other tokens of antiquite'. In 1577, the English Antiquarian and Historian, William Camden began his great work: 'Britannia'; a topographical and historical survey of all Britain, with the intention: 'to restore antiquity to Britaine, and Britaine to its antiquity'. Published in 1586, Camden tells in his work of the ruins of Binchester, still then a familiar landmark: 'For peeces of Romane coine are often digged up there, which they call Binchester penies'.

In the 18th century, Jeremiah Dixon of Cockfield, surveyor and co-founder of the: 'Mason-Dixon Line' in the USA, mapped the area around Binchester. He showed a waterway running from the River Wear, about 150 metres downstream from its junction with the River Gaunless, to the east and then to the north of Binchester; perhaps a Roman canal, completing the defence of the fort.

And a sad story followed the demolition of a grand Hall which had stood since Elizabethan times on the site of the fort. During the lifetime of the Hall, many Roman altars and monuments had been collected and preserved. However, when, in the early part of the 19th century, the Hall was eventually demolished on the instruction of the incumbent Bishop of Durham, William Van Mildert, all these precious reminders of antiquity and of the County's heritage: 'were used in forming the 'stoppings' of a nearby coal pit'.

The fort was forgotten but not lost, until, so the story goes, a farm cart fell through a hole in the ground above the Bath House and into the Hypercaust below. Interest in the fort was renewed. In the late 19th century, the Revd R.E. Hoopell, excavated part of what he described as: 'A Buried Roman City' and a series of subsequent excavations have revealed what can be seen today. More discoveries are being made at Binchester, including three Roman military mausolea, found by TV's *Time Team* in 2007; the first to be discovered in Britain for 150 years. To this day most of the fort, and all of the Vicus, remains underground and ongoing excavations of this major historical site are planned. Who knows what other treasures remain undiscovered?

It is hard to know what the Roman Officer serving at Binchester, having erected his personal monument to the Goddess Fortuna, would have thought if he could possibly have foreseen, that after the passage of 1,600 years, the same elaborately carved stone would be: 'rescued from the mouth of a coal pit', still bearing the inscription, familiar to him: 'M. Valerius Fulvianus, Commander of Cavalry, pays his vow to Fortune'

After almost 400 years, the Roman occupation ended. However, it had been much more than an occupation. During that time, Roman controlled Britain had become a fully fledged member of the Roman world. Conquest had evolved into colonisation. The native Celtic tribes had become Romano British citizens, their tribal leaders' now civic worthies with adopted Roman names. This had been no mere invasion for the purpose of piracy and plunder, no smash and grab raid. It is easy to think of the Roman Invasion in the following terms. They came, they saw, they conquered; and then stayed around for a while and left; a well known, but distant chapter in our long history. However, when we relate the lifespan of Roman Britain to our own place in the timescale of history, it is sobering to think; that if the last Legions were leaving these islands now, the first ones would have marched in during the English Civil War.

Almost 2,000 years have now passed, but perhaps if we focus our minds, shade our eyes and free our imagination, we can still almost see snapshots of life then, and the people who lived that life. The events that took place at the very beginning of recorded history in our County. Perhaps we can look out across the River Wear or the: 'Vedra' as the Romans called it, and see the workers toiling in the fertile fields around Old Durham; the workers who produced the wealth for the most northerly Villa in the Roman Empire and the supplies for the Roman Legions that protected it. Perhaps we can see Marcus Valerius Fulvianus, Commander of Cavalry, having made his vow to Fortune, leading his garrison out through the gates of Vinovium, to patrol the remote, wild lands of the Brigantes. And perhaps we can just still see the child, was it playing or serving its life as a slave? Scampering across the wet clay of the newly laid bathhouse floor at Binchester and leaving a tell-tale footprint that would still be seen over 16 centuries later.

Chapter 2

Lord of Battles

'Then it was that the magnanimous Arthur, with all the Kings and military force of
Britain, fought against the Saxons'.
– Nennius History of the Britons

So the Romans built in stone and marble. They left us a reminder of their Britain in their
straight roads, their written word and their built record; a time that is well documented,
well studied, and well known. However, what followed the withdrawal of the Legions was
a weird, twilight world. A world almost lost to us today. A shadowy world of feuding
warlords and the gradual demise of a Romano-British society struggling to come to terms
with the harsh realities of self-governance and the defence of Sub-Roman Britain against
Germanic aggressors. This was the time, not just of the: 'Tyrant Lord' Vortigern and his
Saxon mercenaries Hengist and Horsa, but also of the Celtic Bards, of legendary heroes,
and of course; of Arthur.

Few figures from popular literature have aroused so much interest or caused so much
debate as Arthur. Seen by most historians as pure invention, or at the very least as an
embellishment by later Mediaeval and Victorian writers of a shadowy figure, mentioned
sparingly in obscure and probably unreliable texts. Perhaps he was a Romano-British
aristocrat; perhaps he was a British tribal leader; perhaps a Celtic king, who fought against
the advance of Anglo-Saxon invaders; perhaps he was a military commander, a Dux
Bellorum, Lord of Battles, fighting a civil war for control of the power vacuum left in the
wake of the departing Legions; Perhaps, …Perhaps,…Perhaps!

Perhaps the figure of Arthur was a literary composite of a number of different Dark Age
war leaders, whose exploits were judged worthy of recall; or perhaps he only ever existed
in the world of imagination.

It is variously argued that he was a figure associated with the south-west of England, or
with Wales, or perhaps with Kent. Perhaps even with the frontier lands of Hadrian's Wall
and the Roman fortifications of the North Country. One constant seems to be, that many
parts of the country lay claim to connections to Arthurian legends. Most want to be a part
of the Arthur story, to have: 'a piece of Arthur'. Many claims have been made for legendary
Arthurian sites and: 'identifiable' place names, which, it is confidently claimed, confirm a
historical connection to the Arthur story, to his battles and to his eventual death. County
Durham is no exception. But can we lay as valid a claim to a piece of Arthur as those others
who claim him as their own? Well, according to some commentators, Arthur may have
fought at least one major battle in County Durham and may have met his death in a grim
slaughter within sight of the Roman Wall.

The traditional stories of King Arthur, the Romances of: 'The Once and Future King',
are part, not just of British, but of European literature. We are familiar with the themes;
The Knights of the Round Table; Guinevere, Arthur's queen; Camelot and Merlin;
Excalibur and the Isle of Avalon; and of course, the Holy Grail. These themes have, over
the centuries, been developed and woven into some of the most famous stories in
European literature. But in the end, that's all they are, just stories.

Bamburgh Castle, Northumberland, the: 'Din Guyardi' of Iron Age Britons.

In 1129, about four years before the completion of Durham Cathedral, a young Welsh cleric, Geoffrey of Monmouth, was also completing his work: *The History of the Kings of Britain*. Described as a: 'Masterpiece of Creative Imagination', it is an invented history, drawn from the works of earlier writers and features Arthurian characters and themes that we are familiar with today. Arthur himself had already made his first literary appearance, as a king, in the: *Chronicles of the Kings of England*, written by William, a monk and librarian of Malmesbury Abbey. This work was based on stories William had been told by the monks of Glastonbury; about the legendary King Arthur and his battles against the Anglo-Saxon invaders.

Merlin was originally a shadowy figure from Celtic mythology, first mentioned under the name Myraddin, who according to Celtic tradition was a prophet, a: 'Seer', and a Court Poet from the north of England; who sang his heroic songs about the North Country. The Holy Grail is a fantasy; the ideal of a spiritual quest, first introduced into Arthurian myth by the 12th century French writer Chretien de Troyes, who also introduced us to Lancelot. The Grail was later given a Christian significance by Robert de Boron, a Burgundian knight and poet. It was he who turned the Grail, originally only a serving dish, into the cup used by Christ at the Last Supper, which, according to Boron, was later used by Joseph of Aramathea to catch the blood of Christ at the Crucifixion. For good measure, it was also Robert de Boron who introduced the idea of the Sword in the Stone, although he originally had it in an anvil, on top of a stone. And it was the Jersey born, Anglo Norman poet, Robert Wace, who would later become a Canon of Bayeux, who added the Round Table to the legendary tales and in his writings turned Arthur's sword into a magical sword, and give it a name: 'Excalibur'.

Later, in the late 15th century, Sir Thomas Malory, while it is claimed, incarcerated in Newgate Prison for rape, weaved together all the fictional story strands invented by the earlier writers and from material he had reduced: 'oute of certeyn bookes of Frensshe', and worked them into his: *Le Morte d'Arthur*. Printed by Thomas Caxton in 1485, it became an instant hit and was later described by the great romantic novelist, Sir Walter Scott, as: 'The best prose romance that the English language can boast of'. It gave to the world the idea of: 'Arthur, the Once and Future King', and was the inspiration for yet another Arthurian revival in the Victorian era, with the publication of Alfred Lord Tennyson's poetic: *Idylls of the King*.

So what connection then, between these fictional romances, the North of England and County Durham?

Malory has Arthur's court at Carlisle, which had in its day, seen a rich Romanised urban life. Indeed, in the year AD685, its citizens conducted St Cuthbert himself: 'around the City Walls to see a remarkable Roman fountain that was built into them'. The mediaeval French chronicler, Jean Froissart, also regarded Carlisle as being Arthur's capital; and the stories tell that it was from Carlisle that Sir Lancelot rescued Guinevere after their secret love had been betrayed by Sir Mordred, and from where King Arthur himself would ride out to besiege Sir Lancelot's castle of: 'Joyous Guard'. Malory even suggests the location of: 'Joyous Guard': 'Some men say it was Alnwick and some men say it was Bamburgh'. Malory knew these places. In late 1462 he had been a soldier, fighting for the Yorkist cause during the Wars of the Roses and had been present when the armies of King Edward IV, had laid siege to Bamburgh, Alnwick and Dunstanburgh castles. The King, as it happened, was forced to stay in Durham City to recover from a bout of measles.

Bamburgh, Malory's: 'Joyous Guard', the castle of Sir Lancelot?

Just south of Kirkby Stephen in the Eden Valley stands Pendragon Castle. Traditionally associated with Arthur's father of legend, Uther Pendragon and mentioned in Malory's: *Le Morte d'Arthur*. A story tells that Uther had the castle built during his northern wars and even attempted to divert the natural path of the nearby River Eden to form a moat around his new stronghold. But his efforts were in vain. An old rhyme goes: 'Let Uther Pedragon do what he can; Eden will run where Eden ran'.

The omens for Uther were not good and it followed that he was killed at his mighty castle of Pendragon, along with 100 of his men, after drinking water from the well, poisoned it was said, by: 'Saxon Dogs'. The current ruins date only from the 12th century but still have an association with infamy; as the histories tell that a great Keep was raised and fortified there by Hugh de Moreville, after his flight from Canterbury Cathedral, as one of the four murderers of Thomas Becket.

The ruins of a Roman Milecastle lie close by the Cumbrian village of Gilsland. Since time unremembered it has been known as: 'The King's Stables', which, it is said, gives a nod to a now long forgotten association with Arthur. Interestingly, it also stands close by the Roman Fort of Castlesteads; thought by some modern scholars to be Camboglanna, possibly the place mentioned in the: *Annals of Wales* as Camlann; the scene of Arthur's final, fatal battle.

But County Durham itself is also home to legendary tales of Arthur. In the Arthurian Romances, Beaurepaire was the name of the castle of Sir Perceval's lover, Blanchfleur. Beaurepaire was also the: 'Beautiful Retreat' of the Priors of Durham, which stands today in ruined form, just outside Bearpark, not far from Durham City. And in the Derwent Valley there is an age old legend about the whereabouts of the: 'Once and Future King'.

'Deep buried under Mugglewick,
King Arthur lies asleep'.

Between Allansford and Muggleswick rises a wooded headland, around which the River Derwent forms a picturesque, steep sided horseshoe. The Derwent Valley tradition tells that the location, known as The Sneep, holds secret, deep within its wooded fastness, a cavern, in which lies the legendary King of the Britons himself, at peace in enchanted slumber. Brought here after the healing of his battle wounds, received at the final bloody slaughter of Camlann; he slumbers still, in this otherworldly place. Fire rises from the centre of the stony hall and around it, reclining on fragrant couches, lie Arthur and Guinevere, surrounded by the King's favourite pack of hunting hounds. On a table nearby are a great sword, a garter, and a bugle horn. But the King and Queen do not lie alone, for all around rest his knights, their warhorses and: 'All the power of his Chivalry'; ready, when the spell of enchantment is broken, to wake from their slumber of ages, to re-emerge from their world into ours and to ride once more to the aid of their country in the hour of direst need.

'The scenes which, all enchanting, threw their spell,
O'er old King Arthur, who, in dreamy state,
Abides for ever caverned in this cell;
Or till the subtle hand that fixed his fate,
Dispels the dear delusion'
Barrass, 'The Derwent Valley.

Tales of similar enchanted subterranean caves are told right across the North Country; at Richmond Castle in North Yorkshire, beneath the Eildon Hills in southern Scotland; under the vast bulk of Blencathra in Cumbria and beneath Sewingshields Crags on Hadrian's Wall.

But do the origins of the Arthur story precede the Legends and Romances by far? Are they, as writers from more distant centuries would have us believe, concerned with an actual historical Arthur. Not the myth of a romantic fantasy king, of chivalry, shining armour and noble quests; but a Leader of Battles, locked in a grim struggle for survival in the bloody civil wars of the Sub-Roman Dark Ages. A very different kind of Arthur indeed, as Tennyson tells:-

'Not like that Arthur, who, with lance in rest,
From spur to plume a star of tournament,
Shot through the lists of Camelot, and charged
Before the eyes of ladies and of Kings'

Those struggles, so the Celtic writers tell us, were the very: 'Matter of Britain' and they probably took place in the last quarter of the fifth century, against invading Saxons, Angles and Picts. So what connection has County Durham to an Arthur, not of legend, but of reality?

Over a period of time almost equal to that between the reigns of the first and second Queen Elizabeth, only three written sources suggest a possible historical basis for the Arthur story. In the sixth century, probably around the year AD540 the Welsh monk Gildas: 'the gloomy dean', wrote his: *On the Ruin and Conquest of Britain*. In his writing he railed against the tyrants and warlords of his day, against the Anglo-Saxon: 'invaders' and against the end of the Roman world, telling the world that in his day there was no man that did good: 'no not one'. It is Gildas who first mentions a major British victory over the Anglo-Saxons at a place called Mount Badon: 'Forty-four years and one month after the landing of the Saxons', and suggests the presence at that battle of a powerful British war leader. He

The great mound of Maiden Castle Iron-Age Hillfort looms over the River Wear near Durham City.

does not, however, give that leader a name. Almost 200 years after Gildas, our very own Bede, in his: *Ecclesiastical History of the English People*, also mentions the victory at Mount Badon, but again, does not mention Arthur. It is likely that resistance to the Anglo-Saxon and Pictish incursions that followed the Roman withdrawal was led by the remaining Romano-British warrior aristocracy. From their number, it is possible that one figure unified the disparate and feuding factions of Post Roman Britain against the aggressors.

When the last Legions left southern England in the early fifth century, never to return, the north of what had been Roman Britain, was still dominated by the Romano-British military which continued to garrison the old frontier forts. A Roman way of life, of sorts, would continue for decades, as would Roman style military service. Fortifications were maintained or rebuilt and it is known that some of the forts on Hadrian's Wall were still occupied into the sixth century. It is likely that, centered on these strongholds, ex-Roman Army Officers and their descendants became local leaders. Gradually, local leaders became local rulers, who became Post Roman War Lords. They would call themselves: 'Regum', King; but Gildas denounced them as: 'Tyranni'.

Could this perhaps have happened at Binchester, the old Roman stronghold of Vinovium. After all it had been both a major military and commercial centre for centuries. Perhaps even at Hamsterley Castles, at South Bedburn; that massive and enigmatic ruin, over an acre in size, which stubbornly refuses to give up its secrets to modern archaeology. Experts suggest that it was built shortly after the Roman withdrawal, and with walls 16 feet thick which would have stood around 11ft high, was this the power base of an ambitious local military despot, one of the 'Tyranni' of Gildas? Or was it perhaps a fortified bolt hole for a mobile cavalry strike force, based at a larger fortification? It is thought likely that military resistance to the Anglo-Saxons and Picts would essentially be a mounted hit and run campaign from fortified cavalry bases. Speed of horse against the normally static formations of an enemy that fought on foot. Of course it has also been suggested that Hamsterley Castles was merely a secure enclosure for livestock.

Taliesin, the semi-legendary Celtic Court Poet and: 'The Chief and most learned of the British Bards', was active towards the end of the sixth century; and it was in: *The Book of Taliesin* that was told the story of Cunnedda, a powerful Romano-British war leader, who, a century before, had led the Votadini, the British tribe from south-east Scotland and north-east England, against Pictish incursions south of Hadrian's Wall.

Taliesin tells of Cunnedda's heroic battle victories and his verse includes the following:
'Between the brine and the high slope and fresh stream water,
men will cringe before Cunnedda, the violent one.
In Caer Weir and Caer Lywelydd fighting will shame the Civitates'.

Caer Lywelydd has been identified as Carlisle, where Cunnedda was victorious in battle around the year AD460. It has been suggested that Caer, the Celtic word for fort or stronghold, taken with the word Weir, signifying the River Wear, may imply that the other battle was fought at, or in the vicinity of Maiden Castle; the Iron Age Promontory Fort sitting atop a wooded hill just to the south-east of Durham City. Originally its strong defensive walls and wooden palisade would have commanded uninterrupted views across the plain to modern day Shincliffe and across the River Wear to the old Roman site at Old Durham. There has long been a local tradition that Arthur himself fought against the Anglo-Saxons at Maiden Castle. Could Cunnedda's battle at Caer Weir have been the origin of that tradition? Perhaps the heroic exploits of Cunnedda were simply attributed to Arthur at a later date.

For it is not until around the year AD830, when the chronicler Nennius gives him a name, that Arthur himself actually begins to emerge from Dark Age legend to become a possible historical character. In his: *The History of the Britons*, Nennius tells us:
'Then it was, that the magnanimous Arthur, with all the Kings and military force of Britain, fought against the Saxons, and though there were many more noble than himself, yet he was twelve times chosen their commander, and was as often conqueror'.

Nennius goes on to give an account of 12 major battles in which Arthur defeated the Anglo-Saxons, culminating in the decisive victory at Mount Badon. Geographical claims to the battle sites have been made right across England and Wales and into southern Scotland, but little agreement has been reached among scholars as to their exact location. However, some of the battle sites have been proposed as being likely to have been northern. According to Nennius, the first battle took place: 'at the mouth of the River Glein'. It has been suggested that this could be the River Glen in Northumberland. The seventh battle was in the Caledonian Forest: 'that is Cat Coit Celidon'. This is usually taken to refer to wooded country north of Carlisle. The battle ground of: 'Mount Agned', was given a second name, Bregomion. This has been associated with the name Bremenium, the Roman Fort at High Rochester in the Cheviots in Northumberland. The battle at the City of the Legion, called by Nennius 'Cair Lion', has been variously suggested as Chester, Caerleon, or York, though never yet as Carlisle.

Perhaps of most significance to County Durham, was the eighth battle described by Nennius; the Battle of: 'Castellum Guinnion'. This has been identified as a site either at or near a Roman Fort, a: 'Castellum'; and it was at this major battle, so Nennius tells us, that:

'Caer Weir', one of Arthur's battle sites?

'Arthur carried the image of St Mary, forever virgin on his shield and that day the pagans were turned to flight and Arthur pursued them all day and a great slaughter was made of them through the virtue of our Lord Jesus Christ and through the virtue of his mother, St Mary the Virgin'.

This place name: 'Castellum Guinnion', is also a name that has caused some debate among scholars. A.L.F. Rivet and Colin Smith, in their work: *The Place - Names of Roman Britain*, take us back to the second century geographer, Claudius Ptolemy, and note that: 'Ptolemy's alternative name for Vinovium, the British (Old Welsh), Uinnouion, brings us very close to the later name set down by Nennius', (Guinnion). Of course Vinovium is Binchester.

So, is it possible then that the two names do indeed describe the same location? There has also been a long, if indistinct, tradition that the battle of: 'Mons Badonicus', fought on a hill, was actually fought at Binchester. The French writer, Edmond Faral, in his three volume: *La Legende Arthurienne*, published in 1929, identified Binchester as the site of the Battle of Mount Badon and suggested that the historical Arthur was a British Chieftain in the north of England. Interestingly, Arthur has traditionally been imagined as a leader of cavalry; an idea which resonates perhaps with the cavalry fort of Vinovium. Perhaps then the tradition does echo an actual event, a battle fought by Arthur in modern day County Durham, but perhaps the battle was not that of Mount Badon, but the Battle of: 'Castellum Guinnion', fought at the old City of the Brigantes, as described by Claudius Ptolemy, the Roman Fort of Vinovium.

So writers and scholars, both old and new, have identified the North of England with the struggles of a possible historical Arthur and even modern day film makers suggest that; here is the place where the legends were born. Of course we may just be falling into the trap of willing those legends to be true; of trying to grasp that elusive: 'piece of Arthur' for ourselves. And yet it is surely easy enough for us to picture the charge of Arthur's mounted warriors across the wild lands around Hadrian's Wall; a landscape, in the past so familiar to the crack units of Roman Cavalry. Or to bear mute witness to the tragedy of: 'the last, dim, weird battle of the west' at Camlann, Camboglana; Castlesteads.

Perhaps we can even see, there on the plateau above the River Wear at the old fort of Vinovium, the shadowy figure of Arthur himself; Dux Bellorum, Lord of Battles, sitting astride his charger and placing his fate in the image of the Virgin Mary. About to face the Anglo-Saxon Shield Wall; or perhaps the massed charge of the Picts; or perhaps some unknown petty king making his own claim to the overlordship of this part of Sub-Roman Britain. For Arthur this would be the eighth time, the eighth battle, the Battle of Castellum Guinnion; the Battle of Binchester.

Well, perhaps!

Chapter 3

The Crozier and the Sword

'Goode Rede, Short Rede, kill ye the Bishop'

So it was, that 137 years after the Romans had deserted the shores of Britain, Ida the Flamebearer, Chief of the Angles, established his dynasty at Bamburgh and over the following centuries the Kingdom of Northumbria would develop into a major power in Anglo-Saxon England. Almost a century after Ida, St Aidan would arrive at Lindisfarne and begin the process of Christianising the kingdom. After the death of Aidan in AD651, a monk named Cuthbert would live, die and be proclaimed a Saint and then another monk, Bede, would write, among many other works his: *Ecclesiastical History of the English People*, a work that King Alfred the Great considered to be: 'most necessary for all men to know'. Lights shone in Dark Age Northumbria.

But successive Viking incursions changed the nature of the country. From the early piratical raids to the full scale invasion of AD865, by: 'The Great Heathen Army' under the command of the sons of Ragnar Lodbrok; Ivar the Boneless and Halfdan Wide Embrace; of whom the chronicler Simeon of Durham tells us:

'On their arrival in England they took possession of it, and wandered over the whole of it, carrying with them plunder and slaughter wherever they went. After having subdued and destroyed nearly the whole of the southern provinces of England, they next attacked the region of the Northumbrians'.

One by one, the Anglo-Saxon kingdoms would be overrun and over the following years the geography and society of England would gradually be changed. The old line of the Northumbrian Kings was lost and eventually, in the year 1016, a Viking would become King of England, Denmark and Norway. From his seat on the throne of Anglo-Saxon England, Cnut the Great would rule over his Anglo-Scandinavian Empire, devolving control of England through the great Earldoms of Wessex, Mercia and Northumbria. In Wessex, Earl Godwin would plot and scheme his family's rise to pre-eminence, and eventual oblivion, at Hastings. Northumbria in the mid 11th century was governed by Earl Siward and he ruled, in the tradition of his own royal Danish bloodline, with a high hand.

Indeed, Siward managed to alienate that other controller of large landed estates in 11th century Northumbria, the already rich and influential Community of St Cuthbert at Durham. In 1042 Siward imposed a monk named Ethelric on the Community as their new bishop. This was unpopular with the Durham monks for, as the church histories recall, Ethelric was: 'an alien who made himself obnoxious to the Community'. He had in fact, been a member of that Community for 21 years. The problem was, that originally hailing from Peterborough Abbey, he was not a Northumbrian, and therefore not one of their own. Quickly making matters worse, he appointed his own brother, Ethelwin, to senior office within the Community and Ethelwin it was, according to Simeon: 'Who took on the management of the whole Bishopric under him with some other monks, all of whom joined with the Bishop in studying how to plunder the church of her money and ornaments and to carry them away'. In only his third year of office the Durham monks

The Church of St Mary and St Cuthbert, Chester-le-Street, from where, found during its early contruction, Bishop Ethelric appropriated a horde of treasure.

tried to expel Ethelric. The church histories tell that he bribed Siward to restore him to office and that Siward, perhaps as his part of the bargain and perhaps also to demonstrate or to remind the Community of St Cuthbert of his own authority, ensured that Ethelric was restored; and the Community who had tried to rid themselves of the alien in their midst: 'Were constrained to be reconciled to the Bishop, whether they would or not, and to readmit him to the Episcopal See'.

Having undertaken to build a new church at Chester-le-Street, Ethelric pulled down the old wooden one and when the new foundations were being dug, a horde of treasure was found, hidden it was thought, by a previous Bishop. The treasure was quickly appropriated by Ethelric and sent to his native monastery at Peterborough, where, in the 15th year of the reign of Edward the Confessor, he followed; but not before securing his brother Ethelwin as his successor to the See of Durham.

At Peterborough, Simeon tells us that Ethelric: 'Employed the money, of which we have already spoken, in constructing through the fenny regions, roads of stone and wood, and churches, and many other things which caused him to be regarded with favour in that country'. However, Ethelric would eventually be called to account for his actions. Condemned for: 'Piracy', he was accused of robbing the Church of Durham but he refused to refund what he had taken. He was sentenced to be held in captivity in Westminster Abbey, and, never to be reconciled with the King, he would live on: 'in voluntary poverty and a wealth of tears', until his death on 15 October 1072.

Siward died in 1055 and his successor as Earl of Northumbria was Tostig, the younger brother of Harold Godwinson. It was with Tostig's support and, so it is said, the support of the King, that Ethelwin succeeded his brother to the See of Durham. He would be the last Anglo-Saxon Bishop of Durham, and his time would see massive change, in which the old order of England would be irreversibly swept away.

When dawn rose over Senlac Field on 15 October,1066, it heralded a new age for England. Through his victory in battle the previous day, the country would have a new king, William, Duke of Normandy. King Harold and the chiefs of Anglo-Saxon England were dead or driven into hiding. With ruthless efficiency and no small measure of brutality, King William, known to later generations, but not to his own, as: 'The Conqueror', quickly made use of the existing machinery of state to underpin his rule.

An Anglo-Saxon royal dynasty reaching back to the ninth century and to King Alfred the Great was ended. Norman aristocrats replaced English thegns as the governing class. King William, who had traditionally appointed all bishops and abbots in Normandy, continued this practice in his new kingdom. After 1070, no Englishman was appointed as bishop or abbot and within a few years nearly all the bishops, both in Normandy and in England, most of whom were extremely capable men, were relatives or friends of William. The English received not just a new Royal Family but also a new ruling class, a new culture and a new language, as Norman French became the language of Government, of the Law and of the King's Court. The Anglo Norman chronicler, Orderic Vitalis, tells us that: 'The native inhabitants were crushed, imprisoned, disinherited, banished and scattered beyond the limits of their own country; while his own vassals and adherents were exhalted to wealth and honours and raised to all offices of state'.

Militarily, however, the conquest was not easily achieved, the Battle of Hastings being merely the first step. For the next five years the Normans lived more like an army of occupation, fighting against a campaign of seemingly never-ending guerrilla warfare. In the north, Edwin and Morcar, the English Earls of Mercia and Northumbria, rose against the King. William himself rode as far as York, where he garrisoned the castle with 500 soldiers. He sent north; with a further 700 men at arms, a Norman noble, Robert de Comines, to impose the King's will on Durham and to further extend the chain of strategic fortifications which had already reached Nottingham, Lincoln and York.

He was met at the River Tees by Ethelwin. The Bishop had already sworn allegiance to the Conqueror, but his role in the northern rebellion has been described as: 'ambiguous' and he attempted to dissuade Comines, unsuccessfully, from entering Durham. The Norman Lord and his men crashed into the City and massacred the inhabitants. But the following morning the tables were turned when rebels stormed the City, slaughtering the Normans, whom they caught drunk and off guard. Comines was killed and the streets were: 'filled with blood and carcasses'. It is said that only one of his men survived. Spurred on by their success at Durham, the rebels advanced south as far as York, where the City was seized and the Norman commander killed; but critically, the castle garrison held out. Once again the King himself rode north, raised the siege and put the rebels to flight, back to their northern stronghold. But now the King demanded retribution, and so began the infamous: 'Harrying of the North'.

The northern counties would be devastated by the Normans. People and livestock were slaughtered, crops ruined, and farming implements destroyed. The whole country to the north of York was laid waste, so that for nine years after, the ground lay untilled. Those who escaped the sword, starved to death.

Of the Bishop, Simeon tells us that on 11 December 1069, 74 years after the arrival in Durham of the Community of St Cuthbert, Ethelwin: 'with the Chiefs of the people', fled Durham: 'in order to escape the King's sword'; taking the body of St Cuthbert, the Lindisfarne Gospels and other treasures of his church, north to the holy island of Lindisfarne. They broke their journey first at St Paul's, Jarrow, then at Bedlington and Tughall in Northumberland. On reaching the coast at night, to their dismay, the tide was high and their safe passage denied but following much prayer, they found that in the morning the sea had retreated and they were: 'afforded the means of passing over, while at every other point the tide was at the fullest'. This they declared to be a miracle and ascribed it to St Cuthbert. After a stay of just over three months they returned, and on 25 March 1070, St Cuthbert: 'with hymns and praises', was restored to his sanctuary at Durham.

Simeon tells that Ethelwin's overriding motivation was no better than his brother's had been, and that he was even more successful in siphoning away the riches of the Durham Church; and now, Ethelwin reasoned, was the time to gracefully depart the See of St Cuthbert. He determined, to leave Durham and to go into exile: 'dreading the heavy rule of a foreign nation', and, it was claimed, taking with him a large amount of treasure. He had a ship made ready to depart at Wearmouth and he waited for a favourable wind. And so it was that when his favourable wind duly arrived, Ethelwin deserted his Office and the Church of St Cuthbert; and the last Anglo-Saxon Bishop of Durham was outlawed by William the Conqueror.

On setting out he cursed the oppressors and declared them separated from the communion of Christians: 'May they be dammed by Jesus Christ'. Of course, had the Conqueror heard, he would have cared little, for: 'William had priests to give the lie to priests, and he had swords to ward off swords'. It was Ethelwin's intention to make his way

The lonely Lindisfarne Causeway crossed by Pilgrims and by Bishop Ethelwin on his flight from William the Conqueror's army.

to Cologne, but his favourable wind betrayed him and drove him back on to the Scottish coast, where he spent the winter. The following year his adventures took him south, to East Anglia and his homelands around Peterborough; and to involvement in another rebellion, that of Hereward the Wake. Hereward had gained a reputation as a fighter of considerable skill, and, basing his rebellion in the Fens, he conducted a guerilla war that was a thorn in William's side. In time he gathered around him a substantial rebel army, an army that included fresh forces and refugees from Northumbria. The 13th century Chronicler, Mathew Paris, gives account that in 1071:

'The Earls Edwin and Morcar, together with Ethelwin, Bishop of Durham, associated themselves with many thousands disaffected persons and rebels against William the First. At first they betake themselves to the forest and the waste plains; then they do what mischief they can to the King's property in various places, and finally seek a place of refuge in the Isle of Ely. There, under the leadership of Hereward the Wake, they make frequent sallies and do much damage'

William made a number of unsuccessful attempts to take the Isle of Ely but he would not be denied. Eventually he surrounded the Isle with his forces and began to build fortifications around the Fens. Any possible escape to the sea was blocked, and the Conqueror began building a causeway: 'rendering the deep swamps passable for man and beast'. Hereward was captured. However, William had been so impressed with the bravery and tenacity he had shown, that his life was spared.

As for the renegade Bishop of Durham, Ethelwin, as far as is known the only Bishop to have joined the rebellion, was taken prisoner and formally accused of stealing treasures from his former See. Placed in the custody of the Abbot of Abingdon and being required to restore to the Church of St Cuthbert, that which he had taken, he denied on oath that he had taken anything; but was betrayed, the story tells, by a gold bracelet dropping down his arm as he was washing his hands: 'and thus the Bishop was convicted of manifest perjury and in his vexation he refused all sustenance, and so died'. It has, however, been questioned whether his fatal abstinence was entirely voluntary. And so, said some: 'ended another Patriot Prelate'. Ethelwin, like his brother, died in captivity, thus marking the ignoble end of the last Anglo-Saxon Bishop of Durham.

Following Ethelwin's demise, the Conqueror appointed the first foreigner to the See of Durham. Walcher of Lorraine was a man of noble birth, of ability and intelligence, but he was not a Norman; he had not been set in that mould and therefore was ill-prepared for the rebellious land into which he was to be sent. A story is told that at his consecration as Bishop, at Winchester, Queen Editha, the widow of Edward the Confessor, on seeing Walcher's: 'white hair, rosy countenance and tall, handsome figure', and thinking no doubt of the wild and fierce race among which he was going, exclaimed: 'Here we have a Martyr'. Nonetheless, soon after his installation at Durham, on 3 April 1071, when the Conqueror bestowed gold upon the church, sufficient to make amends for the thefts of Norman freebooters; Walcher was not above accepting part of the gift for the church, and the rest he: 'in his poverty appropriated for his own use'.

His time was stormy. In 1075 there was yet another rebellion, this time involving Waltheof, then Earl of Northumbria, who three years earlier, under the instruction of the Conqueror, had begun construction of a castle at Durham which would become the seat and stronghold of the Bishop. But a hoped for supporting invasion by the King of Denmark never came and the 1075 rebellion, like all the others, was put down. Waltheof was executed and Walcher was: 'invited' by the King to buy the Earldom of Northumbria, for 400 marks: 'an invidious and perilous addition to the cares of the Episcopal Office'. But Walcher did not win the support and trust of the Northumbrians. He failed to prevent repeated incursions into northern England by the armies of King Malcolm of Scotland. In August and September 1079 the Scots ravaged the countryside totally unopposed. More significantly, he was unable to prevent his soldiers robbing and murdering local people. Reputedly a mild man of gentle disposition, and therefore unlike those who would come after, he lacked control over his Norman household. His closest advisors: 'were violent and unscrupulous, and hated much by the people'. First among these were Leobwin his Archdeacon and personal chaplain; and Gilbert, a relative to whom he entrusted his affairs of the earldom: Richardson tells us that: 'The former plundered the treasures of the church, and the country groaned under the tyranny of the latter'.

Ligulf of Lumley was a local English thegn, connected by family to the old Northumbrian Earls and, as Sir Frank Stenton has told us: 'was fitted in every way to be the intermediary between the Bishop and the Englishmen of his province'. He was a confidente of the Bishop's and, hoping for his intercession, he remonstrated loudly to Walcher about the actions of his household. Leobwin especially hated Ligulf and insulted him even in the Bishop's presence. It was at his instigation that Gilbert formed an armed band and went by night to the house in which Ligulf was staying: 'and slew him and the greater part of his people'. An enraged populace demanded of the Bishop that the culprits be held to account. Walcher dithered, denying any complicity of his own in the murders; declaring that he had banished Gilbert, though he had not, and offering to prove his innocence by his personal oath.

On 14 May 1080, the crisis came to a head when a meeting of all parties was held, at a Wintagemot at a church in Gateshead: 'and thither came a number of persons of consequence from north of the Tyne, with no friendly feelings towards the Bishop'. A petition of wrongs was presented to Walcher, who refused to receive it. Those gathered around became: 'insolent and refractory'. The Bishop and his party, having only a small bodyguard of armed soldiery, retired into the church with some of the protestors and tried to: 'speak peace with their main men'. Negotiations took place but the main demands of the people, namely that the guilty should be punished, were not met. A riot ensued. Outside the church, the Bishop's soldiers were set upon and killed. The mob demanded revenge for Ligulf. The church that was the Bishop's shelter was set alight. Some left its protection to plead mercy; and were murdered. It is said that Walcher persuaded Gilbert to go out and hand himself over; the rioters had their revenge as he was cut down upon stepping out of the church. And as the chief men of both sides tried to restore some sort of order, a chilling cry went up from the rioters, they wanted no more discussion: 'Good rede, short rede, sley ye the Bishop'. Walcher's cause was lost: 'The fire urged him to the swords of his enemies; the latter drove him back to the flames'. Eventually, preferring to face death by the blade, rather than by the flames and leaving Leobwin: 'whose death the crowd above all desired', to be the last to perish; Walcher paused at the church door, covered his face with his cloak, stepped out into the light, and the prophecy of Queen Editha was fulfilled. The monks of Jarrow eventually carried off Walcher's body: 'despoiled and hacked about'. He had been Bishop for just over nine years and his mortal remains were eventually buried at Durham.

The first foreign Bishop of Durham was dead. The local people, fired by anti-Norman feeling, rushed to Durham City and besieged the garrison there. After a few days, however, the seriousness of the situation was realised. They knew the King and what he was capable of, and they dispersed. On hearing of Walcher's murder, the King was determined, once and for all, to stamp Norman authority irreversibly upon the north. He sent his half-brother, Odo of Bayeux, to take summary vengeance and, duly obliging, he: 'ravaged the unfortunate province and confounded the innocent with the guilty in the undistinguishing severity of military execution'.

After Walcher, a new type of Bishop would appear. Men of great influence and ability who would eventually be granted semi-regal powers, and who would rule the North as the King ruled the rest of his realm. Men who would be, as it was put by Sir Timothy Eden: 'no mere puppets, dressed up in the semblance of power, no mere paraders of pomp and purple'. The Prince Bishops of Durham would rule over a land far away from the direct authority of the King, a land where the King's law was not upheld, but the Bishop's law; where the King's peace was not kept, but the Bishop's peace. While never turning their thoughts, and their power, towards directly challenging the word of the King, several chose simply to ignore it and such extensive powers would lead some of their number to become: 'among the most splendidly arrogant figures in English history'.

Part Two

By Divine Providence

The Prince Bishops of Durham

'There are two Kings in England, namely, the Lord King of England, wearing a crown in
sign of his regality, and the Lord Bishop of Durham, who wears a mitre instead of a
crown in sign of his regality in the Bishopric of Durham'
– Master William Boston, Steward to Bishop Antony Bek, 1302

The present day Bishops of Durham can trace their antecedents back, over 1,300 years of
history, to the original early Christian saints of seventh century Lindisfarne.

Their immediate predecessors, the Prince Bishops, or more correctly titled; Counts
Palatine of Durham are unique in English History. From Norman times until the days of
Henry VIII, they wielded semi-regal powers, granted to them by the King, to rule the
County Palatine of Durham as the King ruled the rest of his realm. They derived their
authority directly from the King and in matters temporal, answered only to the King, and
then, sometimes grudgingly. At the peak of their powers they ruled the County Palatine
virtually as an independent Kingdom, protecting the southern realm from invading
Scottish armies.

They were Bishops of the church and Counts of the Palatine lands; as Simeon of
Durham tells us: 'Both Priest and King'. Lords spiritual and temporal, their office
combined the religious authority of the spiritual successor to St Aidan and St Cuthbert,
with the military might of a great feudal lord. None were saints, many were sinners. Some
were pious and scholarly; others were great builders and benefactors to the people. A few
were greedy, ambitious and ruthless and some of their number were among the most
powerful ecclesiastical warlords of the middle ages. They were men of the highest level of
influence in the land. However, the church histories acknowledge: 'It must be owned, there
was much more of worldliness than of religion in the history of the Diocese'.

Their powers were considerable. They raised their own armies, and led them into battle.
They administered civil and criminal law, appointing their own Chancellors, Sheriffs, Judges
and Coroners. They created Barons of the Bishopric, who would in turn be obliged to
provide military service to the Bishop and acknowledge him as their liege lord. The Prince
Bishops levied their own taxes and coined their own money. They had the authority of the
King to pardon treasons and to take arms against, or to negotiate peace with the Scots. In the
great hunting forest, the Caza Magna of Weardale, the supreme jurisdiction was that of the
Bishop of Durham and not of the King. The Bishop had every right within the Bishopric that
the King had across the rest of the country: 'Thus, in theory, the Bishop was as a king in his
Bishopric'.

As their strength grew throughout the Norman and mediaeval years, they built a power
base in Durham, centered on the Cathedral and Castle that would last until the
Reformation. Their times were defined by wars, intrigues, excommunications and almost

constant power struggles with Barons, Popes, Kings and Archbishops; and frequently with the Monks of Durham. Often their backgrounds were widely different; from Antony Bek, Bishop of Durham, Count Palatine, Patriarch of Jerusalem and King of Man, to William Severs, the son of a sieve maker from Shincliffe; from Robert of Holy Island, a Lindisfarne monk, to Hugh of Le Puiset, nephew of King Stephen and, so he alleged, great grandson of William the Conqueror.

So it was that from Norman times, Durham began to acquire something of a reputation for having: 'turbulent priests' as incumbent Bishops. Their ancient authority lives on in their legacy. The Bishop of Durham has precedence over all English prelates except those of Canterbury, York and London. Styled not as Bishops: 'By Divine Permission', as are all other Bishops, but as Bishops: 'By Divine Providence'; sharing that dignity only with the Archbishops of Canterbury and York. And, as in Mediaeval times, so it is today, that at a Coronation, it is the Bishop of Durham, who supports the Monarch's right hand.

'Palatine – a term originating in the palace of the Byzantine Emperors, denotes…

A Governor of a Province with extensive delegated powers…and, at last, when these Governors grew sufficiently powerful to make themselves feared by their masters, a Feudal Prince, who owed little more than nominal subjection to the paramount Sovereign' – **Robert Surtees**

Chapter 4

He Destroys Well, Who Builds Something Better

William of St Carilef
'A Very Political Prelate'

After the murder at Gateshead of Walcher of Lorraine, William the Conqueror appointed the first Norman to the See of Durham.

William of St Carilef, sometimes written as William of St Calais, is chiefly remembered for two things, the removal of the ancient Community of St Cuthbert from Durham and its replacement with Benedictine monks; and the foundation of the great Norman cathedral that we see today. He is perhaps less well remembered for his political intrigues, for his involvement in a rebellion against the King, for being found guilty of treason; and for his role in the creation of one of the most important documents in British history; the *Domesday Book*.

A monk and a man of great ability, he had previously been elected Abbot of St Vincent in the County of Maine, Normandy. Well used to the political intrigues of an unruly border land, his abilities had come to the attention of the Conqueror: 'who found him assiduous in the conduct of difficult business'. A complex character, he would later be described by Simeon of Durham as: 'sober, frugal and chaste, of great eloquence and marvellous powers of memory'. Others, however, considered him an opportunist, a political gambler: 'In public matters his path was not clear, he had no principles to guide him, and his actions were swayed by selfishness'. St Carilef was, it has been said: 'a very political prelate, and in politics his conduct was not pretty'.

Consecrated as Bishop of Durham at Gloucester on 3 January 1081, in the presence of the Conqueror and all the Bishops and nobles of the land, he: 'succeeded to a troubled diocese'. But this was no gentle, ineffectual, Walcher; this was from the beginning a man: 'much in the company of the great men of his time'. Chief Justiciar of England, held in high favour. He continued to be so for the rest of the Conqueror's reign.

At the end of 1082, St Carilef was in Rome meeting Pope Gregory VII on the King's business. He used his time there to gain Papal approval for the creation of a Benedictine Chapter at Durham. He had already sought and received the support of the King and Queen for his actions. It was not an original idea, as his predecessor, Walcher had begun a move towards it in his time, but there may have been more pressing reasons for St Carilef. There was at the time a major monastic revival throughout Norman England encouraged by the King and by Lanfranc, the Archbishop of Canterbury: 'the monastic order had wholly lapsed into worldly corruption'. Rather than a radical reformer, St Carilef may simply have been promoting himself as a faithful implementer of the religious trends of the time. The move was probably more than just that of a new bishop making his mark on the Diocese.

The old Community of St Cuthbert had been in continuous existence since the Saint's death in AD687, and since arriving at Durham it had held great political sway, with links to the ancient royal house of the Northumbrians. That same Community was made up of the successors to the monks that had begun their journey from Lindisfarne over 200 years before and had watched over St Cuthbert's Shrine since their arrival in Durham in AD995. But a religious way of life had lapsed. Clerical celibacy was not strictly enforced. This was a Community in a very real sense of the word, with the clerics having wives and families. Probably more importantly, St Carilef may well have considered the Community a possible rallying point for further English rebellion. The guardians of the holy remains of the Patron Saint still attracted strong loyalties from the Northumbrian people. Control was needed; order had to be restored.

So it was that in May 1083, William ejected the secular Community of St Cuthbert, and 23 Benedictine monks were brought to Durham from Jarrow and Wearmouth; who bound themselves to the service of the Saint: 'the monks were given to the Church, and the Church given to them'; together with the lion's share of its extensive landed estates between the Tyne and the Tees. St Carilef also bestowed churches upon the new Benedictine chapter. Among these was, with no little irony, the church at Lindisfarne and as Richardson tells us, a cell of monks was immediately established on the island: 'and they called the new settlement, no longer Lindisfarne, but Holy Island'. The ancient Community of St Cuthbert, except for their Dean, who alone accepted the invitation to become a Benedictine monk, was dispersed to the collegiate churches of Norton, Auckland and Darlington. From then on, as Simeon records, the Durham monks, perhaps not surprisingly, considered St Carilef a: 'kindly, prudent and wise ruler'; and Durham would remain a great Benedictine monastery for another four and a half centuries.

St Carilef was a clever man, often in the company of the King himself and throughout the reign of William I he was a: 'valued counsellor of the King of whom all stood in awe'. At Christmas, 1085, he was with the King when the Conqueror held his mid-winter court at Gloucester. Almost 20 years since victory at the Battle of Hastings, his military conquest of England was complete; if still precarious. But another kind of conquest was about to begin. There was rumour of unrest, of possible further rebellion in the North of his kingdom; there were even whispers of a possible invasion from Scandinavia. He had to be fully aware of what resources; money, fighting men, feudal obligations, would be available to him, if needed. The King determined to find out exactly who held what in his Kingdom of England, what was due to him and what more could be taken.

The Anglo-Saxon Chronicle, almost lamenting, tells that for five days the King and his chief advisers: 'had much thought and very deep discussion about this country, how it was occupied, with what sorts of people…then he sent his men all over England, into every Shire'. So began a vast taxation survey. England was divided up into seven circuits, made up of groups of Counties. In each circuit, the inquisition would be carried out by Royal Commissioners sitting in Shire Courts, with officers and scribes in attendance. These men would have been high ranking, trusted allies of the King. For the most part, their identity has been lost to the passage of time. But one of the very few names to be handed down, as Commissioner for the South Western circuit, was the Bishop of Durham, William of St Carilef. The survey work was carried out quickly, the first returns being produced in the second half of 1086. The Chronicler tells us that nothing escaped the inquisition of the King's Commissioners: 'for so very narrowly did he have it investigated, that there was no

Lindisfarne Priory: 'and they called the new settlement, no longer Lindisfarne, but Holy Island'.

single hide nor yard of land, nor indeed (it is a shame to relate but it seemed no shame to him to do) one oxen, nor one cow, nor one pig, which was left out'. But the survey was more than just a tax survey. By asking the questions that it did: 'What was there in the reign of King Edward the Confessor? What was given by King William? What is there now?' William was identifying Edward the Confessor as his legitimate predecessor and removing the brief reign of the last English King, Harold, from the written records of state.

At a great ceremony at Old Sarum, Salisbury, on the 1 August 1086, a large number of all the nobles in the land confirmed their oath of allegiance to William the Conqueror. At the same ceremony, the King was presented with the first folios of his completed survey. Its decisions and its contents were final and could not be questioned. So, as the Day of Judgment, from which no man is spared and against which there is no appeal, it would come to be known as the *Domesday Book*. Everything contained in it could be taken or given away by the King. All taxes and feudal duties due to him from his subjects, from the greatest lord to the humblest farmer, were recorded in it; a confirmation of their subjugation. William had been handed his Kingdom of England, in a book; he had conquered the country again.

The *Domesday Book* would be one of the most important documents in English history, still referred to as a source of legal precedent in the 1960s, almost 900 years after its creation. The survey itself had been a massive undertaking, even underpinned, as it was, by the existing and for its time, advanced machinery of state which had been developed by the Anglo-Saxons. Experts have suggested that the *Domesday Book* survey was probably the brain-child of one man, an intelligent, influential and trusted ally of the King. Though none can be certain, a name that has been more than whispered of as being: 'The Man behind the *Domesday Book* Survey', is William of St Carilef, Bishop of Durham.

So Bishop William was probably at the peak of his career and influence at the Conqueror's court. But in September 1087, William the Conqueror died. His second son, William Rufus, was quickly crowned King of England. William of St Carilef, so high in the court of the father, briefly maintained his position in that of the son. But it has been said of St Carilef that: 'in public affairs his subtlety led him into intrigue' and in 1088 his political game playing saw him tried as a traitor and exiled.

A rebellion, led by the Conqueror's half brother and the King's uncle; Odo, Bishop of Bayeux, sought to have William Rufus replaced as King of England by the Conqueror's eldest son Robert, Duke of Normandy. Almost all the major Norman Barons were involved, moved primarily by self interest. By dividing his joint realms of England and Normandy between two of his sons, the Conqueror had created a problem for the Barons. Most owned estates in both England and Normandy. Should there be any future enmity between the two royal brothers; allegiances would be difficult, royal patronage, uncertain; the extensive and valuable possessions of the great Norman landholders, hard won under the Conqueror, would be put under threat.

William Rufus, King of England, was the younger son. He was unpredictable, violent and self-willed. Robert, Duke of Normandy, was the eldest, and as such his claim to overall kingship probably had more weight. Besides his nature was different to that of Rufus, he was more likely to be amenable to the wishes of the Barons. And those wishes were for a single stable kingship to secure the Norman Realm and of course to secure their own landed interests.

For such a formidable array of Norman military power, the insurrection was short lived and there was very little actual fighting. The chronicler, Orderic Vitalis noted: 'The rebels, although they were so many and abundantly furnished with arms and supplies, did not dare to join battle with the King in his kingdom'. A list was drawn up of Norman nobles and magnates who were party to the rebellion, on it only one high-ranking Norman churchman appeared, the Bishop of Durham, William of St Carilef. All the other English dioceses supported Rufus. The reason for St Carilef's defection from Rufus to Robert is unknown. He had begun his career at Odo's cathedral at Bayeux, so perhaps he felt some allegiance to the Bishop. Robert de Mowbray, Earl of Northumbria, also stood against the King, so perhaps St Carilef thought it politically sensible, in this part of the world, to show support for him. He may have simply followed the thinking that in the matter of succession to a Kingdom, the claims of the eldest son were difficult to deny. Perhaps he agreed with the Barons that unless the Conqueror's realm was unified it was in danger of collapse. But St Carilef had a: 'fertile and subtle mind'. Perhaps he thought that if there was going to be a rebellion, Robert, a character certainly more amenable to the Church than Rufus, was simply a better bet. If so, his gamble failed, the rebellion was put down and St Carilef was in serious trouble. The monk and chronicler, Simeon of Durham, gives a full, though hardly unbiased account of the events that followed in his: *History of the unjust Persecution of the first Bishop William; inflicted by King William, the son of the great King William.*

Rufus immediately seized lands held personally by the Bishop, and those held by the Church of Durham and directed that the Bishop should be placed under arrest: 'and many was the snare which he laid for him'. Without any hesitation, St Carilef dispatched a messenger to Rufus, complaining that the King's men had imprisoned his retainers and seized his lands, entreating the King not: 'to treat me so basely and to dispossess me so unjustly', and requested the King to immediately restore his men, his lands and his money. The King did not and decreed that, for his part in the rebellion, St Carilef would be tried, not under Canon Law as a Bishop, but under the King's law, as a Tenant-in-Chief. The Bishop continued to argue from his Durham stronghold and insisted on a trial under Canon Law: 'For it is not the province of anyone to judge a Bishop'. He pleaded the privileges of his order and offered to purge himself of the charge of treason by his personal oath. The King refused and persisted with his demand that St Carilef be tried as a layman. The Bishop of Durham, however, was unbowed, and continued to manoeuvre. The King then instructed St Carilef to come to him and gave assurances of his safe conduct, and of his liberty to return to Durham in safety. But when the Bishop was about to set off in answer to the royal summons, the assurances of this particular King seemed to become something less than reliable.

A request had been made to Ralph Paganell, Sheriff of York, asking him to acknowledge the royal protection granted to the Bishop and his retinue on leaving the Bishopric of Durham. But Paganell refused safe conduct, not only to the Bishop but to all his retainers and messengers; and he confirmed his words with his actions. One unfortunate messenger monk, trying to return from the King's court to Durham, was arrested by Paganell, who after killing his horse, eventually permitted him to escape back to the Bishop on foot. According to Simeon, Paganell also encouraged the King's subjects to cause as much trouble for the Bishop, in whatever way they could and because of this, St Carlief argued, he was unable, safely, to come to the King. But Rufus was not a person to be trifled with. No great respecter of the Church and openly irreligious, of explosive temper, vindictive in nature and ruthless in dealing with those who opposed him; many unfortunate subjects felt the wrath of William the Red.

He commanded the attendance of the Bishop of Durham. St Carilef, undaunted, again wrote back, insisting upon further assurances of safe conduct; for the haughty Bishop of Durham was a man who had not easily bowed before the Conqueror himself; still less before the son. Openly questioning the word of the King he reminded Rufus of the actions of: 'This Paganell', both in refusing him the protection ordered by Rufus and denouncing the Bishop as an enemy, on the King's behalf. Going on, he said that: 'by your writ, you gave me your protection to come to you in safety, to stay with you and return home'. He concluded by requiring the King to restore his property: 'of which you have deprived me without reason and without judgement'. If this was done, St Carilef gave his assurance that he would attend the King's court. So it was that his safe conduct was again granted and the Bishop came at last to the King. But the Bishop again insisted on being tried as a Bishop. The King again said no, he would be tried, as had been the Bishop of Bayeux in the time of the Conqueror, as a Tenant-in-Chief; and after being refused any counsel with his fellow churchmen, St Carilef returned again to Durham.

He wrote further letters to the King, arguing his right to be judged as a Bishop. On their receipt, the King promptly imprisoned the unfortunate Durham monk who had delivered them and sent his soldiers against the Bishop. When the King's men began to lay waste to the Bishop's lands, the intention of Rufus was all too obvious. At last St Carilef had to bow to the inevitable and agree to appear before the King's Court, but only after it was settled that, in his absence, his castle would be held for him by three of his own Durham Barons; and after winning an assurance that: 'if found guilty, he should be at liberty to go beyond the sea'. His trial was set for November 1088.

So it was that on 2 November the court met at Salisbury. Lanfranc, Archbishop of Canterbury, spoke for the King. St Carilef opened by complaining that the King had sent messages to the Durham Barons commanding them to do to the Bishop: 'all the mischief they could possibly inflict'. He continued by raising objections at every turn. He was a: 'skillful lawyer and a clever and copious speaker'. He objected that his fellow Bishops were not allowed to give him counsel, and made the point that it had been made impossible for them to do so as they were sitting in judgement upon him, as part of the court. He declared that he would only answer to Archbishops and he would speak direct to the King; this was denied. Simeon tells us that the King told St Carlilef: 'Consult with your own friends; of our side not one single individual shall confer with you'. To which the Bishop countered: 'These seven men who stand with me, have but little counsel to weigh against the power and the wisdom of the whole of the realm, which I see ranged against me'. St Carilef then requested to lodge an appeal to the Pope; this also was denied, to which the Bishop responded: 'but to Rome I go, to sue for the aid of God and St Peter'. Finally, the King, growing angry and bringing proceedings to an end said: 'Be assured of it for a truth, Bishop, you shall not on any account return to Durham, nor shall your men under any pretence remain in Durham, nor shall you escape from my hands until you have given up your castle unconditionally'. It was clear that, after all his political manoeuvring and his legal arguments, his cause was lost. William of St Carilef, Bishop of Durham, was found guilty of treason and sentenced to exile. With a parting shot at the Archbishops, Bishops and Nobles sitting in judgement against him, he complained about the injustice that he saw being done to him: 'there is not one single

Durham Cathedral: 'He destroys well, who builds something better.'

Bishop St Carilef's Cathedral.

individual among you all, who dares, either as judge or witness, to utter a single word which may be displeasing to the King'

His trial was ended, his fate decided, but still he raised new points; about his safe conduct to Normandy, about the delivery of Durham Castle, about the King's ships which were to take him abroad; he refused to give any assurances about their safe return once they had reached Normandy. Eventually, St Carilef was given a guarantee of safe conduct upon finally giving up Durham Castle. He was allowed to take with him as many of his own men that wished to go with him and he prepared to sail across the sea; but not before managing to negotiate an allowance of money for his own maintenance, while in exile. So it was that on 14 November 1088, Ivo Tailbois and Ernesius de Buron took possession of Durham Castle for King William Rufus. After some further delay, William of St Carilef sailed away into exile. When, as Simeon tells us he: 'passed the sea, and having been welcomed by the Earl of Normandy, spent the three years of his residence with him, in great honour, not as an exile, but as a Father'. Indeed, it is said by some, that Robert of Normandy, eldest son of William the Conqueror, entrusted the Bishop with the management of the whole Duchy.

Of course Simeon was a monk of Durham and he pointedly does not mention in his account of St Carilef's: 'Unjust Persecution' the undeniable fact that the Bishop had in fact sided against the King in a rebellion which sought to put the King's elder brother, Robert of Normandy on the throne of England.

But it has been said that: 'St Carilef's recoveries were as remarkable as his lapses' and eventually he was reconciled with William Rufus. While in Normandy he had raised a siege of one of the King's garrisons, in addition, Pope Urban II had remonstrated with Rufus over his: 'ill treatment' of the Bishop of Durham. Probably more importantly, Robert and William were themselves reconciled by the threat of an invasion of England by the Scots. So it was that in 1091, William of St Carilef was restored to his See and in the September of that year the people of Durham witnessed the return of their Bishop. And what a return it must have been, as the Bishop arrived alongside both Rufus and Robert, on their march north against Malcolm of Scotland. The reputation of St Carilef among his Durham monks was no doubt even further enhanced as, on his arrival with the King of England and the Duke of Normandy, a Scottish army which had been blockading Durham was dispersed.

illief had also returned from exile with lavish gifts for his church, including many valuable liturgical books which would form the basis of a great library, some of which can still be seen in the Cathedral today; and importantly for Durham, a new architectural vision.

The existing Anglo-Saxon cathedral at Durham was less than 100 years old. St Carilef, again following the Norman trend of building larger structures on the sites of smaller Saxon buildings, now began work on a new Cathedral. On Friday 29 July 1093, the Bishop, together with the Prior began to dig the foundations, and on Thursday 11 August the foundation stones were laid in the presence of St Carilef, Prior Turgot and King Malcolm of Scotland, who was on route south to Gloucester for peace talks with William Rufus. Once again St Carilef was high in royal favour, spending Christmas 1093 at the King's Court. Indeed, he had perhaps become the most eminent Norman churchman in England. It is not known if the new Cathedral was of St Carilef's own design, but he certainly would have seen examples of Romanesque architecture during his exile on the continent. He could not, however, have been much at Durham during its early construction because of the demands of his offices of state.

In 1095, a row broke out between the King and the Archbishop of Canterbury. Lanfranc had gone and the new Primate was the monk and ascetic, Anselm of Bec. The dispute was referred to a great council at Rockingham on 25 February of that year. The King's cause was led by the Bishop of Durham. Anselm would not answer to the council, arguing his rights under Canon, not secular law. St Carilef, seemingly without any scruples whatsoever, vigorously promoted the King's arguments against Anselm, the very same arguments that he had so exhaustively argued against in his own case. So much so that he would later be accused by his enemies of having his own eyes on the Primacy, on the successful dismissal of Anselm. But this time St Carilef's eloquence did not succeed, the council was inconclusive, the situation unchanged, and St Carilef's reputation was damaged. In the same year Robert de Mowbray, Earl of Northumbria, rebelled again against the King and was eventually imprisoned for life. Again, St Carilef's role in this rebellion has been described as: 'ambiguous'. He was suspected of complicity and was sent for by the King. Claiming ill health, he refused to go. The King then demanded that he attend the Christmas court at Windsor. He had no choice but to answer the King's call, but he was dying. On Christmas Day 1095, he took to his bed, and: 'in his last illness he was comforted by the great men of the church', including Anselm. William of St Carilef, the first Norman Bishop of Durham, conceiver of: 'the purest and noblest specimen of Romanesque architecture in England', died, at dawn, on 2 January 1096. It had been suggested that he be buried in his new cathedral at Durham, but, according to Simeon, St Carilef did not think himself worthy to lie near St Cuthbert, requesting instead: 'bury me in the Chapter House, where my tomb will always be before your eyes'. His wishes were carried out: 'amid the tears and lamentations of the monks'. With the passing of Robert de Mowbray, the Earls of Northumbria were no more. So it was that their military and civil jurisdiction over the northern lands began to be assimilated by the Bishops of Durham. These extensive secular powers, in addition to the spiritual authority of the guardian of St Cuthbert's Lands would eventually be vested in one man, the Bishop and Count Palatine; known to later generations as the Prince Bishop of Durham.

A Norman noble, Goscelin de St Bertin, summed up the Norman trend in architecture: 'I hate small buildings', he said: 'Frankly, I would not allow buildings to stay standing, even if everyone liked them, unless they were glorious, magnificently big, very tall and spacious and simply beautiful. He destroys well, who builds something better'. At Durham, William of St Carilef: 'a man without principles in public matters', began work on his masterpiece of Norman architecture. But it was more than this, more even than a great church. It was, together with the Castle, a visible symbol of Norman authority. English craftsmen may have built it, and an English saint protected it, but as a symbol of power it spoke loud, and it said: 'Normandy is King and God her suzerain lord'

Chapter 5

Mainspring of the King's Iniquity

Rannulf Flambard
'That Picturesque Ruffian'

So William of St Carilef, the founder of Durham's great Norman Cathedral was dead. The See would now remain vacant for three and a half years. This was a time of intrigue and political in-fighting, in the Church establishment as much as in the King's Court. A time when careers could be made and fortunes could be amassed; by the right kind of people. As William Hutchinson relates to us: 'Justice, temperance and religion, were rare qualities in this era'. And it was onto this stage that appeared the notorious Rannulf Flambard.

He became Bishop of Durham in the summer of 1099; the same summer that saw the capture of Jerusalem by soldiers of the First Crusade and the subsequent massacre of thousands of Muslim inhabitants of the city; and the death in Valencia of the Spanish hero, Rodrigo Diaz of Bivar, known to history, and to Hollywood, as El Cid. But according to the chronicler William of Malmesbury, Flambard became Bishop only after paying the King one thousand marks for the See of Durham.

Described by the Durham Historian, Robert Surtees, as: 'destitute alike of the influences of birth or education and not restrained by the influences of any religious sentiment', Flambard, Chaplain and Chief Financial Minister to King William Rufus, has always had a mixed press. However, Lawrence, the chronicler monk of Durham, suggested that Durham owed more to Flambard than to any other Bishop: 'his was a spirit worthy of Durham, worthy of riches, worthy of honour'. Lawrence continued: 'that was our golden age, under Rannulf our Bishop'. What then are we to make of: 'that mainspring of the King's iniquity…the inciter of his covetousness' Rannulf Flambard?

He came from humble beginnings, from, it was said: 'the dregs of the people'. His father, Turstin, was a monk of the diocese of Bayeux and Rannulf, so the Anglo-Norman chronicler Orderic Vitalis tells us: 'was educated from boyhood with the base parasites among the hangers on' but he rapidly rose in the service of Maurice, Bishop of London. Rannulf was one of the: 'new men' of Norman England, clerical bureaucrats who benefited from royal patronage and who, according to Orderic were: 'underlings, who were exalted by granting them wide honours as a reward for flattery'. Later, after applying to Maurice for the Deanery of London, and being refused, he was by way of compensation so the chronicles record, even though: 'he had scarce any learning, and not so much as an external show of religion', made Chaplain to King William Rufus: 'and from this moment his rise was rapid'. In time, through ability and cunning, he became Chief Minister to the King. Rannulf would have been well aware that for someone in his position, there were unprecedented opportunities. He proved himself to be an excellent administrator and he also has been associated with the Domesday project. Being, as he was, at the centre of the machinery of government, he has been identified by some scholars as possibly being responsible for, or at least taking a leading role in, the collection and amalgamation of information from the Survey and the drafting of the Domesday Documents. So, although it may never be known for certain, it has been suggested that if William of St Carilef was the man behind the Domesday Survey, then Rannulf Flambard was the man behind the *Domesday Book* itself.

But the church historians hated Rannulf almost as much as they hated the King, and it is largely because churchmen wrote the histories that they were both given such particularly black reputations. Rufus was openly irreligious and treated the church as: 'a rich corporation which needed soaking'. Of Flambard it has been said, perhaps understatedly, that in him: 'it was difficult to find any sign of a refined spirituality'. A story, perhaps apocryphal, was told of when after witnessing an Ordeal by Fire, during which those accused had passed through unhurt; Flambard is said to have exclaimed: 'By St Luke's face! I will never again believe, after this, that God is a just judge'. The church histories have recorded that he proved an able and enthusiastic servant: 'the chief agent of the King's will'. Whatever the King demanded of his subjects, Rannulf would exact double what was required. Orderic Vitalis, never it seems, a fan of Rannulf, even accused him of trying to persuade Rufus to revise the Domesday Survey, to enable him to confiscate from his subjects, all that was found above a certain quantity. His name became notorious, he was the King's man and was universally hated, but: 'William congratulated himself on having a minister who cared not whom he displeased, so he served his sovereign's ends'. By 1096, Rannulf had become such a trusted steward of the King that he was exercising vice-regal powers over judicial and financial matters during the King's absences in Normandy. King's Chaplain, Justiciar, and chief tax collector; Rannulf effectively supervised royal administration in England. But a man like Rannulf made enemies and so it was that plotters drew up their plans for his demise.

A certain individual named Gerold, who was known to Rannulf from his time in the service of the Bishop of London, arranged to meet him on the banks of the Thames. He had a message, the Bishop was dying and wished to see Rannulf before the end. Rannulf was persuaded to board a boat to be taken down the river to the dying prelate. The real destination, however, was a ship about to take to sea. Rannulf was held and forced aboard. With no armed guards to protect him, he was quickly separated from his servants but had the presence of mind to break the official seals he was carrying: 'lest some improper use be made of them'. The fate of Flambard seemed clear. He was to be dispatched and cast into the sea. His would be assassins, somewhat prematurely, began to argue over his clothes, their payment for the deed; in particular they coveted his fine cloak. They prevaricated as the ship was made ready for the tide. But the wind changed and a storm suddenly blew up. Perhaps they thought it an ill omen; this was, after all, the King's man. As they dallied, Rannulf, defiant as always, convinced Gerold, through persuasion or bribery, to return him safely to the shore: 'Slave what fearest thou? Knowest thou not that thou carriest the fortunes of Flambard?' So Rannulf escaped his assassins, returned to the King:

'And to the dismay of his enemies, a few days after they supposed they had got rid of him, he appeared again among them'.

After the King, Rannulf was possibly the most influential man in England. William of Malmesbury describes him as: 'Manager of the whole Kingdom'. The histories tell that they suited each other well: 'both of them very clever, both of them very proud, and without a single scruple between them'. Malmesbury goes on to claim that Rannulf: 'skinned the rich, ground down the poor, and swept other men's inheritances into his net'. William Rufus, the second son of the Conqueror was stocky and red faced. The taxes he levied were spent on his military campaigns abroad or bestowed on his loyal followers. In terms of: 'style', his

Court was far removed from that of his father's. Gone were the severe, crop headed: 'Soldiers of God' and in their place were favourites with fine clothes and long hair. Sober brutality had been replaced by decadent indulgence: 'effeminate fashions, vices horrible and unheard of in England, flourished at his Court and threatened to corrupt the nation'. As for Rufus himself, it has been said: 'He every morning got up a worse man than he lay down, and every evening, lay down a worse man than he got up'.

William Rufus' reign was particularly notorious for his exploitation of church revenues, by keeping bishoprics vacant and appropriating their considerable income for himself. An arrangement encouraged and put on a businesslike footing by Rannulf. The wealthy and influential See of Durham had been vacant for over three years when Rannulf allegedly paid the King for the Bishopric. The church establishment was outraged, and Rannulf would later be asked to answer for his actions to the Pope. In the meantime, however, he continued to encourage Rufus's extravagances, and many stories, some, again no doubt apocryphal, grew up around them. It was said that when on a royal progress they would even have their horses' hooves washed with wine: 'They had the claws of a Harpy, the extravagance of a Cleopatra, and the shamelessness of both'. Anselm, the saintly Archbishop of Canterbury, could not countenance Rannulf, describing him as being: 'by profession a priest, but in fact not only a tax collector but the most infamous prince of tax collectors'. He would later despatch to the Pope, a series of charges of crimes allegedly committed by Rannulf, both before and after his appointment as Bishop. The Pope would in turn write to Rannulf, ordering him to clear himself of the charges which, if true, were enough, not only to have the Bishopric of Durham taken from him, but also to have him defrocked. Events, however, were to intervene.

Rannulf's notorious early career came to an end on 2 August 1100, when his patron, William Rufus was killed by an arrow, apparently accidentally, while hunting in the New Forest. Coincidentally, also in the New Forest that day was William's younger brother, Henry, who wasted no time in having himself crowned King Henry I. But the new King had to distance himself from the unpopularity of his brother's reign. He needed a scapegoat, and the reputation of the Bishop of Durham, Rannulf Flambard, served his purpose well: 'for he was universally hated'. Rannulf was arrested on a charge of: 'Malversation'; essentially, misbehavior in office and embezzlement and on 15 August imprisoned in the Tower of London, under the custody of William de Magnaville, the first ever prisoner to be held in the Conqueror's fortress. Rannulf was down, but certainly not out. As well as what friends brought him he was given an allowance of two shillings a day for his keep, so prison life was tolerable. But on 3 February 1101, by a mixture of cunning and raw courage, he made his escape. It has been suggested, rather prosaically, that for political reasons he was: 'allowed' to escape and leave the shores of the new King's realm. It is also possible that he could have simply bribed his was out of custody. But as with the rest of Flambard's life, the story of his escape which has been handed down for posterity is far more colourful than that. It fits well with his reputation; and of course, it might be true.

He had arranged for a large flagon of wine to be sent to him, in which was concealed a length of rope. After getting his guards drunk, celebrating the Feast of Candlemass, he made his move. Fastening the rope to the central pillar of the window and slinging his pastoral staff over his shoulder, the Bishop of Durham climbed through the window and shinned down the wall. The story tells that he neglected to wear gloves and, being a hefty man, his hands were cut to the bone by the rope. The rope was too short and he had to fall a considerable distance to the ground below, being injured in the process. But Flambard's friends were there to meet him, and he escaped to Normandy, taking with him his aged mother who, according to his enemies, was a Witch with one eye. So the Bishop of Durham, the first prisoner to be held in the mighty Tower of London, had become the first to escape from it. He was welcomed by Duke Robert, Henry's elder brother, and proceeded to play a dangerous game of playing one royal brother off against the other. As the historian, H.S. Offler remarked:

'During the next five years, this resilient man conducted himself so deviously as to defeat historians' attempts to elucidate the complications of the double game he played between Henry and Robert'.

It may well have been Rannulf who persuaded Robert to invade England and take the Kingdom from his brother, the invasion landing at Portsmouth in the summer of 1101. But the brothers did not fight. Robert's army marched on London, but at Alton, in Hampshire, negotiations took place and a peace treaty was signed. Robert gave up his claim to the throne of England in return for an annual payment of three thousand Marks and an assurance that: 'the refugees of both courts would be allowed to return and have their former dignities restored'. Flambard was back! Indeed some commentators have suggested that he had more than a passing involvement in the drafting of the Treaty. There were at least 12 Royal Charters concerned with his return. Charters regarding his safe conduct, the restitution of all his possessions and his complete absolution by the Archbishops of York and Canterbury, even though Rannulf had never sworn any profession of obedience to either of them. So most of what Rannulf once had, was returned to him. But one thing he never gained was the trust of King Henry, and much of Rannulf's influence in matters of state was lost to him. His considerable energy was now turned to his Bishopric of Durham.

There would always be mistrust between Rannulf and the Durham monks. They suspected that he might attempt to take for himself the generous endowments of wealth and land granted to them by his predecessor; which he did. In turn, Rannulf was suspicious that the monks had forged charters granting themselves lands and rights; which they had. The plain fact was that unlike his predecessor, Rannulf had little in common with the Benedictine Order.

Nonetheless, for the rest of his career in Durham, this larger-than-life Bishop: 'employed his revenues in various honourable and munificent labours'. Work on the Cathedral advanced, Rannulf redirecting altar offerings and burial fees, which, by right, should have gone to the monks; into financing the work. Under Flambard, the Nave and aisles were completed up to the roof, the great western door added, and the lower part of the western towers built. Eventually, construction of the Cathedral became far enough advanced to allow for the body of St Cuthbert to be moved from its temporary shrine on what is now the Cloister Green. As Bishop, Rannulf would preside over the proceedings. The date was set for 29 August 1104, over 417 years after the death of the Saint. It was also decided that, as befitting such a solemn and sacred occasion, the coffin should be opened before its final internment, to ensure that the body remained in the same blessed state as it had been in AD698, 11 years after Cuthbert's death. The: 'Cult of St Cuthbert' and the continuing pre-eminence and well being of the Durham monastery demanded no less.

So it was that five days before the official internment, the Prior and nine Durham monks investigated. According to Simeon they found Cuthbert lying on his right side, his

Durham Castle towers over Framwellgate: 'Flambard's' Bridge.

body still incorrupt and his joints flexible. It seemed the Saint simply slept. The news was of course, received by the monastery with great joy, and no doubt a certain amount of relief, but there were doubters; Rannulf himself not least among them. Why had the coffin been opened at night? Why had nobody independent of the Durham monastery been allowed to be present? It was agreed that the procedure should be carried out again, this time, in public. Once again the Saint was disturbed but it was clear for all to see that the body was indeed, how it had been described. In front of independent witnesses the arms were again flexed and the body raised up, almost to a sitting position. The doubters were now convinced, the sceptics finally silenced. Final preparations could now be made for the Saint's official internment.

At last the day of the great occasion dawned. Before ceremonial burial, the Saint's coffin, covered in the Bishop's magnificent green cope, richly embroidered with large Griffons, was carried around the outside of the Cathedral with Rannulf himself, holding aloft a copy of the Gospel of St John and: 'various relics of other saints going before'. An immense crowd, including Alexander, the future King of Scotland, had gathered who: 'from very joy burst into tears and fell flat on the ground'. The solemn procession then halted at the east end of the Cathedral, where Rannulf delivered a lengthy sermon: 'The day had far advanced, and the Bishop kept preaching on and on, touching many points, not all appropriate to the solemnity, and fairly wearing out the patience of his hearers by the prolixity of his discourse'.

The wise words of Flambard were only brought to an end by a: 'miraculous' heavy rain shower, which dispersed his congregation and drove the bearers of the Saint's body, with unseemly haste, inside the Cathedral, where St Cuthbert was finally interred, in the place familiar to today's generations, and where he would remain undisturbed for another 437 years.

Rannulf would also make improvements to the City. He built St Giles Church, at Gilesgate; which was dedicated in June 1112 and in the same year he founded Kepier

Hospital for the poor. Three years later he granted land at Finchale to the hermit Godric, who was regarded as a living saint; and he threw Framwellgate Bridge, Durham City's: 'Old Bridge', across the River Wear. He also cleared the growing cluster of dwellings around the Cathedral: 'He made as clear and level as a field the space between the Cathedral and Castle, which had been invaded by numerous dwelling places, lest the Church be soiled by their filth or imperiled by the fires, thereby giving us Palace Green'; or Place Green, as it was originally known. He also began to fortify against attack or invasion. In 1121, work was begun on Norham Castle, in Northumberland, as a forward defensive measure against the Scots. In Durham, he began building the City Wall: 'betwixt the Cathedral and the Castle', the wall that would eventually fortify the entire 58 acre peninsula, which, in the 16th century, John Leland would describe as: 'Alonely caullid the waulled toune of Duresme'. So it was that the walled City of Durham became a military stronghold, where it may truly be said, that the Cathedral stood inside the Castle.

Already a senior figure in the church, Flambard, always restless and energetic, now established himself as a great baronial lord. His personal motto had always been: 'Either first, or up with the leaders'. He granted many gifts of land, mainly to his relatives, but also to other: 'loyal subjects', in effect, founding some of the great family dynasties of Durham; the Barons of the Bishopric. Indeed, it can perhaps be seen that under Flambard, the semi-autonomous status of the County Palatine of Durham began to be defined. He appointed Sheriffs, answerable to himself and not to the King. His hunting rights and Forest Laws were, by Royal Charter of 1107, independent of and as strictly adhered to, as the King's own. Indeed, the Bishop of Durham's great hunting forest of Weardale was second in size only to the King's own New Forest.

Towards the end of his life, Rannulf, perhaps to atone for the misdeeds of his early days, after paying off his debts, began making generous gifts to the monks and to the poor: 'not only when solicited, but also of his own accord'. A story tells that when he thought he was dying or, as some have suggested, pretended that he thought that he was dying, he had himself carried into the Cathedral, to the High Altar, there to offer up his gold signet ring: 'as a pledge of restitution to his bretheren'. When, on 5 September 1128, he did eventually die; he left four sons, all with positions in the church establishment, and a number of assorted nephews, other relatives and friendly barons, all holding large estates in Durham, granted by himself. He had been Bishop of Durham for 29 years, and left the Bishopric considerably wealthier than it had been before he came. On Flambard's death, King Henry immediately seized all his goods and committed the running of the Bishopric to two of his own Barons. Then, as his brother, on the advice of Flambard himself, had done before him; the King kept the See of Durham vacant for five years, before a new Bishop was elected.

Yet the reputation of Rannulf Flambard survived long after his death. Before becoming Bishop of Durham, he'd had a mistress, and Englishwoman named Alveva, who had borne him two of his sons. On becoming Bishop he married her off but remained on good terms with her and her spouse, often staying with them during his journeys away from Durham. On one of these visits he met Alveva's 16-year-old niece Christina, and the story of his behaviour during this particular meeting would be told long after his death. For the young Christina would, in later years, commit to a life of chastity, become a recluse and later Prioress of Markyate, near St Albans. In 1150 the incident was recounted in the: *Life of Christina of Markyate*. In it a claim was made that during Rannulf's visit in 1114, he had tried to seduce her but her quick thinking had avoided the worst. It was alleged that, after

Palace: 'Place' Green, cleared by Flambard lies in the Cathedral's shadow.

ensuring her parents were drunk, Rannulf had the young girl brought to his bedchamber and when his intentions were made clear, Christina suggested that it would be better if she locked the door. This she did, but leaving herself on the outside and the Bishop within. So was the old rogue foiled in his amorous intentions? He has of course been accused of having: 'a great economy of scruples'. Or was the story merely an apocryphal one to demonstrate the piety and chastity of Christina? He was no longer around to defend himself but the reputation of Rannulf Flambard was one around which shadows grew.

It has been said that: 'Flambard's whole life exhibits a tissue of violence and ambition, illuminated by a few splendid traits of generosity and magnificence'.

However, Lawrence, the faithful chronicler of Durham, suggested that: 'Durham demands such a man; great in spirit, liberal in spending, for Durham is no empty shell for the man who holds it'.

H.E.H. Jerningham, writing in 1883, thought that: 'his indomitable pluck and strength of will, his knowledge of human failings, his perseverance, his diplomacy, mark him for ever as one of the greatest prelates of this realm; if indeed, we cannot give him a place among its worthiest'.

Perhaps more importantly, by his grants of land, his building and fortification, his development of the laws and administration of the Bishopric of Durham and its growing independence from the King, this: 'Picturesque Ruffian', laid the foundation for the truly feudal County Palatine of Durham, that the later warrior Bishops would know as their own.

There is a footnote to the career of Rannulf Flambard. When his grave was discovered and opened, it was found to contain the bones of a sturdily built man, who would have stood about five feet nine inches tall. The grave also contained the remains of the Bishop's pastoral staff; his Crozier. Most of the wooden shaft had disintegrated over the centuries

Finchale Priory, built on land granted to St Godric, by Rannulf Flambard.

but the fine Crozier head had survived; silver covered, intricately carved with interlacing animals and thought possibly to have been of Danish origin. There was also present the Bishop's Episcopal ring; gold, with a dark, pyramid shaped sapphire. Both can now be seen as part of the Treasures of St Cuthbert at Durham Cathedral. Looking at them today, it is easy to imagine that very Crozier head decorating the same staff that Rannulf flung over his shoulder during his escape from the Tower of London; and that same Episcopal ring being placed on the High Altar by the Bishop himself, in spiritual restitution to his Durham brethren, as his time drew near.

Also discovered in the grave was a quantity of charcoal, upon which the body was thought to have been laid. The presence in such a burial of charcoal, which would probably have originally been infused with incense, is thought by some archaeologists to have an important symbolic significance; representing penance and the state of the soul of the deceased. Was this, it is to be wondered, a final gesture by the monks of Durham on behalf of their Bishop? An acknowledgement perhaps of his worldly past; and insurance for the salvation of the soul of Rannulf Flambard.

Chapter 6

A New Earl and an Old Bishop

Hugh of Le Puiset
'The Jolye Byshop of Durham'

The time of Hugh of Le Puiset, so we have been told by authors down the centuries, was a time of romantic high adventure; of chivalry, of the Crusades, of legendary characters living in a period from which historical fact has been inextricably entwined with popular fiction. Good King Richard the Lionheart, scheming and cruel Prince John, the heroic Wilfred of Ivanhoe, Robin Hood and his outlaws; Larger than life characters who inhabited both a historical and a legendary world.

Grudging historians tell us, however, that Robin Hood may never have existed at all, or, as with Arthur, his exploits may be a composite of the exploits of a number of different individuals. Wilfred of Ivanhoe was of course a literary creation by Sir Walter Scott and the real life Prince John, though hardly endearing to his subjects, suffered a particularly bad press largely as a result of the inadequacies of his elder brother Richard: 'The least English of all the Kings of England'. And it was through this world, and no less larger than life, that swaggered the son of the Viscount of Chartres, nephew of King Stephen, wealthy and ambitious, the Bishop of Durham, Hugh of Le Puiset; known to posterity as Hugh Pudsey.

Hugh, described as: 'of noble extraction and goodly presence', was only 25 years old and: 'addicted to the pleasures of the world', when he was elected Bishop of Durham. Already Archdeacon of Winchester, Treasurer of York and father to three illegitimate sons, more than one through an: 'alliance' with Adelaide de Percy; needless to say his election was not universally popular with the church establishment of the day. Henry Murdac, the austere Archbishop of York and former Abbot of Fountains Abbey, all sackcloth and damnation, had previously excommunicated Hugh and naturally enough opposed his election, claiming Hugh was not of Canonical age, which he was not; that he: 'lacked the requisite learning', which he may well have done; and that: 'he was by no means strict in his life'; which he seems not to have been.

Murdac refused to sanction Hugh's election; and for good measure, excommunicated the Prior and Chapter, who had elected him. It took the intercession of Theobald, the Archbishop of Canterbury to reduce the severity of their sentence to a penance, and a public flogging at the door of Beverley Minster. But still Murdac refused to consecrate Hugh. It was decided therefore that a petition be taken to the Pope in Rome; and so it was that Hugh, in the style, as Surtees tells us: 'More of the Temporal Prince than of the humble Ecclesiastic', along with Prior Lawrence of Durham, their attendants and: 'A splendid train, as well as of Ecclesiastics as the lay vassals of the Bishopric', set out on his journey. The chroniclers recorded that all that came across them saw: 'what goodly and noble looking persons they were, attracting universal admiration and leading everyone to think that church happy and incomparable which possessed such noteworthy men'.

Before they got to Rome, the incumbent Pope, Eugenius III, was dead, and it was his successor, Anastasius IV, who finally, after some further discussion over Hugh's age, approved his election and on 20 December 1153, Hugh Pudsey was consecrated as Bishop of Durham. Henry Murdac had died in the October and so, without any further domestic opposition, Hugh returned and on 2 May 1154, was enthroned at Durham Cathedral. Fordyce tells us that the population of St Cuthbert's City was: 'dazzled by his rank, influence, and ostentation; for his manners were secular, as well as his priesthood'.

King Stephen, Hugh's uncle and the last of the Norman Kings died the same year and a new era of English history would now begin; as Prince Henry of Anjou was crowned King Henry II of England and head of a vast Angevin Empire which stretched from Ireland and the Scottish Border Lands, to the Pyrenees. The age of the Plantagenet Kings had dawned; the new, young, Bishop of Durham was in attendance at King Henry's Coronation. So began the time of Hugh of Le Puiset: 'proud and magnificent, of grand stature and noble face, ever desirous of titles and honours', the larger than life: 'Jolye Byshop' of Durham. During his episcopate of over 40 years he would quarrel with the Durham Monks, with the Archbishop of York and with King Henry II. He would fall in and out of favour with King Richard I and would: 'intrigue' with the Scots. Not content with being Bishop and Count Palatine of Durham, he would also have himself made Earl of Northumberland and Earl of Sadberge.

Everyone was happy, at least for a while; it seemed that: 'The Lord had mercifully looked down from heaven upon His people, and raised a new Daniel in the land'. As Surtees tells us, the inhabitants of the Bishopric: 'Hoped for protection and security from the vigour of his age and the influence of his rank'. It was soon to change. Wealth and power did not fail to have their effect on the new Bishop. Dissension arose between Hugh and the Chapter, and successive Priors tried to resist, with little success. Relations between the Bishop and the monastery which had become strained under Flambard, now worsened to an all time low. The monks tried to protect themselves against the: 'arbitrary proceedings of the Bishop' by producing documents, probably forged, that set out the rights and traditions of the Durham Monastery. But Hugh paid little heed to old traditions. He also paid little heed to the Barons of the Bishopric, being supportive of those who acknowledged his position as Count Palatine but: 'having found out that all were afraid of him, he failed not to profit by his knowledge'.

In the early days of Hugh's episcopate, much of his time was spent on renewing what had been destroyed during the usurpation of William Cumin. The borough of Elvet was rebuilt, and in 1160, Elvet Bridge was thrown across the River Wear to connect it to the City. Hugh also rebuilt part of the City Walls; however, he was not helped in his designs by a fire which broke out in what is today, Saddler Street; which, fanned by a wind from the north, broke over the battlements and destroyed the north wing of the Castle. Despite the friction between himself and the monastery, Hugh made many generous gifts to the Cathedral and the Bishopric. In the 1170s he would add the Galilee Chapel to the west end of the Cathedral and he would have built a Shrine for the bones of Bede. He built Sherburn Hospital for lepers and ordered the repair and strengthening of Flambard's northern fortress, Norham Castle, by the addition of a massive Keep. He began to be recognised in Durham as a man: 'of great ability and industry, eloquent and prudent' and although he did not remain on good terms with the Chapter, he carefully protected the interests and liberties of the Durham Church, from outside interference and: 'he spared no expense to carry out his designs and to win general approval'.

On the national stage there arose the dispute between Henry II and Thomas Becket, into which Hugh was dragged. Eventually, along with a number of other Bishops, he sided

Le Puiset's Lady Chapel, the: 'Galilee Chapel' of Durham Cathedral.

Elvet Bridge, built by Bishop Hugh of Le Puiset, links Elvet with the Durham peninsula.

with the King, for which he was involved in a sentence of suspension from the Church. However, on the intervention of Becket himself, he was absolved, because, it was claimed, he had not been so deeply implicated as some.

Eventually the sons of Henry II, the future Kings, Richard and John, rebelled against him, and the behaviour of Hugh during the rebellion has been described as: 'ambiguous'. Most of the leading Barons were involved supporting one side or the other but the Church remained loyal to the King; generally. The loyalty of only two leading churchmen has been questioned; Arnulf, Bishop of Lisieux; and Hugh of Le Puiset, Bishop of Durham. It seems that during the King's absence across the Channel, Hugh: 'turned a blind eye' which allowed the army of William, King of the Scots, to march unopposed through County Durham; and purchased a truce for himself from the Scottish King. Preparations were even made at Hartlepool for the reception of mercenary troops from Flanders; troops under the command of Hugh's nephew, the Count of Bar, who would eventually garrison a strengthened Northallerton Castle. However, the royal rebellion was put down and the King returned suddenly. Henry: 'displeased' at Hugh's actions, or inactions, demanded his attendance before him. As punishment, his castles of Durham, Norham and Northallerton were forfeit to the King. It was to be a while before he regained Durham and Norham. Northallerton was razed to the ground. Throughout the remainder of Henry's reign, Hugh continued to fall in and out of favour with the King. Many times he would spend at Court, with the two on friendly terms but when the Archbishop of York died in 1181, the King asked Hugh to account for 300 marks that he'd been given by the Archbishop for charitable purposes. Hugh refused, and once again paid the price of the King's anger, with the confiscation of his castle of Durham.

Following the killing of Thomas Becket, in December 1170, the murdered Archbishop began to be revered as a Saint. A shrine was erected at Canterbury Cathedral and pilgrims in their thousands flocked there to leave their gifts and offerings. The Shrine of Thomas Becket was rapidly becoming the most important religious site in England. This was not good news for the monks of Durham, or for their Bishop. A lessening in importance of the Shrine of St Cuthbert would mean a lessening of income. Hugh tried to counteract this state of affairs. He decided to send out a group of Durham monks, with some: 'relics of St Cuthbert', to 'tour' England and parts of Scotland and: 'spread abroad the praises of St Cuthbert'.

Hugh also had an idea, worthy almost of Flambard himself, about how to reduce the cost of strengthening Norham Castle. A story was spread about of how a young boy who had been imprisoned in the deepest, vilest dungeon in Berwick Castle, had prayed for the assistance of St Cuthbert. Miraculously, he had been freed and physically transported over land and water, though he knew not how, to Norham Church, where he was found and where the manacles that had held him captive in the castle dungeon, were left hanging on the wall as witness to the truth of the story. The intercession of St Cuthbert was acknowledged and it was held that: 'in such a place the relics of the Saint himself would be much venerated'. So it was that Hugh: 'allowed' his engineer to travel north with a fragment of St Cuthbert's burial shroud that had been kept safe by a Durham monk. But the chronicler, Reginald of Durham tells that the relic was stolen by an: 'envious Frenchman', who tried to burn it. The holy cloth, however, could not be damaged by the flames; again and again the Frenchman returned it to the fire, but: 'The relic stood up as white as snow and it was purified like gold from the blazing furnace'. Fearful and remorseful, the Frenchman returned the sacred cloth to Hugh's agent and for a time: 'all those who gave him aid, were rewarded with a view of the relic'.

So the northern stronghold of the Prince Bishops of Durham was duly strengthened with the aid of St Cuthbert. There was even 20 shillings a year set aside for a permanent chaplain to reside at the Castle. However, those appointed cared little for residing on the potentially dangerous Scottish Border and preferred to stay at Durham:

'And though a Bishop built this fort,
Few Holy Brethren here resort.
Even our good chaplain, as I ween,
Since our last siege I have not seen;
The Mass he might not sing or say,
Upon one stinted meal a day,
So safe he sat in Durham's aisle,
And prayed for our success the while'.

Lawrence, the Prior of the monastery of Durham, wrote several books recording the days of Bishop Hugh. His words were recounted in the Victoria County History and paint an interesting picture of the time. With a constant stream of the faithful, bringing offerings and riches to the Shrine of the Saint, St Cuthbert's City had become: 'a highly developed franchise'; a state of affairs that Hugh encouraged with his: 'sumptuous and magnificent enrichment of Durham'. Visitors to the Shrine of the Saint also brought good business to the people of his City, for the needs of Pilgrims had to be catered for and Lawrence tells us that Hugh: 'greatly increased the attractions of Durham as a place of pilgrimage'.

Lodging houses made money, as did the shops in the Market Place and those fronting on to the streets. As Count Palatine, Hugh granted the City a Charter to hold a weekly market and Saturday then, as it still is today, was Market Day in Durham City. Two Feasts of St Cuthbert were held, in March and September, to commemorate both the Saints death and the translation of his body to his Shrine. On these days the holy relics would be exhibited for public view. Lawrence tells us that these fairs brought great crowds of people into the City and profited those who catered for their needs. Visitor attractions were on offer, not only in the Cathedral itself, but outside, where sports and games were held. Obviously these occasions encouraged trading on a large scale and the money from that trade plus that gained from: 'Booth Silver'; paid by travelling shows to set up their stands in the Market Place enriched the City and: 'brought no little gain to the Bishop'.

As for the City itself, we are told that it was circled with crosses about a mile from the Cathedral, which marked the limit of the right of Sanctuary. Kepier Hospital as well as caring for the sick, also acted as a shelter for pilgrims before entering the City itself. To do this from any direction the City Walls had to be passed through. A final, muddy approach across Palace Green, from where the ringing Cathedral Bells could be seen from outside, brought them to the main entrance, then, as now, the great North Door. Once inside, the pilgrims would file along a marble pavement, surrounded by statues of Saints and Kings until they reached the guarded inner gates that led to St Cuthbert's Shrine itself.

The massive gates of the Castle were constantly guarded by a porter and penants fluttered high over sentinels, who kept permanent watch from the battlements. Prisoners were housed in the Bishop's prison, probably on the west side of Palace Green. Across the river gorge, the houses of Allergate and South Street could even then be seen. An official Town Crier plied his nightly trade and the Master of the Bishop's Mint was a busy man. Unfortunately, the Castle, Cathedral and Monastery, perched upon the wooded rock, high above the River, could not easily make use of the natural cleansing benefits of its stream and the contents of the latrines had to be ejected over the banks, the effects of gravity and the distance of the drop deciding the amount washed away and the purity or otherwise of the Monastery air. And, as is recorded in the Victoria County History: 'With the River low, as it often is in summer, and with a prevailing westerly breeze, the defects of mediaeval drainage must have been constantly and painfully apparent'.

The chronicles record that in 1183:
'Lord Hugh, Bishop of Durham, caused to be written down in his and his men's presence, all the returns of his whole Bishopric, fixed rents and customs as they were then and had been before'.

So was written the Boldon Buke, Durham's own Domesday; which recorded all the duties, labour and rents owed to the Bishop by his tenants across the Palatine Lands. Unlike Domesday, the Boldon Buke; called so because Boldon was the first place described in it, does not include dues owed by the Bishop's military tenants. But in its pages are recorded glimpses of the lives, not just of the great Lords, but of the ordinary people of 12th-century County Durham; of people like Ralph the Crafty and the Bishop's villeins of Aucklandshire.

In 1188, King Henry held a Council to consider the consequences of the fall of Jerusalem and Bishop Hugh took the opportunity to renew his Crusading vows. A royal decree was issued across England, requiring a: 'tenth' to be levied on all Bishops, Abbots, Earls and Barons, to finance a Crusade. However, there was a: 'get-out' clause, which stated that if any of these elected to actually serve in the forthcoming Crusade, they were to be allowed to keep the 10th for their own use. The King proposed to go himself and Bishop Hugh, now in his sixties, but no doubt considering the possible rewards, decided to go with him. However, Hugh's idea of Crusading did not necessarily follow the ideal of hardship, sacrifice and personal courage. He made: 'most magnificent and costly preparations'. He provided ships for the journey, which were: 'gorgeously furnished'. In his own ship he had made a: 'silver throne, for himself, of wonderful workmanship'. Even the kitchen utensils and tableware were made of silver. King Henry, however, died in July, 1189. His rebellious son Richard would now take up the cross and Robert de Stockton sailed from Hartlepool with Hugh's glittering ships, to London and the King's service.

So it was that, as he had been at the Coronation of his father, Hugh of Le Puiset, Bishop of Durham, was present at Westminster Abbey, on Sunday 3 September 1189, at the Coronation of Richard the Lionheart; and walked at the right hand of the King. The ceremony, probably much to Hugh's satisfaction, was a glitteringly ostentatious affair: 'unsurpassed in magnificence'; Richard resplendent in gold with a golden sword, golden spurs and a golden crown upon his head. However, the sight of a bat, disturbed from its slumbers and flying round and round above the head of the new King, was taken by some to be a bad omen.

King Richard I inherited an empty Treasury. He needed money for his Crusade and began to sell off land, castles and titles. He sold Berwick back to the Scots and said that he would even sell London, if only he could find a buyer. Roger of Howden wrote: 'In this manner, the King acquired a huge amount of money, more than any of his predecessors is known to have had'. Bishop Hugh, rich and: 'of boundless ambition' proved to be very useful to the King. From Hugh's point of view it was more opportunity for: 'advancement'. He bought from the King, the Earldom of Northumberland and the Earldom of Sadberge; the King commenting that he had indeed: 'made a new Earl out of an old Bishop'.

But it seems that Hugh's Crusading zeal had now deserted him. He first got a dispensation from it for three years, and then he just gave it up altogether. In September 1189, Richard held a Council at Pipewell Abbey in Northamptonshire. He took the opportunity to remove from office the incumbent Justiciar of England, a former friend and confidant of his father; and replace him jointly with William de Mandeville, Count of Aumale and Earl of Essex; and Hugh of Le Puiset, who, for the past 35 years had been Bishop and Count Palatine of Durham, but had also paid the King a thousand marks for his new office. Critically for Hugh, Richard appointed his favourite, William Longchamp, as the new Bishop of Ely and Royal Chancellor. However, it was not long before Mandeville died and Hugh, probably hoping for the sole Justiciarship of the Kingdom, was to be disappointed by the King. Instead, Richard gave to Hugh, Justiciarship of only the northern half of the country together with the Wardenship of Windsor Castle. Responsibility for the southern half of the country, custody of the Tower of London and the safekeeping of the Royal Seal, was given to Longchamp: 'An obscure foreigner of unproven ability and loyalty', according to William of Newburgh. But Longchamp had qualities of critical importance to the King; he was fiercely loyal, brooked no opposition to the King's wishes and excelled in making money for the Lionheart. And so it was that Richard departed on his Crusade and left Hugh and Longchamp in effective control of his Kingdom of England.

Relations between the two were not good. Neither trusted the other. Hugh was aristocratic, of royal blood: 'tall, handsome, eloquent and affable'. Longchamp, in contrast was of humble origins, small and bent. Gerold of Wales describes him as being: 'more like an ape than a man', considered by some, and probably by Hugh, as an upstart, allegedly the grandson of a runaway serf, who openly professed to despise the English. Arrogant, intolerant; he was deeply unpopular, condemned by William of Newburgh: 'The laity found him more than a King, the clergy found him more than a Pope; and both an intolerable tyrant'. But Richard trusted him; he probably did not entirely trust Hugh. And it was indeed Hugh who first: 'murmured at the limitation of his powers'. Longchamp refused to admit him to the Exchequer. He would not recognise Hugh's claims as the: 'new' Earl of Northumberland, it seems the Bishop had: 'neglected' to forward the payment for his title. When they met to discuss the situation Hugh set out his written commission as Justiciar; dispenser of the King's justice. But Longchamp was Chancellor, the King's Man and he was cunning; seeing an opportunity he deferred to a second meeting, decoyed Hugh to London and had him arrested on a trumped-up charge of treason. When Hugh remonstrated Longchamp produced his own commission, of a later date, and told Hugh: 'You have had your say at our last meeting, now I shall have mine. As my Lord King liveth, you shall not quit this place until you have given me hostages for the surrender of all your castles. No protest, I am not a Bishop arresting another Bishop, I am the Chancellor, arresting his supplanter'. Hugh was imprisoned and forced to surrender Windsor and Newcastle. Eventually the requested hostages were delivered and Hugh was released but he was made to agree that from now on he would restrict himself only to his northern jurisdiction. Longchamp was now Chancellor of England, Justiciar and Papal Legate and Hugh's days on the centre stage of national affairs were effectively over.

When, in 1194, Richard eventually returned from the Third Crusade, after his captivity in Germany and the payment of a huge ransom, said to have been 34 tons of gold, to secure his release, Hugh met him at Nottingham Castle and was well received. But by and by the old Bishop found himself held gradually less high in royal favour, even though he had contributed a large sum of money towards Richard's ransom; on the pretext of which, it was said, perhaps apocryphally, that he had extorted a much larger sum from his Durham taxpayers, and pocketed the difference himself. Eventually, never fully regaining the King's favour, he was obliged to resign the Earldom of Northumberland: 'and trembled also for Sadberg'.

He was around 70 years old when he undertook a journey to the King in London to: 're-negotiate' his titles. He was taken ill at Craike, allegedly after partaking too freely of a Shrovetide Feast. He pushed on as far as Doncaster, but from there could go no further and was taken by water to Howden. So it was that Hugh of Le Puiset realising the end of his life was in sight, confessed his sins, and made restitution to the Durham monks for: 'whatever wrong he had done them'. It was said, that 20 years before, Hugh had been warned by the hermit, St Godric of Finchale, that he would be blind seven years before his death. Obviously, Hugh had taken the message literally and had taken the greatest care of his eyes from then on. On his death bed therefore he said that Godric had deceived him. Someone made so bold as to suggest that he had long been blind to his pastoral duties, seeking as he had done, after Earldoms and other: 'worldly' honours. The magnificent Hugh of Le Puiset, finally closed his earthly account in March 1195. Immediately his body arrived back at Durham for burial, Hugh Bardolf seized the Castle for the King. Two years were to pass before the arrival of the next Bishop, during which time; the keys of the City were hung above St Cuthbert's Shrine.

Fordyce referred to Hugh's character in the following terms: 'It was as remarkable as it was imperfect. Exalted into a Prince Bishop, he played the first character to admiration but marred the last...his personal conduct was similar; he was licentious, luxurious and ostentatious, but often generous and munificent.' In his time, Hugh of le Puiset, a man with: 'inate vanity and natural ambition', had quarrelled with the Prior and monks of Durham; with fellow Bishops, with Archbishops and with Barons. A century later, however, one would come after; who could barely stand even the suzerainty of the King of England himself.

Chapter 7

The Power and the Glory

Antony Bek
'The most splendid and dangerous churchman, of a splendid and dangerous church'

It was dawn on 22 July 1298. Two armies faced each other. The Scottish War of Independence had reached a critical impasse. An English host of 15,000 men under the command of King Edward I had made a dash northward towards Falkirk to face down his opponent. The King was bent, not just on victory but on annihilation. Facing him, across a mile or so of open ground, the 10,000 men of Scottish hero, resistance fighter and victor over the English at the Battle of Stirling Bridge; the: 'Guardian of Scotland', Sir William Wallace of Ellerslie.

In the distance the Scots could be seen preparing for battle. Four great hedgehog like formations: 'Schiltrons', each made up of 2,000 densely packed men, brandishing 12ft spears, triple tiers of which pointed outward, like a steel wall, to repulse over two thousand mounted English Knights. Their spear tips could be seen glimmering in the early morning sun; the faint voices of their commanders carried on the breeze over the Westquarter Burn, glinting and rattling its sinuous way across the battlefield.

The English host had spent a restless night in full armour, in readiness for the events of the dawn. The King himself had been trampled by his own warhorse as he lay asleep on the ground and now mounted for the attack with two of his ribs broken. All holy rights had been done; Antony Bek, Bishop of Durham had said Mass for all those about to go into battle. Edward's army was now divided into four divisions; the vanguard was commanded by the Earl of Lincoln, behind him, the King himself commanded the centre, the left hand division was led by the Earl of Surrey. At the King's right hand, was Antony Bek, who, as Bishop, had so short a time ago performed the sacred religious offices. He now mounted his own warhorse as Count Palatine and leader of the right hand division. Perhaps more a warrior than a prelate, the first Bishop to carry his own Coat of Arms into battle, Antony Bek now assumed the role for which he was most fitted; as the Prince of the Prince Bishops of Durham. He wondered not, how he had come to so high a station.

Bek was of noble birth; the third son of Walter, Baron of Eresby in Lincolnshire. His rise in favour with King Edward I had probably as much to do with his prowess as a warrior, as it did with his piety and chaste lifestyle. Whether offering Edward advice as the King's Counsellor, Secretary or Ambassador; or spiritual guidance as a man of the cloth, he had long been a friend and confidant to the: 'Hammer of the Scots'. By the time he was 30 and with a considerable personal fortune, he had entered the service of Edward's father, King Henry III, as a King's Clerk. He accompanied the young Edward on Crusade, acting almost as a guardian on the King's behalf. Henry died while Edward was away and the young Prince returned as King of England. Bek then held various posts in the royal household, including Constable of the Tower of London. He had a prominent role in Edward's campaigns in Wales, including raising money to pay his armies. It was the King's wish that

The Gatehouse of Durham Castle.

Bek, already Archdeacon of Durham, should be appointed Bishop and he was consecrated at York, in January 1284, in the presence of King Edward: 'and a great concourse of the nobility'.

Trouble started almost at once when matters came to a head over an ongoing dispute between the Prior and Monks of Durham and the Archbishop of York, over Durham's continuing refusal to allow the Archbishop his claimed right of Ecclesiastical Visitation. Both the Bishop and the Monks of Durham owed obedience, at least in theory, to the Archbishop and Province of York. However, in Durham the view seems to have been generally taken that while the Bishop may have owed obedience; the Count Palatine certainly did not; and York was largely ignored. The Durham monks also refused to acknowledge the supremacy of the Archbishop of York. Indeed, only shortly before, the Archbishop had been refused entry into Durham Cathedral by the Prior. He was forced to take shelter in St Nicholas' Church in the Market Place where he began to preach sermon. He was about to begin excommunicating the Prior and Monks, when he was set upon by: 'some of the young men of the City'. Escaping through a narrow alleyway by the Church, he made his way, via the Sands, to the relative safety of Kepier Hospital; but not before his horse's ears had been clipped by the crowd of roughs. The story may be apocryphal that, to add to his humiliation, the Archbishop was tied on his horse backwards. So it was that the day after Bek's consecration he was instructed by the Archbishop of York, on his, at least theoretical, obedience to the Primate, to excommunicate the Prior and Monks of Durham. Bek refused, saying: 'Yesterday, I was consecrated their Bishop, and shall I excommunicate them today? Nothing will induce me to do so, on account of any obedience'. So began the career of Antony Bek; largely as it would continue. Indeed, there would be further trouble over his enthronement at Durham Cathedral. The Prior of Durham, insisted, by virtue of his office, that he should perform the rights. The Archbishop of York demanded that it should be himself. Eventually, Bek, impatient and imperious; ignored them both and had his own brother, Thomas, the Bishop of St David's, carry out the ceremony; on Christmas Eve, 1285. Early signs perhaps, for those who heeded them, that this was no Pudsey; no: 'Jolye Byshope'.

The Episcopate of Antony Bek was inextricably entwined with the Scottish War of Independence. On the night of 18 March 1286, Alexander III, King of Scotland, had died accidentally, leaving no surviving direct heirs. The only remaining claimant was a granddaughter, Margaret, whose mother, the queen of King Eric II of Norway had died giving birth to the child in 1283. So it was that the infant: 'Maid of Norway', the last of the royal house of Canmore, stood in line to succeed to the Scottish Throne. A Council of Regency was appointed to administer the Kingdom in her minority.

King Edward, perhaps wishing to unite the Scottish and English crowns for the greater good, or perhaps seeing an opportunity to expand his Plantagenet empire, proposed a future marriage between the: 'Maid of Norway' and his own son Edward, Prince of Wales. It may also have been the case that an approach was made to Bek and others by the Scottish Guardians, suggesting such an arrangement. Edward then instructed Antony Bek to act, along with the Scots, as a Joint Guardian of the infant Queen and was employed by the King as a member of the deputation sent to negotiate the marriage. The first stage of the negotiations took place at Salisbury in November 1289, where Bek acted as the King's chief negotiator. The arrangement was accepted by the Scots on condition that Scotland would continue as an independent Kingdom and Bek was instructed by the King to act as his lieutenant in Scotland, to hold the administration of the country on trust, jointly for both Margaret and the Prince of Wales. However, the infant heiress died in September 1290; the question of Scottish succession was once again thrown open. A rush of: 'Competitors', staked their own claim to the throne of Scotland, and, with a fear of all out Civil War, Edward was invited to intervene in the issue. New possibilities were surely not lost on the English King and he agreed to do so, if he received acknowledgement as Overlord of Scotland.

The Prince Bishop's Castle of Durham, in which Antony Bek built a Great Hall.

Edward rode north in 1291, reaching Darlington in April. From there he issued orders for all his chief subjects to join him at Norham Castle. After spending Easter at Newcastle, the King reached Norham on 9 May and from there he required all the competing Scottish magnates to bring their cases to him at the end of the month. The King was evidently determined to make an impression to the Scots. H.E.H. Jerningham, in his 1983 book on Norham Castle, tells us that: 'If Norham had once before seen a pageant worthy of remembrance, all was eclipsed by the splendour of the present gathering'. The account of a contemporary chronicler, described the scene.

The court of King Edward glittered with all the trappings of English wealth, power and chivalry. The King himself, his six feet two inch frame resplendent in a robe of Scarlet silk, covered by a Tabard, richly embroidered with the Arms of England and France; a golden brooch at his breast and precious jewels around his shoulders; a golden crown upon his head. As well as his chief lords, the King was surrounded by clergy no less grand. By Abbots in ornamented gowns of scarlet and green; by Monks, their tunics edged with fur and: 'their hoods fastened beneath the chin with a golden pin and bells on their horses bridles, jingling as they rode'; by Friars, whose appearance the chronicler noted, was: 'not that of a poor man in a threadbare cape, but more like the Pope himself'. And onto this splendid stage, attired like a Knight, with a long sword in a broad belt, rode the no less splendid, Antony Bek. His Bishop's Mitre: 'embellished with pearls like the head of a queen, and a Staff of gold set with jewels as heavy as lead', all covered with an outer tunic, with a hood ornamented with precious stones.

So it was that at Norham Castle, Edward and his Counsellors heard the claims of all the claimants to the Scottish Throne. One of the foremost was John Balliol, an Anglo-Norman nobleman with estates in Scotland, England and France. Balliol may have turned to Bek for support for his claim. Antony Bek probably knew him well, Balliol being, as he was, Lord of Barnard Castle and a subject of the Prince Bishop. Indeed, it is likely that Bek's was one of the loudest voices advising Edward on Balliol's claim. Eventually, on 17 November 1292, Edward decided in favour of Balliol, who was then required to render fealty to Edward of England, which he did three days later at Norham Castle. On St Andrew's Day, at Scone, Bek placed him on the Stone of Destiny, and Balliol, the Bishop's Durham vassal, was crowned, King John of Scotland. But Balliol was weak and his support among the feuding Scottish nobility was uncertain. Edward made increasingly humiliating demands of him, emphasizing Balliol's position as the King of England's feudal vassal. Both were factors in the events which would lead inevitably to war. When King Edward began a campaign in France, he demanded feudal service from the Scots. Balliol refused, deferred to the Scottish nobility and sought assistance from England's French enemy.

Sending a message to the Scots, in the autumn of 1295, Edward appointed Bek, along with John de Warrenne, Earl of Surrey as custodians of all the shires north of the Trent, their task, to militarise the north of England. And early in the November, Bek and Warrenne summoned all of the northern knights to York to receive instructions on defence. The following month, 200 writs were issued to military tenants, to muster at Newcastle on 1 March 1296. Finally, Balliol renounced his allegiance to England altogether. King Edward, clearly would not let this situation lie. A contemporary chronicler tells us that Balliol was: 'a lamb among wolves, who dared not open his mouth', and now he was to lead his countrymen against Edward Plantaganet. The Scots crossed the border: 'burning houses, slaughtering men and driving off cattle'. Edward's army, with Antony Bek leading his military tenants, besieged Berwick and more atrocities were carried out, this time in the name of England. The English then made for Dunbar Castle and on the 27 April they came across and attacked the main body of the Scots army. The Scots were defeated and their Castles were handed over without any further fighting; Stirling Castle, symbol of Scottish resistance, was abandoned and the keys left with the porter, to hand over to the English. After Stirling, the English campaign became a simple: 'mopping up' exercise, with Bek, riding at the front of his own force, and some way ahead of the King, accepting Scots leaders on the King's behalf, as they came forward to offer homage.

Balliol himself finally surrendered on 10 July, at Brechin Castle and Antony Bek, who had stood alongside him as he was crowned at Scone, was deputed by the King to receive Balliol's submission and take him into custody. Bek had proposed a deal, in which Scotland would be given to Edward in perpetuity and in return, John would be given an English Earldom, abased round his large northern estates, mostly in the Bishopric. But Edward would have none of it; he demanded total surrender, and humiliation for John Balliol. So it was that it was firstly before the Bishop of Durham and not Edward that King John of Scotland was ceremonially deprived of his crown, robes and regalia. His royal coat of arms was stripped from his Tabard; his Tabard was now bare, divested of honour and dignity, and it would be as: 'Toom Tabard', that history would remember him. King Edward took the Stone of Scone south, there to have it incorporated into the English Coronation Chair. It seemed that Scottish claims to the Scottish Throne were ended.

But it was not long before a new Scottish champion emerged. William Wallace, the almost mythical Scottish patriot, hero and woad smeared freedom fighter of recent cinema, was in fact the son of a minor Scotish aristocrat and in 1297 he began his campaign. In August of that year, King Edward sailed with an army for Flanders, taking most of his chief men, including Antony Bek, with him. The following month, Wallace inflicted a disastrous defeat on the English at Stirling Bridge. His way was now free to devastate the northern counties of England.

Wallace made his way south with about 3,000 foot and 100 horse and on 7 November Hexham Abbey was plundered, but Wallace gave to the clergy, letters of protection and his personal guarantee of safety, before his force moved west into Cumbria. There he blockaded Carlisle and: 'burnt the country for thirty leagues around'. With winter worsening he turned east again making for Durham, from where the Prince Bishop was absent, abroad with the King. Crossing Stainmore, he got as far as Bowes, where he was halted by a severe snow storm. A proposed attack on Newcastle took him back into the Tyne Valley and back to Hexham. A story is told that, Hexham Abbey was being sacked and the monks: 'persuaded' to tell the Scots, where the remainder of the church's treasures were hidden, when William Wallace himself appeared, dispersed his men and requested a Mass to be said. The monks of course complied. Wallace, it is said, even assisted: 'with great reverence and devotion'. At the: 'Elevation', Wallace retired from the church to remove his armour. At this, his soldiers overpowered the officiating priest and carried off the precious altar vessels. On his return, Wallace ordered the culprits to: 'be sought out and put to death'. To the brethren of the Abbey he said: 'My people are full of mischief, and I cannot keep them in order'. The Abbey was now left alone but his Scottish host then spent another two days: 'ravaging the neighbourhood with fire and sword'. Abandoning the attack on Newcastle, Wallace turned his force for home and on his return was made: 'Guardian of Scotland'.

The situation had once again been forced. King Edward returned from Flanders in March 1298 and immediately set about organizing his campaign against Wallace. He moved the centre of Government to York and while there, made a pilgrimage to the shrine of St John of Beverley. At Durham the Prince Bishop made ready his own forces and he was joined by the King when Edward rode into Durham on 12 June. The time had come to deal with William Wallace.

So it was that Antony Bek marched out of Durham: 'in all the pomp and splendour of a Prince Palatine', with his own Palatine Army marching behind him: '26 Standard Bearers of his household and 140 Knights formed his train'. Following them went 1,000 foot soldiers and 500 cavalry, all marching under the sacred Banner of St Cuthbert, held aloft by Henry de Horncastre: 'A monk of the House of Durham'. The glint of shining armour, the colour of bright surcoats and shields and the fluttering of pennons above them. Down through the narrow streets and out across the River Wear. What a sight that must have been!

They rode from Durham to Newcastle, then to Alnwick, and on to Roxburgh, where the English host was assembled; and from there, crossing the border on 3 July; north into Scotland. Expecting an attack, Wallace employed a: 'Scorched Earth' policy, destroying all that could sustain the English Army. It worked; lack of supplies became a serious problem. The English halted at Kirkliston, near Edinburgh. Edward had arranged for supply ships to sail up the coast and meet the army on the Forth. But the winds had not been favourable and the supplies were late. Edward was delayed for nearly a fortnight and decided to use the time to capture three castles held by the Scots and he asked Bek to do the job. So the Prince Bishop, with no siege engines, made for Direlton Castle, one of the most formidable castles of its time, standing on a rock outcrop, surrounded by a deep, water filled ditch. His men surviving only on what they could forage from the fields. Under the circumstances, the castle was too strong and was holding out, and Bek sent John Fitzmarmaduke to request further instructions from the King. Edward sent back a message: 'Go back and tell Antony, that when he is acting as Bishop, he is a man of peace, but now he is a soldier and must forget his calling'; to Fitzmarmaduke he said: 'You, on the other hand, are a cruel man and oft have I rebuked you for being too cruel and for the pleasure you take in the death of your enemies. But now go and exert all your frightfulness, I shall not blame but praise you…take care you do not see my face again, until all three castles are burnt'. Asked how this was to be done, with no siege engines and an army racked with hunger, the King replied: 'You will do by doing it, and give me your promise that you will'.

Eventually, Bek took Direlton Castle and the two others in East Lothian were left empty by the Scots. During the wait, things in the English camp got worse. A provisions ship had at last arrived, its cargo, 200 barrels of wine, was duly liberated and partaken of by the troops. The inevitable happened and a serious fight broke out between Welsh and English contingents of the army, with deaths on both sides. Things, it seemed, could get no worse but as Edward considered retreating to Edinburgh, news came of the whereabouts of Wallace's army; no more than 20 miles away. The King was warned that the Scots meant to seek him out and harry his retreat, to which he replied: 'I will not trouble them to seek me; as God lives, they need not pursue me, for I will meet them this day'. And so the advance began towards Falkirk. The night before the Battle, east of Linlithgow, the English Army camped in full armour, ready to move at any moment. The chronicler, Walter of Guisbrough tells that they lay: 'arranging their shields as pillows and their arms as coverlets. Their horses too, tasted nothing save hard steel, and were tethered each one hard by its Lord'. After a short and restless summer night, the English host rode out toward Falkirk before the break of dawn.

So it was that Antony Bek, Prince Bishop of Durham was once again at the right hand of the King; and at the head of one most glittering arrays of English nobility ever put into the field: 'the contemporary roll of Falkirk is a roll call of the chivalry of England'. Edward, wishing to rest his men and horses had proposed making camp but was dissuaded by his advisers: 'for between these two armies there is nothing but a very small stream'. Across the valley the Scots were now arrayed on the sloping hillside opposite, to their rear, a possible escape route through Callender Wood. The English began their ominous advance towards those glittering Scottish Schiltrons and as they did, the legend tells that William Wallace rode out in front of his host and said: 'I have brought you to the revel; now dance if you can'. The mounted English Knights, heavily armoured and thought to be unbeatable in open combat, increased their pace. Antony Bek charged at the head of his division; two Earls, and almost 450 Knights followed him. They rode headlong down the sloping ground to where the Westquarter Burn flowed but could not see into the waterlogged valley bottom. Their descent would lead them to boggy ground and they were forced to veer away to the right. The pace of their charge had put them a good way ahead of the King's division and they were in danger of becoming isolated and exposed.

Bek reigned in, to await the advance of the other divisions and maximise the impact of the attack. But one Knight, Sir Ralph Basset of Drayton: 'a rough soldier', would have none of it and told Bek: 'It is not your office to instruct us in the art of war; to thy Mass, Bishop, and teach not such as us as how we are to behave in the face of the enemy'. Bek's response either at the time, or after the Battle, is not recorded but could perhaps be guessed at. Eventually the advance was reordered and the English engaged the Schiltrons but with: 'Their spears point over point, as sair and so thick, and fast together joint, to see it was ferlike as a castle they stood that was walled with stone'; for a time, they withstood the mounted Knights. However, for a reason that has been little understood, the Scottish Cavalry suddenly left the field of battle, seemingly driven off, without striking a blow. They were probably no match for the heavily armoured English and were in any case outnumbered about four to one, but suspicions have been held about their withdrawal; and there have since been whispers of betrayal.

With the Scottish Cavalry gone, the English turned on the now totally exposed Scottish Archers and those who did not find protection within the massed ranks of the Schiltrons were quickly cut down. Now Edward ordered his own Archers to fire at the Schiltrons, for spears were no defence against a storm of arrows, and death rained down upon Wallace's army. Where the dead fell, gaps appeared in the defences. The English Knights took due advantage and eventually the defences broke. Those Scots that could, made for the protection of the woodland. Most were cut down. Wallace's army was utterly defeated. The: 'Scalacronica' relates that: 'more than ten thousand' Scots were killed, though this is an exaggeration. But fall they did; as an English chronicler recorded: 'like blossoms in an orchard, when the first fruit has ripened'. Wallace and his close associates made his way from the battlefield. He resigned the Guardianship of Scotland and went into hiding; to France, and then, it is thought, to Rome. Eventually returning to Scotland, it would be another seven years before he was finally betrayed by his fellow countrymen, arrested near Glasgow and, on 23 August 1305, died a traitor's death.

Antony Bek was probably now at the peak of his power and influence. The Durham chronicler, Robert de Graystanes, described him so: 'This Antony was of lofty disposition; second to none in the Kingdom in splendour, dress and military power; concerned rather with the business of the Kingdom rather than the affairs of his Bishopric; a strong support to the King in war and provident in Counsel'.

Things, however, were to change. A man such as this, it would seem, would inevitably clash with those that opposed him, and one such would be King Edward himself.

Initially, Bek, by refusing the Archbishop of York's command to excommunicate the Prior and Monks of Durham, had indicated his support for them. Peace, however, did not reign for long between them. In the year 1300, trouble arose between the monks and the Prior of Durham; Prior Hotoun. The monks were dissatisfied with the Prior's administration and the Bishop proposed to hold a visitation. The Prior refused; it was a bad move. Bek, infuriated, excommunicated and suspended Prior Hotoun. The monastery was divided. Some, knowing the Bishop, aligned with him, some, equally knowing the Bishop, sided with the Prior; others, perhaps more politically astute, remained: 'neutral'. Bek, wishing to rid himself of this upstart Prior, began to employ strong-arm tactics. His men: 'began to annoy the Prior and his servants in every way, and would, but for the interference of some monks, have put him in prison'. The situation became so serious that the King himself interfered and a temporary peace was accommodated. The Prior would retain his office, the Bishop was allowed to visit; and Edward warned them both that he would take part against either one who broke this peace.

Bek also upset the Barons and men of the Bishopric of Durham. As Count Palatine he had required them to fight under him in the Scottish wars. Some, not relishing the thought of a prolonged campaign north of the border, had simply returned home. The Bishop had them imprisoned. The men pleaded the ancient right of the: 'Haliwerfole', The: 'Holyman People'; the guardians of St Cuthbert. They stated that as such, they were legally bound to give military service to the Count Palatine, only between the Tyne and the Tees and could not be called upon to serve either Bishop or King elsewhere. Lord Neville of Raby was the most powerful Baron to support this claim and the case was brought before Edward's Parliament. Of course, in the dispute between Bishop and Prior, the Barons then took: 'a favourable view', of the Prior's side of the argument. Bek, however, was undaunted. He called the monks together and required them to elect a new Prior. They refused. Bek then appointed one himself, Henry de Luceby, the Prior of Lindisfarne. There: 'then ensued a strange scene of violence'. Bek brought in some of his hired heavy's, his: 'men from Weardale and Tynedale'. He told them to expel the old Prior and install his new one. The Cathedral was besieged, with the old Prior and his monks trapped inside. No provisions were allowed in, the gates were broken down and a monk who ventured out to fetch water from the well in the cloister yard, had his pitcher emptied and smashed. The Prior and 46 monks were shut inside for three days, with only: 'six loaves and 16 herrings'. On the third day, a Tynedale man was sent in to physically remove the Prior from his stall in the Cathedral. However, this man, clearly not hired for his gentle and sympathetic disposition, on seeing the Prior in prayer, was nevertheless: 'so awed by his venerable appearance that he dared not lay a hand on him'. Bek, of course, had no time for this nonsense, and a monk, one of his own supporters, and with significantly fewer scruples than the Tynedale tough, was sent in to get the Prior. It worked. Prior Hotoun was seized and imprisoned, and Henry de Luceby installed. For his part the new Prior made his peace with the monks.

Indeed, so much so that they said that: 'If he had come to the Office in a legitimate way, he ought to have been reckoned a very excellent head of the House'.

Bek no doubt, considered himself vindicated. More trouble, however, was on the way. For the Prince Bishop himself was imperious and Prior Richard Hotoun was: 'a man of monumental arrogance and stubbornness'.

In the best traditions of the Durham clergy, Prior Hotoun escaped from prison. He immediately made his way to King Edward, who was at Lincoln and put his case before him, reminding Edward of the accommodation arrived at following his previous intercession. Needless to say, Bek was not in the King's good books. To make matters worse, there was at the time a dispute between the King on the one side and the Earl Marshal of England and the Earl of Hereford on the other. The nobles were disputing the King's increasingly arbitrary rule. Edward summoned Bek to him. The Bishop duly answered his call, complete with his usual retinue of 140 knights. The King asked him where he stood in the dispute, no doubt relying on his old allegiance. Bek replied that if the noblemen were acting: 'for the profit and honour of the realm and the sovereign, then he held with them and against the King'. From then on there was no love lost between the two. So it was that Prior Hotoun, with the full support of the King and commendatory letters from him for Pope Boniface VIII, now set out for Rome to further his claim against the Bishop. He received a: 'favourable decision'. Representatives of the Bishop tried to argue that the Prior had voluntarily resigned, but the Pope replied to them that: 'no one who knew what it was to be Prior of Durham would ever resign his Office of his own accord'. Hotoun returned to Durham in triumph: 'and was received with joy', but not by Bek. Bek's man, Luceby, and his supporters, were forced to withdraw, but not without first attempting to carry off some silver plate from the Cathedral.

Now it was Bek's turn. He had previously chosen not to appear before the Pope, sending only envoys instead. Now he was summoned again, under a threat of deprivation of his See. So Bek decided that if he had to go, he would go in style, and show everyone just who they were dealing with: 'Upon this he betook himself to Rome with such a retinue and such magnificence as to raise wonder everywhere'. Stories began to make their way back of exploits during his journey; stories that seemed to sum up the magnificence and the arrogance of Antony Bek, Prince Bishop of Durham. In one place he came to, his retinue became involved in a: 'tumult in a north Italian city'. The dispute got out of hand and inevitably, it turned violent. A group of local law enforcement officers forced their way into Bek's chamber armed with swords and clubs, and, as if Bek were a thief, demanded: 'yield thee, yield'. Completely unabashed Bek replied with contempt: 'You have failed to tell me to whom I am to yield, certainly to none of you'. This of course made matters worse and: 'on this occasion he would have been slain but for timely help'.

The display of magnificence that Bek and his entourage showed set out for all to see, that this was no man to be trifled with. This was the Bishop of Durham and Count Palatine who thought nothing of standing up to, and publicly disagreeing with the ruthless King Edward I of England, so when it came to standing up to and publicly disagreeing with the Pope and his Cardinals; it was no contest. Everywhere he went he demonstrated the wealth and power of the Bishop of Durham. A tale is told of a merchant who boasted about some fine expensive cloth he was selling, saying that it was too costly, even for the Bishop of Durham to buy. News of the conceit reached the ears of Bek, who ordered his men to go and buy up all of this prized cloth, and then, in front of the merchant, to cut it up to make blankets for the Bishop's horses. When in Rome it was said that a citizen asked: 'Who is this?' to which came the reply: 'an enemy of money'. Another story tells that a Cardinal had admired the Bishop's horses. Bek sent the Cardinal two, so that he could choose one as a gift. The Cardinal kept them both. Bek remarked: 'he has not failed to keep the best'. He thought nothing of giving a benediction in the presence of a Cardinal, when he should have deferred to the superior office and when, in private audience with the Pope, instead of demonstrating appropriate humility, Bek would amuse himself and distract proceedings by playing with a hawk on his hand.

There was no danger of someone like this losing his case in front of the Pope. The previous decision was overturned, Prior Hotoun's complaint dismissed as frivolous and Bek: 'Was treated with all honour and respect by Boniface and his Cardinals'.

Meanwhile back in England, the Prior's complaint was receiving more attention from King Edward, who, still infuriated with Bek, who had left England to go to Rome without his permission, seized the temporalities of the See and appointed his own Chancellor and Justiciary to hear the grievances of the Prior. The case was heard in front of men chosen from Northumberland; the men of the Bishopric suspected as having a likely bias for the Bishop. The words of Master William Boston were now brought against him at the Royal Assizes at Durham, held in the name of the King. But the Prior was successful and the Bishop was ordered to pay heavy damages. Bek was not finished yet. When the time came of the death of Pope Boniface VIII, he again accused the Prior and directed his accusation at the new Pope; Benedict. Unfortunately for Bek, the new Pope died shortly after and the Bishop lost all his expenses incurred in the prosecution of his complaint. Benedict was succeeded by Pope Clement V, and a new opportunity arose for Bek; another complaint was laid against the Prior. This time Bek was successful; the Pope suspended the Prior and within a year, made Bek, Patriarch of Jerusalem.

King Edward now stepped in again. He encouraged the ageing Prior to appeal in person to the Papal Court and this time the: 'goodly and venerable presence', that had previously so impressed the Tynedale heavy, now equally impressed the Pope and his Cardinals. As did a payment of a thousand marks. The Pope now found in favour of the Prior. However, Hotoun was never again to see Durham Cathedral. He died before beginning his journey home and all his possessions, money and jewels were: 'confiscated to the Pope's chamber'. News of his death, and the fact that his escorting monks had been unable or unwilling to vote for a successor reached England, a situation which now unusually brought agreement between King Edward and Bishop Bek, who both favoured William de Tanfield, Prior of Wetherall. He was duly appointed, but not before having to pay three thousand marks to the Pope and another thousand to the Cardinals. Seizing the harmonious moment, Bek made submission to the King and was restored to his See but apart from this brief meeting of minds, and ego's, all was still not well between Bishop and King. Citing Bek's rejection of his mediation in the case of the Prior, Edward took from the Bishop, Barnard Castle, previously forfeited by Balliol, and Hartlepool, previously forfeited by Bruce.

On 7 July 1307 King Edward I, finally died, at Burgh on Sands, on the Solway, not far from Carlisle; at the beginning of another campaign into Scotland, this time against Robert Bruce. With the old King succeeded by his son, Edward II, Antony Bek, was now back in royal favour. Visiting the Durham monastery soon after, he made use of his time there to suspend all the old Prior's supporters for 10 years. Edward II bestowed upon Bek

Auckland Castle strengthened and extended by Bek, now the seat of the modern day Bishops of Durham.

the sovereignty of the Isle of Man. So it was that when he died, on 3 March 1310, after a pontificate of 28 years; Antony Bek was Bishop of Durham, Count Palatine; Patriarch of Jerusalem and: 'King' of Man.

He was laid to rest, not in the Chapter House but in the Cathedral, the first Bishop to be buried there since St Cuthbert himself; none before, out of reverence to the Saint, being granted that privilege. So it was that Antony Bek was placed in his tomb in the northern end of the Chapel of the Nine Altars and there he lies still; his grave, on which can be seen a small brass memorial plate, lies hard by the splendid marble monument to William Van Mildert. During his life he spent profusely, yet as a measure of his wealth, when he died, he did so still in possession of great riches, of treasure, money and of land. More of a Prince than a Bishop, and more of a soldier than either: 'He was a man of unbounded pride and ambition, impatient of contradiction, inveterate and implacable in his resentments'. His position as Patriarch of Jerusalem, the only Englishman ever to hold that office, effectively gave Bek the rank of

The grave and memorial of Antony Bek, in the Chapel of the Nine Altars, Durham Cathedral.

74

senior prelate in England and as such he was nominated in 1308, as principal inquisitor into the affairs of the Knights Templar in England Scotland and Ireland.

He built a chapel and hall at Bishop Auckland: 'which he turned from a manor house into a castle'. He founded a collegiate church at Chester-le-Street for a Dean and seven Prebendaries, and another at Lanchester. He built a magnificent Great Hall in Durham Castle, where it is said that he had placed for himself a double throne; two: 'Seats of Regality', emphasizing his dual capacity; one as the Bishop, one as the Count Palatine.

The story is also told that in 1309, Bek, while holding the Barony and Castle of Alnwick in trust for an illegitimate son of William, Lord de Vesci, sold it, for around four thousand marks, to a Yorkshire family; the Percy's, to whom it has belonged ever since. Questions have been raised as to whether it was actually Bek's to sell, but a deed witnessing the sale was signed by: 'some of the principal persons of the time' and confirmed by King Edward II. Allegedly selling the trust because he had been offended by language the youth had reportedly used in respect of the Bishop, Bek sold it: 'with many scornful words'. Although it has also been alleged that the Bishop: 'appears to have appropriated the Barony to himself for many years before he sold it'.

The death of Bek saw perhaps the end of the greatest of all the mediaeval Prince Bishops of Durham. A man who, as Professor Arthur Bryant noted: 'maintained a magnificence strangely at variance with the See's founder, St Cuthbert'. But a generation on, and another in the mould of Bek would arise; another Warrior Bishop and Counsellor to the King of his day. The King, whom it was thought, would be the: 'New Arthur', would be Edward III; grandson of Bek's own Liege Lord and sparring partner, Edward I. The Bishop would be Thomas Hatfield, who would in his day, send emissaries to measure the height of the Pope's throne in Rome, so that he could erect his own throne in Durham Cathedral just that little bit higher. So it was that the throne of the Prince Bishop of Durham would come to be known, as the: 'Highest Throne in Christendom'.

Chapter 8

The Highest Throne in Christendom

'Yon kingless throne is now for ever bare'

As a final chapter to the great Prince Bishops of Durham, we now look at a few more individuals and events that have added both renown and notoriety to that office. In order to do so, we must go back and begin again at the year 1197. More than 12 months had passed since the end of the Episcopate of Hugh of Le Puiset, and: 'evil days came to Durham'.

Philip of Poitou, sometimes written as Philip de Pictavia, had long been a close royal confidant. In his early career he had accompanied Richard the Lionheart on the third Crusade and it is said that he was Richard's most trusted Clerk and constant companion. Indeed, on 12 May 1191, he had been present at the Chapel of St George, Limassol, Cyprus, at the wedding of Richard to Berengaria of Navarre. He would later be appointed by Richard as Archdeacon of Canterbury. A trusted royal servant, Philip also spent a large proportion of his time on diplomatic missions and he had been one of the emissaries who travelled to Germany with Richard's ransom. Although not in Priests: 'Orders', he had to be ordained a priest before his consecration as Bishop, his rise in favour continued when he was: 'at the urgent desire of the King', appointed Bishop of Durham. He was consecrated at Rome on 12 May 1197.

But the loyalty which Philip showed his royal masters would eventually be rewarded upon his death, with burial, without Christian rights, in an obscure, unconsecrated piece of ground. A Prince Bishop of Durham declared Excommunicate and damned in the eyes of the Church. For the next king that Philip considered worthy of his loyalty was Richard's brother and successor, King John: 'he of ignoble memory', as one Durham chronicler recalled. For John was disliked, distrusted and would himself eventually be excommunicated: 'foul as it is, hell itself is defiled by the fouler presence of John'.

At Durham, so the monks record, Philip was a divisive and unpopular figure. Quickly installing his nephew, Aimeric, as Archdeacon both of Durham and Carlisle, he continued it seems the tradition of his predecessors and his relationships with the Durham monks were troubled. Of course we have to remember that the recorders of these events were the monks themselves and according to their chronicles, Philip: 'oppressed the convent'. Shortly after his consecration the quarrels began. Aimeric claimed that certain rights belonging to the Bishop were being usurped by the Prior and monks. The Prior, Bertram, claimed that the rights were theirs by Royal Grant. Things soon deteriorated. Accusation turned into violence. Following another dispute over a vacancy at St Oswald's Church, a number of monks occupied the building in protest. The Bishop sent in armed men who lit fires around the church and eventually smoked out the reverend, but recalcitrant brethren.

The Bishop next obtained letters from Rome, granting him rights as Abbot. The Prior protested against them, made an appeal to Rome and to the ecclesiastical courts and it is

St Oswald's Church, Durham, from where Bishop Philip of Poitou had rebellious monks: 'smoked out'.

said, obtained confirmation of his own rights, from the King. The Bishop did not give in: 'and proceeded to take very rough measures' against the monks. He closed the road to their Mill, confiscated their supplies of food, destroyed their fish weirs at Finchale, diverted their water supply and slaughtered their cattle at Bearpark. Following a refusal of his demand of access to the Chapter House, Philip promptly excommunicated the Prior and the entire Chapter. On the autumn Feast day of St Cuthbert, when the City was thronged with visitors, the Prior attempted to say Mass. The Bishop, who had issued a proclamation forbidding anyone to be present in the Cathedral, ordered his attendants: 'some of whom were Priests', to stop him. The Bishop's men entered the Cathedral as Mass was being said, seized the Prior, and the altar linen. The monks, understandably dismayed, also grabbed the cloth and: 'a most unseemly struggle ensued', with the Bishop's men pulling at one end of the altar linen, and the monks at the other. The poor Prior was wrestled out of the Cathedral altogether and the monks feared that the Bishop would even: 'throw down the Altar'. According to the chronicler: 'worse doings never before were seen in a church, except at Canterbury when the Archbishop was slain'. However, all, it seems was resolved. Mediation took place, the dispute was settled and, according to the chronicler: 'there was a great calm'. The: 'great calm', of course, would not last.

When, in 1205, Hubert Walter, the Archbishop of Canterbury, died, King John became involved in a dispute with Pope Innocent III. The monks of Canterbury had claimed the right to elect the new Archbishop but this was an immensely powerful position and both the Bishops and the King had vested interests in who should get the job. When the dispute could not be settled, the monks just went ahead and elected one of their own. The King imposed another. The Pope declined them both. It was claimed that the Pope was disregarding the King's authority: 'in the selection of his own vassals'. The King was supported in his resistance to the Pope by the English Barons and many of the Bishops, including the Bishop of Durham, Philip of Pouitou. King John then expelled the Canterbury monks and the Pope retaliated by ordering the serious ecclesiastical sanction of an Interdict against the whole Kingdom of England. Churches were closed; there were no masses, no baptisms and no bells. Religious offices were deprived to those being married and to those being buried. John immediately ordered the seizure of church property: 'for failure to provide feudal service'; from Durham his men took 61 silver plates and had them melted down and made into money. The dispute would go on until 1213, the King himself being excommunicated; and throughout that time King John had the unswerving support of the Prince Bishop of Durham.

Philip may well have been an unscrupulous and violent man: 'excessive in his full blooded rages', so at least those monkish chroniclers tell us. But perhaps this was less to do with Philip himself, and more to do with the unscrupulous and violent times in which he lived and operated. Nevertheless, when he died, the monks of Durham refused a Christian burial for their Bishop.

The See of Durham was now again vacant and over a number of years, efforts were made to find the: 'right man', for the job. The first candidate, elected secretly by the monks of Durham, was Richard, Dean of Salisbury; his election, however, was not approved by the King. The next candidate, who was acceptable to John, was John Grey, Bishop of Norwich but he was already dead by the time his election was confirmed by the Pope. Next was the Prior of Beverley, but he was an illegitimate brother of King John. This, it was considered, could constitute a: 'bar' to his election. However, the Pope offered to confirm his election, if he changed his name to that of his mother's husband, but he refused.

By and by, late in 1217, Gualo, the Papal Legate conferred the Bishopric of Durham on Richard de Marisco, or Richard Marsh, Lord Chancellor of England. The new Bishop, it was said, resembled in character his former royal master, King John, and he began his career in Durham by taking up largely where his predecessor had left off. He contested the privileges claimed by the Durham monks and demanded to see their originating charters. The Prior refused. As tradition would seem to dictate, a: 'deadly feud' arose between Bishop and Chapter, and, just for good measure, Richard swore that the Church of Durham should never have peace as long as he lived. Things clearly, were not harmonious. Richard went on to decree that, if a monk was found beyond his cloister, he should lose his head. It was further alleged, by the monkish chronicler, that when the Bishop's servants: 'grievously assaulted' a monk of the Chapter, the brethren had the temerity to complain to the Bishop; who was heard to exclaim: 'it was a pity that they had not killed him'.

This was too much. The monks made their usual journey to Rome and to the Pope, where they also accused Richard of Sacrilege and of: 'Simony'; the selling of religious favours and the inappropriate use of religious funds; and of many other acts equally: 'inconsistent with his Office'. He was a Bishop, they claimed, who lived his life licentiously. A lengthy litigation followed, with enormous sums of money being spent by both parties. However, Richard de Marisco would not live to see the end of that litigation. For, after a stormy reign as Bishop of Durham and on his way to London in prosecution of his suit against the Durham Chapter, he suddenly expired at Peterborough Abbey; found one morning dead in bed. Apparently no one knew how, or why and according to Surtees: 'The monks, who regarded his death as the interposition of Providence in their favour, have loaded his memory with every species of reproach'.

When Bishop Richard Kellaw died, on 9 October 1316, there was, as usual, keen competition for the wealthy See of Durham. The Queen, Isabella, requested that her kinsman, Lewis de Beaumont, be appointed Bishop. The Chapter of monks, as usual disagreed. The Pope was subsequently petitioned in favour of Beaumont, who, as well as being related to Isabella, was also kin to the King of France. For its support of the petition, it is said that such a large payment was requested by the Papal Court, that, despite the vast revenues of the See of Durham, it took Beaumont 14 years to pay it. Described variously as a: 'Popinjay'; weak, masterful, uncouth, vain, handsome, unlearned, obstinate and: 'lame in both feet'; a major bar to his selection, as far as the monks were concerned, was his ignorance of Latin. At his consecration he stumbled over a solemn Latin vow and shouted out in French: 'Let it be understood as said'. Later, at an ordination, again unable to relay part of the Latin verse, he exclaimed in a loud voice: 'By St Lewis, he wanted courtesy who wrote that word here'.

His Episcopate got off to a less than edifying, but probably predictable start, considering the rough and lawless nature of the Bishopric in the years following the Battle of Bannockburn. Travelling to Durham with his brother and two Cardinals on their way to meet with the King of Scots: 'And a great array of Ecclesiastics', he was ambushed at Rushyford, by the local: 'Robber Baron', Sir Gilbert Middleton and his own private army of freebooters and thugs. The Cardinals were relieved of their valuables and left to make their way to Durham. The Bishop was kidnapped, taken to Middleton's stronghold, Mitford Castle near Morpeth, and held there for ransom. The monks of the Durham monastery were obliged to pay for his release and they reluctantly no doubt, but nonetheless fully, handed over: 'a great deal of money', for a Bishop they had not even wanted in the first place.

Middleton was eventually arrested and so notorious was he, it is said that the King, Edward II, himself devised his execution. His feet were tied beneath his horse and he was dragged through the streets of London for a couple of miles to the gallows. There he was hanged until he was half dead, then cut down and beheaded. His heart was cut out and burned. His body was then quartered and the parts sent for public display to Newcastle, York, Bristol and Dover.

If the monks of Durham were expecting a Bishop's gratitude, not for the first time, they were in for a big shock. Beaumont of course knew that they had opposed his election and had not supported his petition to the Pope. The grudge was very firmly held. He told them he disliked them intensely: 'Do nothing for me', he said: 'As I do nothing for you. Pray for my death, for while I live, you shall have no favour from me'. The Chapter of Durham, so the Chroniclers tell us, tried to conciliate by lavishing gifts on the Bishop, but still he: 'encroached on their rights, and oppressed them by his exactions'.

His episcopate was troubled by the endless lawlessness of the day and by the relentless border raiding of the Scots. But if this was not enough, he also developed a dispute with the Archbishop of York about the Archbishop's claims of visitation rights on Durham. The situation worsened to such a degree that Beaumont, we are told, brought in hired thugs to stop the Archbishop, and was, so the chroniclers say, quite prepared to kill him. Such were the church relations of the day. However, the Archbishop, in an effort to hit the Bishop of Durham where it would really hurt, in his purse; kept up a deadly game of: 'cat and mouse' by evading the Bishop's men, who Beaumont had to keep paying, in order to keep them in the field and in the hunt. The Bishop of Durham then produced a Papal Bull, empowering him to appoint as Prior, any member of his own household he chose to, and assigning to himself a quarter of the Prior's revenue for the duration of the Scottish Wars. Of course it was eventually discovered that these had been obtained under false pretences and he was unable to enforce them.

There remains, however, a paradox to the reign of Lewis de Beaumont, Prince Bishop of Durham. For all his clashes with the monks, and, as we are told: 'He is plainly one of whom the Church of Durham has no reason to be proud', when he died in 1333, there was not for Beaumont an anonymous burial in unconsecrated ground. This Prince Bishop was honoured with a magnificent funeral, and still lies today in his grave in front of the High Altar in Durham Cathedral. Perhaps then, there was more to the episcopate of Lewis de Beaumont, than has been recorded for history by the monks of Durham.

Unlike Lewis de Beaumont, Richard de Bury, or Richard de Aungerville, was a scholar, writer, Bibliophile and a true: 'Patron of Learning'. He was also; it was said, implicated in the intrigues surrounding the deposition and murder of King Edward II.

After this, on the accession of Edward III, whose tutor he had been, he achieved rapid promotion, eventually becoming Chancellor of England, Keeper of the Privy and Secretary to the King. In 1333, the King appointed him as Bishop of Durham, against the wishes of the monks. Nevertheless, he was enthroned at the Cathedral, in the presence of the King and Queen of England, the King of Scotland, and: 'many high dignitaries'.

But the tradition of fighting Bishops would be restored when, in 1345, Richard de Bury died and another Warrior Ecclesiastic would assume the Bishop's Throne. King Edward III himself nominated Thomas de Hatfield for the Bishopric of Durham.

Considered: 'rather light on religious qualifications', but well versed in martial pursuits, in his time he would also be Keeper of the Privy Seal, Secretary to the King and Counsellor to the King's son. Hatfield would indeed be a great favourite of King Edward. Since the 1330s, he had been: 'Keeper of the Chamber', responsible for raising money for the King's French Wars. But he had also been a soldier, fighting in the King's service, with his own: 'substantial military retinue'. However, there had been serious objections to his appointment as Bishop, mainly from the Cardinals who made accusations of: 'significant lobbying' by the King, on Hatfield's behalf. Nonetheless the Pope, Clement VI, countered by telling them that: 'if the King of England petitioned for an ass for Bishop, he would be accommodated'. Thomas Hatfield was subsequently enthroned at Durham, on Christmas Day, 1345.

In 1346, Edward III invaded France; Hatfield went with him and when the English Army eventually marched on Paris it advanced in three divisions. The first Division, the Vanguard, was under the command of the 16-year-old, Edward: 'Black Prince' of Wales. This was followed by the main body of the army, which was commanded by King Edward himself; then came the third division, the Reanguard, with the Earls of Warwick and Northampton assisting its overall commander; Thomas Hatfield, Prince Bishop of Durham. In the August he fought alongside King Edward at the Battle of Crecy again in joint command of the Reanguard of the Army and had come to the aid of the young Black Prince who had become: 'hard pressed' in the fight. When the victory had been won, Hatfield the warrior assumed the role of Hatfield the Bishop and officiated at the funeral of John, the blind King of Bohemia who had fallen in the Battle. Following the victory at Crecy, Hatfield remained with the King and took part in the Siege of Calais. So it was that in the October of that year, the Bishop of Durham was not present at the defeat of King David II of Scotland and his army at the Battle of Neville's Cross; his place having been taken by the Archbishop of York.

The Warrior Bishop fought on and towards the end of 1355, he was back in France, alongside the King, with 100 of his own men at arms. The following year Hatfield was one of the King's men charged with the defence of England's northern border, and he was present at the negotiations that culminated, in October 1357, with the final release of King David of Scotland. Fourteen years on, at David's death, Hatfield, still the Warrior Bishop was again instructed to guard against expected Scottish incursions.

Unlike some of his predecessors, Hatfield's relationships with the Durham monks were generally good; perhaps, however, this was something to do with his lengthy absences. The formal relationship between Bishop and Convent had been regulated by Bishop Richard le Poore, who had drawn up a binding agreement: 'Le Convenit'. Originally sealed in 1229, it had been mutually acceptable to both sides and the agreement was ratified by Hatfield in 1354. However, in his dealings with the Archbishops of York, we are told that Hatfield: 'maintained the animosity common to his forebears'. His relationships: 'were not harmonious'. In 1349, he was suspected of being behind an armed attack on the Archbishop's men, a: 'disgusting disturbance' in York Minster. Following an inquiry, however, the King himself issued an official denial of Hatfield's involvement in the attack. What it was to have friends in the highest places! Eleven years later and Hatfield instructed his Chancellor to publish a protest, declaring his complete exemption from obedience or subjection to the Archbishop. Relationships remained strained. Indeed when Alexander Neville, Archbishop of York, attempted to visit the Durham Diocese in 1376, the King himself prohibited his action as: 'being likely to promote disturbance'. The chronicler William Chambre praised Hatfield's attitude and generosity towards the Durham monastery, telling us nonetheless that this Prince Bishop of Durham was: 'A formidable figure, who strove to be foremost among the magnates, was tenacious of the rights of his See, open-handed to the poor; and conscious of his own importance'.

Indeed, Chambre goes on to colour Hatfield's character with phrases such as: 'just and beneficent; haughty and untractable; tenacious of rank and impatient of control'; and we are told by the same chronicler that in physical appearance Hatfield was: 'Tall, unbending under the load of years, grey headed, of venerable aspect, with a lofty and commanding presence'. During his time he ordered the erection of the present: 'Cathedra', the Bishop's throne in Durham Cathedral; symbolising both the ecclesiastical and secular authority of the Bishop. Perhaps rather, as Chambre pointed out: 'conscious of his own importance', Hatfield had emissaries sent to Rome, to measure the height of the Pope's throne. He then had his own throne at Durham built just that little bit higher. Because of this, it is said that the Bishop's throne in Durham Cathedral, is the highest throne in Christendom. The story is perhaps apocryphal, that on hearing what the Bishop of Durham had done; the Pope sat on a cushion. If indeed a Prince Bishop rather: 'light' on religious qualification, he weighed in with substantial military prowess. He claimed that he had been brought up under the protection of Edward III and had acted as Tutor to the Price of Wales. He was proud, haughty and overbearing. One of the most powerful of the Prince Bishops, Hatfield remained in Office for almost 40 years. He instigated major building programmes and his personal spending was considerable but despite this he remained a wealthy man, at one point even making a loan of two thousand marks to the King; and throughout his career he would remain, in the tradition of preceding Counts Palatine: 'jealous to excess of any infringement on the privileges of the Church'.

Eventually, Thomas Hatfield requested the prayers of the monks: 'for his soul's salvation', and after a: 'tedious illness', he died in London, on 8 May 1381. His last journey back to Durham was made on a funeral chariot. In his will he instructed that on the day of his burial and for the following eight days, 100 marks be provided for the poor of Durham. So it was that on the day of Hatfield's funeral, 50: 'poor men', with lighted torches, acted as his official mourners as he was finally laid in his tomb, under his own Cathedra, his Prince Bishops throne, a sketch of which would be made in the 18th century by the splendidly named, Samuel Hieronymous Grimm. It was: 'The highest throne in Christendom'; and there Hatfield lies to this day.

And so we move on towards the end of days for mediaeval Warlords and Robber Barons and approach the demise of the Counts Palatine of Durham. The Tudor age issued in a new breed of royal: 'Favourites', and strong, militarily minded men were neither needed, nor wanted, as Bishops of Durham. The Tudor preference was for: 'Clever Administrators'.

On St George's Day, 23 April 1509, Thomas Ruthall, Lord Privy Seal, Chancellor of the University of Cambridge and Dean of Salisbury, was nominated to the See of Durham and it was during his episcopate that the last throes of the old Scottish Wars were played out, on Flodden Field, near Branxton in Northumberland. After a blessing, the Banner of St Cuthbert was unfurled in Durham Market Place. It would be carried into battle again and for the last time in the open field. The almost mystical Banner which it was said: 'had never been carried in vain, or displayed in an unjust cause'. The Banner which had seen so many victories for those that had carried it, for it was claimed: 'Whoso fights against St Cuthbert,

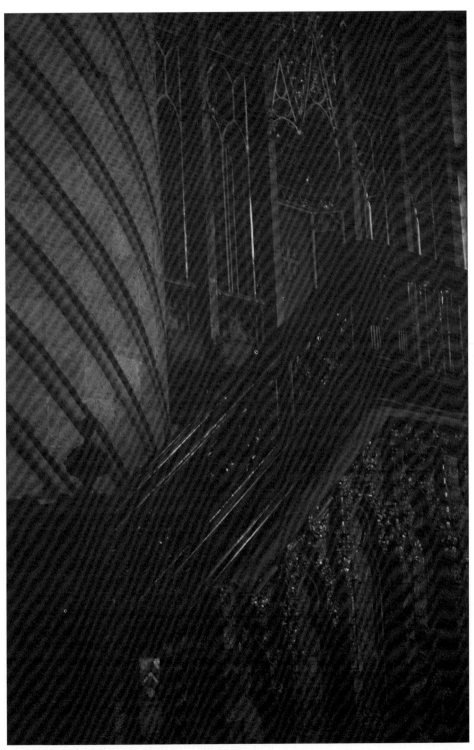

The Durham: 'Cathedra', the Bishop's Throne.

The tomb of Bishop Thomas Hatfield in Durham Cathedral.

fights against right, and cannot prevail'. So it was that St Cuthbert's Banner flew at Flodden Field and was witness to the tragedy that was played out there. It is said that the lament: *Flowers of the Forest* was written to commemorate the Scots dead of that day. As well as the King of Scotland, 10,000 of his men were killed, including two Bishops, two Abbots, 12 Earls, 13 Barons: 'and gentlemen of name beyond the counting'.

Back in his own Diocese, there is little to be said of Ruthall, save his immense wealth, accumulated mainly from the revenues of the See of Durham. However, as the chroniclers record: 'His riches were to prove his ruin'.

Ruthall had received a royal command from Henry VIII, to draw up an account of all the lands and revenues held by the Crown in different parts of England; this, Ruthall had done. In another work, Ruthall had drawn up an account of all his own possessions as Prince Bishop of Durham. Unfortunately for him, it was this account which was mistakenly sent to Henry. The mistake was discovered by Cardinal Wolsey, who, we are told: 'treacherously pointed out to Henry, that if his Majesty wanted money, he now knew where to get it'. In the end, Henry made no use of his new found knowledge but the matter troubled Ruthall considerably. Knowing the nature of the King, and of the King's Chancellor, it hung like the Sword of Damocles over his episcopate: 'The matter sank into the Prelate's own mind, and the mortification he felt at his unintended disclosure is believed to have hastened his death'. Ruthall died in 1523, responsibility for the Bishopric of Durham was handed to Wolsey, who continued to hold it for six years, together with the Archbishopric of York. During those six years Wolsey never once set foot in: 'his' Diocese and in 1528 he simply exchanged it for Winchester.

The long line of Prince Bishops of Durham finally ended with William van Mildert. Born in 1765, the son of a distiller, he was of Dutch origin. Formally the Bishop of Llandaff, in 1826 he came to the See of Durham and: 'the distiller's son found himself to

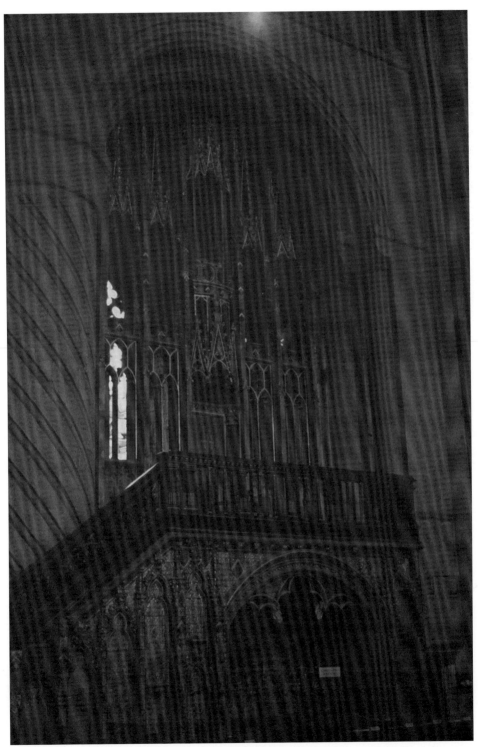

Hatfield's Throne: 'The Highest Throne in Christendom', sits atop his own tomb.

Bishop William Van Mildert, last of the Prince Bishops of Durham.

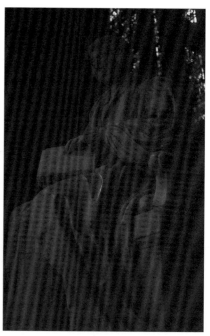

be a Prince as well as a Bishop'. And it was perhaps as a response to memories from his formative years, of the American War of Independence and of the French Revolution that he strenuously resisted the popular political and social reforms of his day, and because of this, was burned in effigy outside Auckland Castle. Within his Bishopric, however, he instructed his clergy to: 'educate the ignorant and attend to public education', as well as to carry out their spiritual ministrations. Van Mildert enjoyed a huge income as Bishop of Durham and he used money from the Episcopal Revenues to: 'give generously to these ends'. The last Prince Bishop is mainly remembered in relation to the establishment of the University of Durham. Brought into being in only two years, between 1831 and 1833, Van Mildert's: 'own energy and money', went into its creation. He gave to the new University a number of buildings; and his own seat, the Prince Bishop's Castle of Durham, to be its first College. He also donated 160 volumes to the new University Library.

On 21 February 1836, William Van Mildert died; the heir to saints and warlords. According to the: 'Diocesan History of Durham', it was a dark and dismal day, when the last Count Palatine was laid to rest: 'As if the very elements felt that there was glory departing'. A memorial to him was erected at the north end of the Chapel of the Nine Altars, hard by the plain brass tomb cover of Antony Bek; the last of the Prince Bishops of Durham to stand over one who was perhaps the greatest of their number.

'The herald breaks the wand, while he proclaims
The sainted Palatine's puissant names
Yon kingless throne is now for ever bare
....
There is a glory less upon the earth'.

With the end of Van Mildert, the Prince Bishops of Durham were reduced by Victorian statute and became simply Bishops. Seven and a half centuries of their rule in the County Palatine of Durham was ended. None had been as the saints of old, many had been sinners. Among their number had been warriors, scholars, politicians and a few downright villains. Some were scheming and ambitious and some were genuinely pious. Perhaps the following picturesque description by Sir Timothy Eden, in his 1952 book about the County of Durham, will serve as a colourful final word on their line:

'They built like gods and they fed like hogs, they dressed like angels and they probably stank like badgers. They threw a fortune at one man and loaded another with fetters at the bottom of a dungeon. They fasted and scourged themselves to the dust; and they glittered through the world like peacocks'.

Part Three

Chapter 9

A Sword and a Serpent

'This place, which had hitherto been so highly honoured, now became a terror to all, and
was surnamed: The Place of the Tortures of Hell'
- Simeon of Durham

If you go to Durham Cathedral and visit the Treasures of St Cuthbert, you will see an item
there which at once seems out of place among the holy relics and religious artifacts on
display. For the item is a curved sword, a Falchion, pronounced Fal-shun; in style
reminiscent of the Scimitar of Turk and Arab, with a blade two and a half feet in length,
and a bronze pommel: 'decorated with serpents and armorials'. Legend would have us
believe that this is the very sword with which: 'in awncient tyme', the noble Conyers fought
and slew one of the terrible legendary beasts of Durham: The Sockburn Worm.

On 29 April 1891, the same sword was exhibited by its then owner, Sir Edward Blackett,
at a meeting of the Newcastle Society of Antiquaries. Attached to its hilt, for the benefit of
Society Members, was a memorandum outlining the weapon's pedigree:

'Sir Edward Blackett now represents the person of Sir John Conyers, who, in the year
1063, in the fields of Sockburn, slew with this Falchion, according to the ancient story, a
Dragon, Worm or Flying Serpent, which devoured men, women and children. The owner
of Sockburn, as a reward for his bravery, gave Sir John the Manor of Sockburn for him and
his heirs forever. On condition of his meeting the Lord Bishop of Durham, with his
Falchion, on his first entrance into his diocese after appointment'.

So what of the origins of the story. What was this: 'fiery, flying serpent'? Who really was
the hero of the tale? The gallant warrior who slew the dreaded beast. To begin we must first
travel back to a time not too long after the Norman Conquest, for it is in those turbulent
and bloody years that our tale is likely to have had its roots.

The chronicles record that one Roger de Conyers was, by William the Conqueror, made
Constable of Durham Castle: 'and keeper of all the arms of the souldiers within the castle,
which was passed after him, the saide Roger, by deede to him and his heires mailes for ever,
under the great seal of William de Sancto Carilepho, Bishop of Durham'. Later, in 1126, St
Carileph's successor, Rannulf Flambard granted to the Conyers family, the Manor of
Sockburn, a grant which was confirmed by the Prior and Convent of Durham and by King
Henry I. Indeed, the chronicles tell that the House and lands of Sockburn were the
inheritance of the Conyers family, having been granted to their Norman ancestor, on
account of, it is said: 'some valiant action performed by him'. So the Conyers were a noble
family, seated in the south of the Bishopric before the troubled accession of King Stephen
in 1135. They ruled the lands around the Tees, as Lords of Sockburn and Bishopton, before
even the completion of Durham Cathedral.

The Sockburn peninsula, near Neasham, is the southern most tip of County Durham. A rural area, the peninsula is formed by a loop in the River Tees, reminiscent of the loop of the River Wear around Durham. A pleasant place the chroniclers record, even in those violent days. A place: 'especially consecrated by Dame Nature to perennial peace'. The River Tees meandering gently amid green countryside and fertile fields. A restful place indeed for the Lords of Sockburn. But the tale tells that into this gentle corner of the Prince Bishop's realm came a horror. A ravaging dragon which brought death and destruction to all around. None could face it. Those who were brave enough to try were killed and devoured. The manuscripts tell of: 'a monstrous and poysonous vermine or wyverne, an ask or werme, which overthrew and devoured many people in fight, for that the sent of that poison was so strong that no person might abide it'.

The Sockburn Worm of which the tale tells was, like its neighbour the Lambton Worm, a hideous serpent like monster. But unlike the beast of Lambton, this horror bore a dreadful resemblance to the dragons of heroic myth. It was endowed with wings: 'and its poisonous breath was death'. The beast, as did its northerly counterpart, laid waste to the countryside around. A scourge, which devoured both people and livestock and brought a reign of terror to bear on the lands of Sockburn. No Knight could stand against it. And it roamed fields and forest at will. However, they do say that: 'cometh the hour, cometh the man' and the hour came when the hero of our story, named in the tale as Sir John Conyers, prepared to do battle with the dread beast. Unlike: 'Young Lambton', however, he did not first consult a: 'Wise Woman', instead he sought the assistance of a higher power: 'But before he made this enterprise, having but one sonne, he went to the Church of Sockburne in complete armour, and offered up his only sonne to the Holy Ghost'. So it was that after due prayer and penitence, our hero left the Church, mounted his horse and rode out of history into legend. He knew something of the habits of the monster. It was said that some days, after slaking its thirst by draining a trough of milk put out as an offering, the Worm could be seen sunning itself on a large rock, the: 'Greystane', in a field near to Sockburn Church. It did not take long before the foes came face to face and all the countryside around knew that only one would see the sun rise the next day.

Battle was joined and for a long while the combat raged. At length Conyers' strength began to fail, soon the beast would have the mastery and he began to see his fate in the jaws of the Dragon. He made one last desperate assault on his enemy. Furiously he tried to smite the beast around the neck with his great sword. But the Dragon was swift and the glancing blows were of no effect, serving only to enrage the beast: 'at which indignant, wide he flapped his wings'. But as the monster reared up, Conyers noticed underneath, near the place where the heart should be, a patch of soft, unguarded skin. Breaking off from the combat he swiftly loaded a dart into his bow; again the Dragon roared and reared, and foul air breathed from its flapping, membranous wings. But as it stretched wide, Conyers let go his dart. A short swift journey and it found its mark. The beast swayed, roared out one last time and crashed to the ground, mortally wounded. The triumphant Conyers strode forward and with two great hews of his sword, separated the monster's head from its body and brought its foul life to an end. The battle was over. Conyers was triumphant and the country folk around rejoiced: 'The vanquished serpent closed his glaring eyes, and like a blasted oak, in ruin lies'.

There are clear parallels between this story and other: 'Worm' stories of the North Country; the Lambton Worm has already been mentioned. The common general form is particularly noticeable. A terrible monster, a curse upon the populace. The hero of the story, a chivalrous knight of a noble family who goes in search of the dragon. Who eventually and at great risk to himself and his future heirs, locks the beast in mortal combat and after a terrible struggle, wins the day. Slaying the monster and freeing the people from its tyranny. There are even more common themes in the details of the stories. It is tempting and easy therefore to imagine, that through the passage of centuries and the telling and re-telling of the tales, the threads of both stories have become intertwined and each has been added to by the other.

Does then this story belong solely to the realms of legend, or is there perhaps some hidden truth from which the tale has later developed. Some chroniclers in later centuries have said that the story is pure allegory. Penant, was of the opinion that the figure of the Sockburn Worm or Dragon was merely symbolic; probably a representation of an invading army which had settled in the area and had systematically pillaged the surrounding countryside, committing: 'various enormities' against the peasantry. He goes on to suggest that the most likely culprits were the Scots, who regularly raided as far south as Durham and beyond. Hutchinson in part agreed with this theory, but he championed the idea of a Norse war band. It would seem, however, that at the time in which the story is set, a marauding Viking army is likely to have been a thing of the past. Nonetheless, there is a striking similarity between these explanations, and those put forward by Sir Cuthbert Sharp, to explain the story of the Lambton Worm and as has already been said, the central themes of both tales bear an obvious resemblance. The noble knight of both stories achieving victory over the enemy and therefore bringing an end to the ravaging of the monster: 'Slaying the Dragon'.

If, however, the reader does not necessarily subscribe to either of these theories, nor indeed to a zoological explanation, there is another alternative, which, in the early 19th century was subscribed to by the celebrated: 'Historian of Durham', Robert Surtees. But in his explanation the killing and destruction associated with the Sockburn Worm was attributed, not to some mythical dragon like monster, nor to marauding armies or ravaging invaders, but were laid squarely at the feet of one man. A man who for his cruelty and treachery, was greatly despised throughout the Palatine Lands. A cleric with a blind, ruthless ambition, who usurped the See of Durham and brought about much suffering on any who opposed him.

When King Henry I died in 1135, with no direct male heir, his son, Prince William had drowned in the sinking of the 'White Ship' in 1120; controversy surrounded the succession. His only surviving, legitimate child, was a daughter, Maud, sometimes written in the Latin form; Matilda. Prior to his death, she had been named as his successor and the Barons of England and Normandy had sworn and oath of allegiance to her. Her cousin, Stephen of Blois, had sworn the same oath. Stephen was only a nephew of Henry but he was one of the richest landowners in England and his mother was Adela, the youngest daughter of William the Conqueror. So both claimants could demonstrate a direct line of succession from the Conqueror himself.

When Henry died, Maud was in France with her husband; Geoffrey, Count of Anjou, and was pregnant with their third child. She was in no position to act in defence of her succession and Stephen moved quickly to take the throne of England. When faced with this situation, the Barons, fearing under Maud, an Angevin, rather than a Norman succession, and not really wanting a woman ruler; despite their oaths of allegiance to her;

switched loyalties to Stephen. He was crowned King of England on 22 December 1135. As a ruler, Stephen was amiable, forgiving; as far as the Barons were concerned, weak.

Never failing to seize an opportunity, the Scots, led by King David I, moved south, ostensibly in support of Maud, she was after all David's niece. But because of the instability in England, a perfect opportunity had showed itself for the Scots to extend their territorial claims. Early in 1136, the Scots crossed the border and advanced as far south as Durham. Stephen, however, responded immediately, bringing north a substantial army. David was forced to negotiate, and a Peace Treaty was signed by both Kings in Durham City. According to the Victoria County History, David then withdrew his troops, with which he had: 'meditated the reduction of the City and the annexation of the Patrimony of St Cuthbert'.

When, in 1139, Maud eventually did invade England in pursuance of her claim to the throne, the country was torn apart. King Stephen lost control. Barons took the law into their own hands and rule by despots became the norm. So began what was called: 'The Anarchy', a largely forgotten dark and violent period of English history, during which the biggest losers were the common people. The Anglo-Saxon Chronicler records:

'I know not how to, nor am I able to tell of, all the atrocities nor all the cruelties which they wrought upon the unhappy people of this country…and men said openly, that Christ and his Saints slept'.

Stephen's position gradually became weaker and a second Peace Treaty between Stephen and David was signed in Durham, on 9 April 1139. It was witnessed by the Archbishops of Canterbury, York, St Andrews and Glasgow, with in attendance, according to Fordyce, the Empress Maud, with her young son, Henry of Anjou; the future King Henry II, and: 'many of the Scottish Barons and Nobles'. This new Treaty gave the Scots control over large swathes of the North of England and Durham became, for a time, part of a zone of Scottish influence which extended as far south as the River Tees.

St Giles Church, Durham, fortified and garrisoned by Roger de Conyers during the: 'Anarchy'.

And it was during these violent and uncertain times that Geoffrey Rufus, Bishop of Durham, died. The See became vacant. A certain William Cumin had been Chaplain to the Bishop, had connections in the Scottish Court and was a: 'zealous adherent' of the Empress Maud. The story tells that Cumin had his own designs on the Bishopric of Durham. As Bishop Geoffrey lay dying, Cumin we are told, journeyed to Scotland, to seek support for his enterprise from King David. On hearing that the Bishop had finally died, Cumin sent messages back to Durham, telling his supporters to withhold the news of the Bishop's death until he'd returned. This he did in haste, after receiving the support of the Scottish king. So it was that Cumin returned, seized Durham, and took the Bishop's throne for his own. Simeon recorded these events; telling us that Cumin: 'violently intruded into the See of Durham, and carried himself with a high hand'. From the outset, the Durham clergy were against him. Ranulf the Archdeacon vehemently opposed him and was banished; along with Roger de Conyers, hereditary Constable of Durham Castle. The Barons were called to swear fealty before Cumin and all who were against him were expelled from the Bishopric, their lands and property confiscated. As a result of his brutal methods of persuasion, Cumin eventually received homage from most but not all of the local nobility. One who would not swear allegiance to the usurper was Roger de Conyers and many times over the following three years Cumin tried to: 'persuade' him by force of arms, and violent clashes between their two forces took place.

During this troubled time, some of the clerics managed to escape the Durham Monastery and petitioned the Pope over the authenticity of Cumin's claim; he had after all produced Papal letters proclaiming him, Bishop of Durham. These had been forged. The Pope declared Cumin a usurper, with no right to the throne of Durham and he instructed the delegation to arrange for the immediate election of a new Bishop.

So it was that in March 1143, the Dean of York, William de St Barbe, was lawfully elected as the next Prince Bishop of Durham. Eventually he rode north to pursue his claim. He was met and lodged at Bishopton by Roger de Conyers, who was in the process of fortifying the house. Together they rode on Cumin at Durham. After: 'a deal of fighting and no small amount of sacrilege', there was stalemate. The rightful Bishop and the rightful Constable of Durham Castle held and fortified St Giles Church, in Gilesgate, and for a time based their small garrison there. They tried to dislodge Cumin but the usurper was secure in his castle stronghold and: 'neither anathema nor seigecraft could dislodge him'. All their actions did not break the deadlock and eventually the allies were forced to return to Bishopton. Cumin still held Durham. After this failed challenge to his authority, Cumin and his supporters gave full vent to their anger and cruelty. They stole, murdered and destroyed and brought much suffering to the people of Durham. Simeon relates:- 'Just as effectually as locusts give proof of their presence by nipping off the leaves and flowers from a tree, so wherever these men passed, it became a wilderness. Their insolence was not confined to ravages and plunderings only, but was extended to the most cruel bodily torments, inflicted not in secret, and in the darkness of the night, and upon a few individuals, but perpetrated openly, and in the sight of day, and upon men of nobler rank'

Do we see perhaps in this persecution, cruelty and laying waste to the Bishopric, the inspiration for the tale of the ravening monster, later to be represented as the Sockburn Worm? Could the real object of the hatred of the people be that thing: 'so dread, so fearful to behold', the instigator of the calamity and the actual foe of Roger de Conyers; William Cumin?

Storm over Durham Castle: 'A Den of Thieves' during William Cumin's usurpation.

The tortures went on. In the winter time, Simeon tells us, Cumin's men amused themselves by breaking the ice on the River Wear and throwing in their victims who had ropes tied around them, so as to enable their tormentors to drag them out and throw them again and again, naked, back into the freezing water. A particular favourite was to suspend their victims from high walls by a rope around their middle. Heavy armour or large rocks were then tied to the neck, wrists and ankles, so that the extremities were pulled down towards the ground. The darkness that Cumin, the: 'savage and rapacious tyrant', had wrought, descended and lay on the Bishopric for 16 months. Simeon tells that the City of Durham echoed with the groans of the tortured and the dying. So at the time in our history when the famous but fictional, Brother Cadfael of Shrewsbury Abbey, was making sense of murder and mayhem in the violent, but essentially just, border lands of the Welsh Marches; in Durham City the murder and mayhem was a terrible reality and justice was no refuge for Cumin's oppressed victims:

'In consequence of such horrible proceedings, this place, which had hitherto been so highly honoured, now became a terror to all, and was surnamed: The Place of the Tortures of Hell'.

Cumin by this time knew that none recognised any legitimate claim of his to the Prince Bishop's throne. He therefore attempted to hold it by force. The chronicles record that in the Cathedral: 'the voice of prayer and praise was silenced' and the Castle was reduced to being: 'a den of thieves'. As for Durham itself, we are told that: 'The misery of the City was so intense…it was as if all the Tyrants that had ever injured it at different times, had united to do their worst'. Outside of the City, Cumin's supporters began fortifying other strategic sites; and it was this action that was to trigger the final act of the drama.

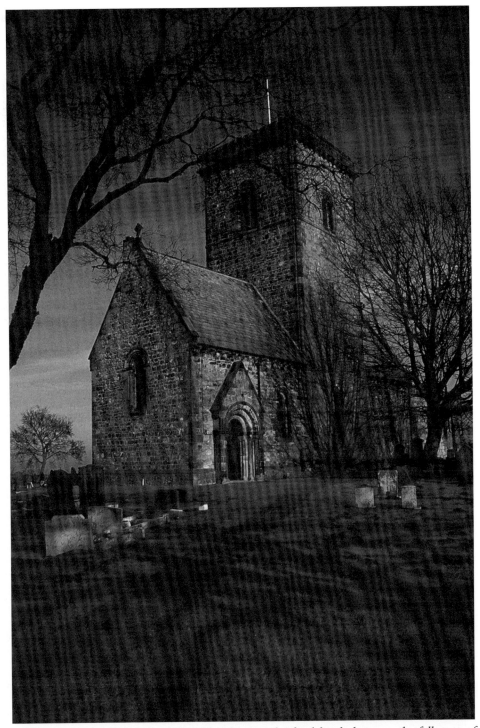

St John's Church, Kirk Merrington. The site saw the fatal battle between the followers of Cumin and Conyers.

One of these sites was the Church of St John, perched high on the ridge at Kirk Merrington, and news of it came to the ears of Roger de Conyers. For some time he had been mustering his forces about him and had gathered the support of other nobles wronged by Cumin. So it was that in the autumn of 1144, Roger de Conyers, supported by Geoffrey de Escolland and Bertram de Bulmer, with whatever forces they could gather together, marched north to strike the usurper. They attacked at Merrington, as Cumin's men were in the process of fortifying the Church. Sykes records the actions of that day: 'Some fled, others barred themselves in the church around which they had nearly completed a fosse, and manning the tower and out works, which they had finished, vainly strove to drive off the assailants with darts and arrows; but the besiegers, reckless of wounds or death, forced their way through the windows, and hurling firebrands on the offenders, were quickly masters of the place'.

So Conyers led his force to the capture of the Church and the scattering of Cumin's men. It is said that those of the usurper's followers who were taken prisoner: 'became suddenly mad, gnawing their own tongues till they died'. Conyers then led his victorious force from Merrington to Durham and eventually took control of the entire City apart from the Castle itself. All the usurper could do was to barricade himself in and await the coming of the rightful Bishop. Cumin's reign of terror was over, his power was gone, the people of the Bishopric rejoiced that the tyrant was captured, his evil forces smashed: 'the vanquished serpent closed his glaring eyes and like a blasted oak, in ruin lies'. Conyers was declared the hero and, we are told, was given back what had been taken from him; the Constable's Staff and the Wardenship of Durham Castle.

Is this then the real tale of Conyers of Sockburn and his fight against: 'The Dragon'? Whether the answer to that question is yes, or no, the story of Cumin's usurpation and of the part played by Sir Roger de Conyers is recorded fact; yet another chapter in the sometimes violent history of Durham. As for the legend and significance of the Worm itself, that must be left for the reader to contemplate upon. Conyer's Falchion, claimed to be the sword that slew the Worm, now hangs among the Treasures of St Cuthbert. The armorials it bears on the pommel are, on one side, the three lions of England; on the other, somewhat fittingly, a winged beast, though thought not to be a Dragon, but a black eagle, perhaps the arms of the Saxon Earl, Morcar. The eventual fate of the Sockburn Worm itself is given to us in legend. After its death, the carcass was taken up and buried in the field near Sockburn Church under the: 'Greystane'. The large boulder serving as a permanent marker for the Dragon of Sockburn.

Dragon Lore is deeply embedded in English mythology. Indeed the Country's patron saint, became so because he: 'Slew the Dragon' of his day. For centuries, stories have been told of the ravages of terrible serpents, winged or otherwise, all seemingly semi-magical and almost invincible, apart, usually, for one particular and fatal weakness. Such stories have been handed down from times more ancient than the early mediaeval days in which this story is set. From the days of: 'Beowulf' and the earliest Anglo-Saxon tales, they have been told, listened to and repeated, and have remained with us, surviving even into the literature of our own century and the realms of J.R.R. Tolkien's: 'Middle Earth', and works similar.

'Legends connected with these pestiferous monsters, excited the imagination of the people who sometimes furnished them with wings as well as feet, converting the 'Worms' into 'Dragons'; and are current from Cornwall to Caithness, as may be seen in any good collection of British folklore'.

Perhaps, however, more than anything, these stories were a way of perceiving and preserving a truth, and a method of passing on that truth, in the form of legend. Whoever or whatever Conyers destroyed, the event was certainly celebrated. The Falchion may later have been presented to the family as a reward for that very deed. And whether or not the modern day reader chooses to believe the legend of the slaying of the Worm, the ceremonial presentation of Conyer's Falchion to a new Bishop of Durham on first entering his Bishopric is beyond doubt and is said to date from the 12th century and the time of Bishop Hugh of Le Puiset, the Bishop who succeeded William de St Barbe. The presentation ceremony itself, originally took place on the ford in the River Tees at Neasham. Later, however, it would be carried out in the middle of Croft Bridge. In 1660, Dr John Cosin a former Prebendary of Durham Cathedral in the days before the English Civil War became the first Prince Bishop of Durham following the Restoration of the Monarchy. In a letter, he described the ancient ritual, as the Sword of Sockburn was presented to him as Lord Bishop:

'At my first entrance through the River of Tease, there was scarce any water to be seene for the multitude of horses and men that filled it. Then the sword that killed the dragone was delivered to me with all the formality of trumpets and gunshots and all acclamations that might be made'.

The formal presentation of the Sword was then made by the Lord of Sockburn: 'My Lord Bishop, I hereby present you with the Falchion wherewith the champion Conyers slew the Worm, Dragon or Fiery Flying Serpent, which destroyed man, woman and child; in memory of which, the King then reigning gave him the Manor of Sockburn'. The weapon was then accepted by the Bishop, who immediately returned it to its owner, wishing the Lord, 'Health and long enjoyment of the Manor'. The ceremonial presentation of the sword ended with the last Prince Bishop of Durham, William van Mildert but was revived in 1984 for the entrance into his Bishopric of Dr David Jenkins. Again, in July 2003, the new Bishop, Canon Tom Wright strode out into the middle of Croft Bridge to receive the ancient sword of Conyers.

To many it might appear merely as just another quaint old custom, common enough throughout England. But it was a custom which, in the 19th century, was known about by a young man, whose family lived only a short distance away, at Croft Rectory. The young man's father, the Reverend Charles Dodgson, was Rector of St Peter's Church, Croft. The family had lived in the area since 1843 and the young man in his formative days, had taken a lively interest in local customs and traditions. He would have been aware of the legend of the Sockburn Worm and the significance of Conyer's Falchion. That young man was Charles Lutwidge Dodgson, who, as Lewis Carroll, would in 1872, publish the sequel to his: *Alice in Wonderland*, and in the pages of: *Through the Looking Glass*, would lurk the beast with: 'Jaws that bite and claws that catch'; the Jabberwock. A dragon like creature which killed and devoured its victims, and which was eventually defeated by a gallant hero who went in search of the beast and did battle with it in a wood, finally emerging triumphant, after cutting off the monster's head with two strokes of his great sword.

So the sword now resides with the Treasures of St Cuthbert. The beast now lies under the: 'Greystane'. The tyrant usurper William Cumin: 'A shivering penitent'; after pleading for mercy, surrendered Durham Castle into the custody of Roger de Conyers: 'to be held in trust for St Cuthbert'. He was pardoned, walked away a free man: 'And was thenceforward hidden from historians in a penitential obscurity'. But what of Conyers himself? In the family chapel, part of the old Parish Church of Sockburn, lay the effigy of a knight of the Conyers family; at peace, with a sword upon his breast, and at his feet, the carved figure of a fabulous, dragon like beast.

The later generations of: 'One of the most honourable houses in the north', were to fade into obscurity and the sad tale of their ultimate demise was recorded by Surtees. Sir George Conyers had, throughout his lifetime, squandered what remained of the riches and land that had been his inheritance. Early in the 19th century he died without an heir and upon his death, the succession went to his uncle, Sir Thomas Conyers. He was a man who had known an unfortunate life, who had descended into anonymity and whose circumstances were poor. Unsuccessful in business, he had even spent a number of years at sea. He was 72 years of age when he received the Conyers inheritance, and it was Sir Thomas who would be the last representative of the Conyers family. A family who came, as Boyle remarked: 'From the very remotest antiquity'. When he was eventually traced, this last descendent of Roger de Conyers, Constable of the Castle of Durham, by order of William the Conqueror; was found: 'Solitary and friendless, a pauper in the parish workhouse of Chester-le-Street'. A sad fall indeed, as Richardson related: 'Such is the mutability of human affairs, that this man, whose ancestors were lords and inheritors of extensive lands; broke stones upon the Turnpike'.

Having a deal of sympathy for noble Durham families whose light shone less brightly than once it did, Surtees, with the aid of the Reverend Patrick George, Curate of Bishop Middleham, went to the aid of the last Conyers. But the native pride was still strong in his heart and according to Surtees: 'Accustomed as he was to hardship and labour, he wished for neither affluence nor luxury, but his then humiliating situation he felt severely'. Having been made aware that the old man's subscriptions were due to be paid on 26 February 1810, Surtees and Reverend George offered financial assistance to Sir Thomas, which would have enabled him to leave the workhouse altogether. But the old man refused saying: 'I am no beggar Sir, I will not accept any such offers'. However, after much persuasion he agreed to allow his new found benefactors to arrange private lodgings for him. They subscribed the sum of 100 pounds and five shillings to lodge Sir Thomas on a permanent basis, at the house of Mr William Pybus of Chester-le-Street. But his relief from the rigours of poverty was to be short lived. Quite soon after, his health began to deteriorate and he quickly realised that his death was approaching. Thus he made all his farewells and, we are told, that on the day of his death he went to bed at six in the evening, his usual time for retiring, and almost immediately passed away without pain. So died the last of the Conyers male line: 'whose origin may be traced back to a period of high and romantic antiquity'. And so, with the: 'extinction of the noble and ancient race of Conyers', we reach the end of our tale. The story of the Conyers family and of the Sockburn Worm remains alive now, only in the history and legend of County Durham. Surtees certainly mourned the passing of a once great Durham family, of whom he lamented that: 'Though descended, in a long lineal procession, of gallant knights and esquires, who held Sockburn till the reign of Charles I, while the younger branches of this stately cedar shadowed both Durham and Yorkshire: all are now fallen'.

Chapter 10

Death on Flambard's Bridge

'And who shall be the Greater Lord?'

It was the winter of the year 1318. From Durham Castle, Prince Bishop Lewis de Beaumont ruled over his Palatinate. England was subject to the uncertain, weak reign of the unpopular King Edward II. In Durham City, Framwellgate Bridge spanned the River Wear, just as it still does today. Built 200 years earlier, Rannulf Flambard's bridge provided guarded access to the western side of the fortified peninsula. And it was on Framwellgate Bridge, in December 1318, that an incident occurred, the consequences of which would change the course of history, certainly for the County of Durham, perhaps even for the Kingdom of England.

Edward's England had been defeated and humiliated four years earlier at the Battle of Bannockburn, by the army of the Scottish king, Robert the Bruce. The north of England had all but been abandoned and raids by Scottish forces were commonplace; some for plunder, some simply to instill terror into the northern population. Sykes tells us they partially destroyed the Prior's seat at Beaurepaire near Bearpark; the Prior, we are told, being surprised when at Mass and being chased by the Scots, all the way to the gates of Durham City. The Scots had eventually reached the City itself, attacking on Market Day: 'cruelly killing all who opposed them', carrying away everything that they could, razing the suburbs but leaving the defended peninsula untouched. Robert the Bruce himself had led another force from which, while the Bruce stayed at Chester-le-Street, his Marshalls were sent to Hartlepool, the main port of the Bishopric and previously Bruce's possession, to sack the town and bring back hostages.

The aim of the Scots does not seem to have been a campaign of territorial conquest but a terror campaign, to harry, slash, burn and loot; to ruin the livelihoods of the populace and bankrupt the economy, and the poor people: 'were washed to and fro in the rough tide-way as the storm flowed or ebbed'. Whatever their intentions, the Scots had more or less free reign across the Northern Counties of England and for years now this had been the miserable experience of the inhabitants of County Durham. The situation was lawless and desperate. The Victoria County History tells us that when the Scots retreated north there was still no respite, for then: 'the ways were infested with robbers who did much damage'. However, Durham itself had generally fared better than other places, the rich Bishopric being more able to sue for Truce. In 1312, a complaint was made to the King from the: 'Commonality of the City' that they had unjustly been required by the Bishop to pay a tax towards paying off the Scots; not only did the King show no sympathy with the protestors, he demanded the Bishop to exact the tax. Three years later the same King wrote to the Bishop, acknowledging that: 'The men of your liberty of Durham have suffered loss beyond calculation owing to the constant ravages of the Scots, who have pillaged and burned excessively in those parts'. So the people of the City were caught in a cycle of paying off Bruce's armies with money raised from the local populace, much in the same way as: 'Danegeld' had been paid centuries before.

Parleys were held between Bruce and the English. And for the Scottish king, there was one very useful contact in St Cuthbert's city.

The Steward to the Bishop of Durham, Richard Fitzmarmaduke was the chief English negotiator with the Scots, he was also a cousin of Robert the Bruce. He was a Baron of the Bishopric, a wealthy landowner and a major player in the feudal power struggles of the day. So it came about that on that December day in 1318, on entering the City to take his seat at the County Court, Fitzmarmaduke, arguably the most powerful man in the Bishopric after the Bishop himself, rode on to Flambard's bridge and came face to face with the brash, reckless, vain and unpredictable, nominal head of the only serious rival family to Fitzmarmaduke's own: 'The Peacock of the North', Robert Neville. Both men were ambitious; both families had aspirations to the feudal overlordship of the Palatinate, under the Bishop. Tensions between the two had, for some time, been running high. Now the day had come. Scores were finally to be settled. One of them would die.

The rise of the House of Fitzmarmaduke had begun in 1127, during the episcopate of Rannulf Flambard. The Bishop had given to his nephew, Richard, large estates in the Team Valley. So it was that Richard of Ravensworth began the line of Fitzmarmaduke and so it was that Richard Fitzmarmaduke could trace his Durham lineage back to Flambard himself. Over the years his ancestors had acquired or had been granted, more land in the east of Durham. With land came wealth, power and influence. When his great-grandfather had succeeded as head of the House, he had done so as a prominent member of the feudal community of Durham, with a seat at the Bishop's Court. In 1208, seven years before Magna Carta, he had been one of a group of Knights who had bought from King John, a Charter of Liberties for the Durham Nobles. Seven years later, he was implicated in a rebellion of northern Knights, against the same King. But it was Richard's grandfather who had attained the status of pre-eminent Baron in North and Eastern Durham, with a substantial personal following of subordinate Knights and landowners.

Richard's father, John Fitzmarmaduke, Baron of the Bishopric, was a warrior. He had fought with King Edward I in the Welsh wars and had been a: 'Banneret', a Knight of senior rank, in the army of Antony Bek; which had been instrumental in the defeat of William Wallace, at the Battle of Falkirk. Notorious for his ruthlessness and fighting prowess, it was during the Scottish campaign that, King Edward, 'Hammer of the Scots', himself hardly known for his meekness and charity, had urged Fitzmarmaduke to use all his cruelty during Bek's siege of Direlton Castle. John Fitzmarmaduke died as Governor of Perth, in the winter of 1310. His wish was to be buried at Durham Cathedral, but it was impossible to return his body through miles of hostile territory; the right of: 'Mos Teutonicus' was therefore invoked. This had been considered a great honour, an entitlement for: 'the highest in the land' that had died or had been slain away from home. It entailed the disemboweling and dismemberment of the body, with the remains then being boiled in a vat of wine, water or vinegar until the flesh dropped from the bones. Finally, the bones were collected and returned home for ceremonial burial. The right had originated in the Crusades but in 1300 had been made, by a Papal Bull of Pope Boniface VIII, a forbidden practice. Nonetheless Fitzmarmaduke's followers carried out his wishes and boiled his flesh from his bones: 'till an opportunity for burying them in the Cathedral Yard of Durham presented itself'.

Through his high profile within the Bishopric and his distinguished military service to the King, it was John Fitzmarmaduke who made the transition from Baron of the

Bishopric, to Baron of the Realm. He married twice, his second wife being Ida, a former member of the House of Neville of Raby; a marriage which was to be the source of future bad feeling between the two families. His first wife had been Isabella, a member of the Bruce family. So it was that when their son, Richard Fitzmarmaduke was born, he would grow up cousin to the Scottish king, Robert the Bruce. This then was Richard's pedigree and his power base, and from the beginning of the 14th century, his father had led the Durham feudal community, together with Rannulf Neville of Raby.

The origins of the family of Neville began with the Norman invasion of 1066. The first of that name, a cousin, it is said, of the Conqueror himself, was we are told by Surtees, a naval commander during William's invasion. Over the years, a succession of well chosen marriages had secured lands and property and the family had become a major force in the feudal community in North Yorkshire and Durham. By the time Robert Neville's father, Rannulf, had assumed the mantle of head of the House, his title was, Lord of Raby, Brancepeth, Middleham and Sheriff Hutton. But his father, known as: 'Rannulf the Indolent', had, we are told, little interest in the affairs of his own estates, being pre-occupied with self-indulgence. In 1313, when long past middle age, he had been found guilty of incest with his daughter, Anastasia, and had been excommunicated by Bishop Kellaw. So it was that Robert Neville, called: 'The Peacock of the North', because of his arrogance and love of finery, had for some time been acting in his father's stead, and had been handed the responsibility of restoring honour and pride to the House of Neville.

Richard Fitzmarmaduke was not, it seems, universally popular. Ambitious, unscrupulous, from 1312 he had played the chief part in peace negotiations with his Scottish cousin. In 1314 he had been appointed as: 'Seneschal' or Steward to the Bishop. It was his responsibility to raise the money to buy peace from the Scots. He was, it seems, very efficient. He kept the money flowing. When voluntary contributions dried up, he used other methods of collection, including house to house searches and forcible seizure of money: 'on promise of future repayment'. He was suspected of taking some of the money for himself. Because of this, and because of his seemingly mutually beneficial relationship with the Bruce, he had been openly accused by Robert Neville, of Treason. As an Episcopal Councillor, he was retained by the Bishop at a higher rate than secular Baron, Robert Neville. Another dent, no doubt, to the pride of: 'The Peacock'. Fitzmarmaduke also refused to acknowledge the legal right of his stepmother, Ida, the former, highly esteemed member of the Neville family, to her customary widow's grant of lands following his father's death; another matter that rankled with the Nevilles. However, the gravest injury to: 'The Peacock of the North', was that Richard Fitzmarmaduke was the most powerful Lord in the Bishopric.

So now, the heirs of their respective families came to their fateful meeting on Framwellgate Bridge. Only a short description of the actual event is recorded. They fought, so the chronicles say, to determine: 'Who shall be the greater Lord'. Fitzmarmaduke was slain: 'On Flambard's own bridge did his kinsman die, shattering the landed family he had created, five generations earlier'. It seems that Robert Neville was assisted in the deed by his younger brother, John, who was granted a Royal Pardon four years later. After his death, he died without an heir, the estates of Fitzmarmaduke were broken up and the rank and status of his family accordingly diminished. There was now no obstacle to the Neville family assuming the role of overlord Barons of the Bishopric.

There seems to be no record of any serious calling to account for Robert Neville. According to Richardson, the general punishment which awaited similar offences, if

Flambard's Bridge, scene of the murder of Richard Fitzmarmaduke.

committed by persons of high rank and power, were seldom more than ecclesiastical censure, soon redeemed by: 'some slight mulct of penance gold'. But: 'The Peacock' did not enjoy the fruits of his deed for long. It is said that because of the murder, Robert Neville incurred the displeasure of Edward II and the: *Scalacronica* relates that because of this censure and in order to regain the King's favour, Neville began to serve in the King's struggle against the Scots and: 'In his pride and wantonness, got together a gang of excommunicated thieves and vagabonds, intending to take prey in the marches of Scotland'

So it was that in June 1319: 'The Peacock' was at the Scottish Border, seeking renown against the formidable Scottish leader, Sir James: 'The Black' Douglas. The chronicles relate that Neville had been particularly irritated by the fear and renown in which Douglas was held: 'and had pledged his knightly word to assail him whensoever he should see his banner displayed'. In turn, Douglas had been made aware of the pride of: 'The Peacock' and made an overnight march towards Berwick, where Neville was encamped, burning villages as bait to lure Neville from his stronghold. The bait was willingly taken and Neville rode out into the countryside with his men, eventually taking up a strong position atop a hill, in full view of Douglas; who attacked without delay. The Scottish chronicler, Barbour, related in colourful verse, the actions that followed:

'Then with a rush they made attack,
The sounds of smashing spears arose,
As each on other dealt his blows,
And blood burst out from gashes wide,
The fight was fierce on every side,
For each man fought with might and main,
To drive his foeman back again'.

At length, the two leaders came face to face and the day ended with their single combat; and the death of: 'The Peacock of the North'. His brothers were captured and held for ransom. Ralph Neville, now head of the House, bought his freedom for two thousand marks. Well into 1320, his brothers were still captive.

Over the following years the Nevilles began establishing their dynasty, eventually securing their position as the most powerful family in mediaeval Durham. In 1346, Ralph

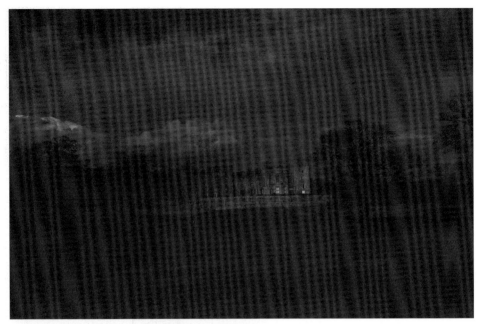

Raby Castle, ancient stronghold of the Neville's.

Neville led the English army which defeated King David II of Scotland, son of Robert the Bruce, at the Battle of Nevilles Cross. He became a hero, the first layman to be buried in Durham Cathedral. His son, John, would become Lord High Admiral of England, Warden of the East Marches, and: 'Seneschal' of Bordeaux. In 1379, he obtained a Licence to Crenellate, and began fortifying what we know today as Raby Castle. Ralph's grandson was created first Earl of Westmorland and Earl Marshall of England. He fought alongside King Henry V, at Agincourt. With their motto: 'God Bless the Bull of Westmoreland', the Neville supremacy in Durham was unchallenged; a supremacy which would last until Tudor times.

A memorial effigy was placed in St Brandon's Church, Brancepeth, to: 'The Peacock of the North', Robert Neville, of whom Wordsworth later wrote: 'He who in bold prosperity of colours manifold and bright, walked around, affronting the daylight', and of whom Surtees commented: 'His character may, from the appellation, be tolerably estimated'. His effigy still lies in a quiet corner of the same Church, surviving as it has the ravages of long years and fierce fire.

Of Fitzmarmaduke, it is said that Robert Neville, despising of the rank of his victim, disposed of his body by throwing it off Framwellgate Bridge, into the River Wear below. Perhaps to this day his bones still lie on the river bed, beneath the passing feet of townspeople and tourists, encased now in the accumulated sediment of almost 700 years.

It is interesting, however, to ponder the consequences if the outcome of the incident on Framwellgate Bridge had been different. If instead, Robert Neville had been slain. If Fitzmarmaduke had been the victor and through his victory his family had secured preeminence in the Bishopric, relegating the Nevilles of Raby to the role of subservient Lords. Perhaps then history would have witnessed a different chain of events. For as we have seen, when Robert Neville was succeeded by his brother Ralph, the Nevilles, now unchallenged

St Brandon's Church, Brancepeth, where lies the effigy of Robert Neville: 'The Peacock of the North'.

in the Bishopric, began to grow in strength and power; as did their influence in national events. Over time, the Lords Neville, with the Lords Percy of Northumberland, would become the two great feudal powers in the North of England. Ralph Neville's great granddaughter was Cecily Neville, who married Richard Plantagenet, Duke of York and two of her sons would become Kings of England; Edward IV and Richard III. Perhaps then, it could be argued that this particular Royal succession would never have come about, if the outcome of an incident involving the Prince Bishop's Steward and: 'The Peacock of the North', on Framwellgate Bridge, in Durham City, on a December day in 1318, had been different.

'God Bless the Bull of Westmoreland'.

Chapter 11

So Tolled the Blanchland Bells

'They came! the nameless, bloody men, they came
Whose long-nursed vengeance stilled the voice of prayer'
-Barrass

A tradition tells that during the Middle Ages a Scottish army crossed the border with England bent on plunder and destruction and turned its eyes southward towards County Durham. The monks of remote Blanchland Abbey, nestling in the upper Derwent Valley on the boundary between Northumberland and Durham, rejoiced that because of the good fortune of a heavy fog, the Scottish host had passed their house by and they had been saved from slaughter. To celebrate their deliverance, they rang out the Abbey bells. The Scots, however, were encamped close by and guided by the tolling Blanchland Bells they reached the monastery, put the brethren to the sword, took what treasures they could and committed what was left to flames. The tradition suggests that this event took place during the unstable, violent years following the defeat of the English army at the Battle of Bannockburn.

The year was 1327. King Edward I: 'Hammer of the Scots', and nemesis of William Wallace, had been dead for 20 years. His son, the hapless Edward II, had been deposed and imprisoned after a disastrous reign and the humiliation of Bannockburn.

The young King, Edward III of England was only 14 years old. But he was King in name only and during his minority England was being governed by a Council of Regency, led by Roger Mortimer, the lover of Edward's mother, Queen Isabella: 'The She-Wolf of France'. Young Edward was excluded from matters of state and publicly humiliated by Mortimer, who, through his influence over Isabella, virtually ruled England himself. But much was expected of this King. He was after all, the grandson of Edward I and the weight of the nation rested upon his young shoulders; it would be his charge to rebuild England's fighting power, its pride and prestige. This boy, it was predicted, would exceed the achievements of his grandfather; he would become: 'the new King Arthur' and would march under the banner of St George, thus associating himself personally with England's two greatest heroic figures. This was to be his destiny and the day would dawn of a new age of high chivalry. However, the reign of the boy King, Edward III, would get off to a less than auspicious start, with a desperate pursuit of a phantom Scottish army across the wild Durham moors and a military humiliation at Stanhope, in Weardale.

Sir James Douglas, the: 'Black Douglas', was 41 years old and was thus described by the poet and chronicler, John Barbour: 'in visage he was rather grey, his hair was black, I've heard them say'. His father had been a supporter of William Wallace and from the early days he had been an ally and close friend of Robert Bruce, fighting alongside him in the Scottish Wars of Independence. Douglas had been knighted on the field before the Battle of Bannockburn and over the years had gained a reputation as a renowned leader, astute military tactician and utterly ruthless soldier. To the Scots he was: 'The Good Sir James', to the English: 'The Blak Dowglas, mair fell than wes ony Devill in Hell'.

Jean le Bel was born in Liege, the son of a Burgundian knight. Already in his late thirties, he was a career soldier with a force of fighting men under the command of the renowned John of Hainault, hired as mercenaries to aid the young Edward in his fight against the Scots. As a chronicler, writing in French instead of Latin, Le Bel is thought to be the first to incorporate eye witness accounts of contemporary events into his record. He compiled his: *True Chronicles*, as a record of the events of the reign of Edward III. And it is Jean le Bel's: *True Chronicles* that tell us today of the events in County Durham in the summer of 1327.

After the English disaster at Bannockburn, Scottish raiding across the border went unchecked. The problem for the Scots had always been the disadvantage of fewer resources and less equipment compared to the English, so they had successfully developed a new type of combat with smaller, fast moving forces; agile and lightly provisioned they avoided pitched battle and defended strongholds, and conducted what was known as the: 'Secret War'. And it was in the art of this secret war of the Borders that the reputation of Douglas was cemented, being victorious both in attack and defence, in raid and counter raid. In Durham he was particularly remembered for slaying Robert Neville, the: 'Peacock of the North', significantly altering the history of the County. As his reputation grew so did his standing. He was made Deputy for the Kingdom of Scotland, two years later, Guardian of the Realm.

A truce between England and Scotland had been signed in 1323. Four years later, however, the instability of the English monarchy and government was too good an opportunity to be missed by Robert Bruce. By raiding deeper and more frequently into northern England, he tried to force more concessions from Mortimer and Isabella, with the ultimate aim of having himself formally recognised as King of an independent Scotland. In addition, in an action calculated to be provocative, on the very day of Edward's coronation, a Scottish army had attacked and taken Norham Castle in Northumberland. The English did not want another war with the Scots, the Treasury could not afford one; but the truce had been broken, a show of force was necessary and Edward himself was spoiling to prove himself in battle.

Negotiations were held at York but they broke down. The order was given to muster the English army there, where it was joined by the men at arms under John of Hainault, who had been granted an annual pension by the English for his mercenary services. Initially, however, things did not go well for the: 'allies'. On 7 June a banquet was held at the expense of the young king and his mother: 'for those of rank'. Within the common soldiery however, a dispute over a game of dice broke out between the Hainaulter mercenaries and English archers from Lincolnshire. The dispute soon developed into a full scale riot which spilled out onto the streets. The Hainaulter knights armed themselves to clear the rioters and the violence escalated. It is said that order was only restored after Edward himself and his senior commanders took to the streets on horseback. There were many deaths. According to wild English claims, 500 Hainaulters were slain and a further 136 drowned in the River Ouse. According to our witness, Jean le Bel, 316 Lincolnshire archers lay dead, who, it was said, were: 'buriede under a stone in Seynt Clementis cherche, haw in Fossegate'. An inquiry was ordered to establish exactly what had happened and who had been responsible, and: 'It was founden by Enquest of the Citee, that the Englisshmen biganne the debate'.

So it was that mistrust replaced respect in the allied camp. There was even a suggestion that the Hainaulters should be sent home. Morale was at rock bottom. It did not bode well for the forthcoming campaign.

On 17 June intelligence was received that the Scots had crossed the northern border and on the 1 July the young Edward III, at the head of what John Leland would later describe as: 'The fairest host of Englischmen that were ever seen', left York, under their fluttering banners of St George, with all the trappings of a great chivalric host. The: 'New Arthur' was come to realise his destiny. A fact not lost on the Scots. But the: 'fair host' had been hurriedly prepared. Provisions had been: 'requisitioned' from unwilling York traders. John of Hainault complained that his men had only enough food for one night's march. Nonetheless, march they did, north through Northallerton and Darlington. Newcastle was their initial objective but before they got to Newcastle there would be one last stop for the English army; and on 15 July 1327, a 14-year-old boy king led his host to Durham City. To John le Bel, Knight of Liege, it seemed that this place was the very last outpost of civilization, as he tells us in his chronicle, beyond Durham lay only: 'A region called Northumberland, which is a savage land full of desolate wastes and great hills, and barren of everything except wild beasts'.

At Durham the English planned their strategy. They thought at first that Carlisle was the main Scots target, or that they may try to outflank the English and make for York, where the rest of the English Royal family were in residence. Then further intelligence reached Durham. The Scots were advancing in three battalions, under the Earls of Mar and Moray and Douglas himself. James Douglas, along with the Earl of Moray, was already ravaging Weardale: 'In this manner were the Scots entered into the said country, and wasted and burned all about, as they went, and took a great number of beasts'.

It was decided to march out from Durham immediately and the host was organised into

three battalions of foot soldiers, each flanked by mounted Knights; a force that would greatly outnumber the Scots. So it was that the young King's heavily equipped army set out from St Cuthbert's City in rigid military formation, to pursue a light, mobile Scottish force, which, according to Le Bel: 'Could scarcely be brought to an engagement, save of their own choice, or in the unlikely event of their being taken by surprise...There were four thousand Knights and Squires mounted on good horses, and another ten thousand men of war, armed after their manner, right hardy and fierce, mounted on little Hackneys'.

The Scots forces moved south from Weardale and were reported near Barnard

Sunderland Old Bridge, near Croxdale, here the army of the young King Edward III crossed the River Wear in pursuit of Sir James: 'The Black' Douglas and his Scots invaders.

Castle. The English followed and by the 17 July had crossed the River Wear at Sunderland Bridge and regrouped at Tudhoe. Two days later they were at Bishop Auckland where they received further intelligence that the Scots had doubled back.

Eighteen hundred banners of St George were ordered to be sent to Stanhope, to where the English army moved to engage the Scots; but their quarry did not appear. At a Council of War, the English commanders conceded that they were chasing shadows as all they saw of the Scots was the red glow in the sky, marking the progress of their burning and destruction. Then they received further news that the Scots had again struck camp and a decision was made, not this time to try and follow, but to move the army north to cut off a suspected Scottish retreat.

'It was determined by great advice and counsel, that all the host should remove at midnight, and make haste in the morning, to the intent to stop the passage of the River Tyne from the Scots, whereby they should be advised by force, either to fight, or else to abide still in England, to their great loss and danger'.

The English commanders knew that there were few places where a large force could safely cross the River Tyne. Discounting the obvious bridges, the English were to make for a ford in the river at Haydon Bridge, about seven miles from Hexham. Speed was of the essence and crucially it was decided to leave behind the baggage train: 'Every man was warned to be ready at the first sounding of the trumpet, and at the second blast every man to arm himself, and at the third, every man to quickly mount on his horse, and to take with him but one loaf of bread, and to truss it behind him on his horse'. It was a major risk, force marching such a large army across the wastes of the Durham moors. Slow, inflexible, heavy, but buoyed up, despite the lack of food and supplies, with the thought that surely they would pass through the: 'tireless, miserable wastes; region of mists and birth place of the storm', into which they were going and engage their enemy in battle the next day.

'So they advanced forward in all haste, through mountains, valleys and rocks, and through many evil passages without any plain country, and on the highest of these hills, and on the plain of those valleys there were marvelous great marshes, and dangerous passages, that it was great wonder much people had not been lost; for they rode still ever forward and never tarried one for another, for whosoever fell into any of these marshes, with much pain could they get any aid to help them out again'

Clearly, the journey was not a smooth one. They travelled over trackless terrain with a force so big that when those in the vanguard raised their voices at the starting of a deer or other wild animal, those following thought the Scots had at last been sighted and charged forward to support, causing pandemonium in the English ranks.

But on they marched as Edward led his great host out across the Durham wilderness, and all they saw was the moors and the mist. 'Thus rode forth all that day the young King of England, by mountains and deserts, without finding any highway, village or town, and when it was again night, they came to the River Tyne'.

After a night and day's forced march their objective had been reached. They crossed the ford at night and prepared to wait for the retreating Scots. It began to rain heavily and incessantly. The rain swelled the river. Edward and his army were now cut off from the road southward. And they waited in vain, for the enemy did not come and worse, they now had no idea where the Scots were.

The highly mobile Scots force was made up of mounted troops who rode on small horses called Hobbins, giving rise to the name: 'Hobelar', to both horse and rider. They foraged for food where they could from the surrounding countryside or took it otherwise by force. Thus, not needing a supply of provisions, they travelled lightly and quickly: 'They take with them no purveyance of bread or wine, for their usage and soberness is such, in the time of war, they will pass a great long time, with flesh half sodden, without bread; and drink river water without wine'.

As the English had abandoned their baggage train it was they who were now short of food and supplies. From the local: 'poor folk' it was ascertained that supplies could be got from Newcastle. The King declared that anyone bringing food from there to his host would be paid a good price and his army would not move until they had news of the Scots position. Of course, this was an opportunity not to be missed. Merchants picked their way along the Tyne Valley from Newcastle to sell their wares to the hungry host, arriving, as Le Bel tells us: 'Charged with bread, evil baked in Panniers, and small pear wine in barrels, and other victuals to sell to the host, and that was not overmuch, poor provisions at high prices'

Morale, already low, sank further. It was still not known where the Scots were, the English force remained hungry: 'And besides all these mischiefs, it never ceased to rain all week'. The rain sodden bindings of saddles, saddle straps and bridles, began to fall apart. Horses began to develop sores on their backs. More went lame, with the spare shoes needed to re-shoe them left far behind in the discarded baggage train. They had no cover from the incessant rain apart from: 'Green bushes and their armour', and after the wet,

followed the cold, with no dry tinder to light fires. This continued for eight days. So desperate did it become that Edward proclaimed he would grant a knighthood and an income of £100 a year to anyone who could locate the Scots. Fifteen men took up his challenge. As the 15 rode off, the English Commanders decided to move the army upstream and on 28 July they arrived at Haltwhistle, where, at last, one of the 15 volunteers rode back with news of the Scots. They were encamped at Stanhope. The King was true to his word, Thomas Rokeby became Sir Thomas Rokeby and the English recrossed the Tyne. Halting at Blanchland: 'A monastery of white monks, which had been burnt, and which was called, in King Arthur's time,

Blanchland Abbey, destroyed by the Scots and where the English army heard Mass before eventually facing their foe at Stanhope.

107

Blanche Lande', the King ordered masses to be said in the remains of the Abbey: 'to housel such as were devoutly inclined' as their horses were turned free to feed in the surrounding fields. Then, as the Blanchland Bells tolled once again, they set out across the wild lands: 'where nought was heard except the wild wind's sigh, or savage Raven's deep and hollow cry'; and on to Stanhope and the Scots.

On 30 July the armies met. The English approached in seven battalions. The Scots stood to arms in three, under their three commanders. The rapidly flowing River Wear passing as a barrier between them. The English host descended from the hills to an area of flat ground hard by the swollen river. Soddened by the recent rains, this low lying area was dangerous, especially for heavy mounted Knights. The English reorganised and advanced slowly, in three groups, toward the river. The Scots looked down on them from raised ground on the opposite bank. Most of their forces high on an inaccessible rock outcrop and well out of reach of English arrows.

The English halted and young Edward rode out and addressed his army. The problem was what to do? A direct frontal attack across the river against a high, defended position would be suicidal. Archers were brought up supported by a force of mounted knights and a limited crossing was attempted. Douglas countered by moving his cavalry to block it. The advance was called off. Edward's frustration grew. Heralds were sent across the river to the Scottish commanders: 'inviting' them to come down and join battle. Le Bel tells us that the Scots taunted the young King: 'Sirs, your King and his Lords see well how we be here, in this realm, and have burned and wasted the country, and if they be displeased therewith, let them amend it, for here we will abide so long as it shall please us'.

As night began to fall, the order was given to hold position and the English settled down in a wet, uncomfortable camp. It would be a sleepless one too, as the Scots, as if to increase their taunting of the massive but impotent English host, banged drums and blew horns all through the short summer night: 'so that it seemed like all the devils in Hell had been there'.

'Thus', says Le Bel: 'These two hosts were lodged there'.

It was clear that the English needed another strategy. Skirmishing and starvation, it was decided, may be the answer. Raiding parties would be sent out to gradually weaken the Scottish force which would be held in its high place and starved into submission. On their part, the Scots were well fed and well rested but the English were weary and poorly provisioned and Le Bel tells us that the canny local merchants from Stanhope made a good profit, as had their compatriots at Haydon Bridge, by charging extortionate prices for their meager supplies. The English could neither starve the Scots, nor feed themselves.

Inconclusive skirmishing did take place and the Scots chroniclers tell of new innovations, both in warfare and in: 'style', that were seen at the Stanhope encounter. 'Crakkis of Wer', used by the English; primitive gunpowder weapons, a kind of prototype field gun; and mounted knights wearing helmet crests: 'Tymbrys for Helmys'; as part of their regalia. But the night time taunting of the English continued, with the Scots lighting great fires that would burn throughout the dark hours, and it was eventually under cover of these fires that the Scots simply slipped out of their stronghold and relocated two miles away, to an even stronger defensive position which Douglas had identified, just south of Eastgate. At daybreak, realising what had happened, the English moved out and positioned themselves, once again, opposite the Scots, on the north side of the River. It was obvious that the Scots could not be forced into a pitched battle and it would be the English who

The River Wear at Stanhope; then in spate, it formed a dangerous barrier between the two armies.

would be the victims of a first strike, led by Douglas, with the intention of taking and holding for ransom the teenage king. Jean le Bel described the events:

'The Lord James Douglas took with him about 200 men at arms, and passed the river far from the host so that he could not be perceived: and suddenly he broke into the English host about midnight, crying 'Douglas! Douglas! Ye shall all die, thieves of England' and he slew 300 men, some in their beds and some scant ready: and he stroke his horse with spurs, and came to the King's tent, always crying 'Douglas!' and stroke asunder two or three cords of the King's tent and so departed'.

There was vicious, hand to hand fighting around the King Edward's own pavilion: 'Has St George no ward?' cried Douglas mockingly, before cutting a swathe out of the English camp and back to the safety of the Scots position. The young King was unharmed but badly shaken and: 'wonder sore afraide'. Needless to say, the number of guards was increased. The Hainaulters took part in the guard but also posted additional guards around their own forces, as they feared the actions of the English archers as much as they feared the Scots. The: 'debate' at York, had been neither forgiven, nor forgotten and there was: 'unconcealed enmity' between the two.

On the night of 6 August the Scots again built up their fires and according to Le Bel, left trumpeters to blow throughout the night. While under cover of the fires and the noise, their host retreated, casting down tied bundles of branches and brushwood to form a temporary causeway for man and horse over the moorland morass to their rear. They melted away in the darkness towards Barnard Castle, then over Stainmore and into the west, before returning home to Scotland. By the time the English realised what had happened, they were miles distant. The next morning, our chronicler, Jean le Bel, Knight of Liege, together with a force of Hainaulters, crossed the River Wear, entered the deserted Scottish camp and saw the waste left behind.

Five hundred cattle slaughtered; a thousand wooden spits loaded with meat for roasting; 300 cauldrons made from the skins of the slaughtered cattle, still with the hair on them, filled with water and suspended over fires for boiling; about 10,000 shoes, newly made from rawhide and: 'Five poor Englishmen bound fast to certain trees, and some of their legs broken'.

No attempt was made to follow the Scots. To prepare for what now seemed likely to be a long, drawn out campaign, Edward issued writs from Stanhope on 7 August summoning a Parliament to Lincoln for 15 September. According to Le Bel, the young king, wept with vexation and frustration: 'And it was ordained by the King, and by the advice of his Council, that the whole host should follow the Marshall's banners, and draw homeward'. So in the end, the young English king and his great army had been outwitted, outrun and ultimately humiliated by the Scots under Douglas. The banners of St George never flew over charging knights at the Battle of Stanhope, for the Battle never happened. And so it is today that there is no battlefield memorial, nor any listing of the site on any heritage trail. No doubt, the Weardale fiasco left a lasting impression on the: 'New Arthur'.

The King turned east, made his way back to Durham City and, as Surtees tells us, stayed a night at the Prior's retreat at Beaurepaire near Bearpark, with his troops encamped in the surrounding fields. From there, accompanied by his nobles, he visited Durham Cathedral. The baggage train had also found its way back to Durham and Edward allowed his troops time to rest and enjoy its welcome, if belated, luxuries. After a stay in the City, they marched on to York where the English forces were stood down and disbanded, while the

The lonely remains of Beurepaire, the Prior of Durham's lodge near Bearpark, where the English rested before re-entering Durham City.

Hainaulters returned to their former quarters and: 'enjoyed the festivities of the Court'. It only remained to pay for the summers proceedings.

About £40,000 was needed to pay the wages of the men at arms. Another £28,000 for the replacement of horses, lost in the campaign.

The need for cash was desperate. Most pressing was the need to settle, as a matter of honour, the account of John of Hainault, both for his recent and for his previous services. To do this, over £19,000 was required for wages, over £21,000 for lost horses. In addition, an extra £600 was needed to pay for ransom money, demanded by the Scots for the release of Hainaulter hostages and for medical supplies for those injured in the York: 'debate'. It was a vast amount of money. The situation was so critical that Edward himself took out personal loans and an order was given to offer the King's jewels, in pledge to certain merchants, for the supply of money. Even the Hainaulters realised that their account could not be settled at once. But they had had enough. After their acceptance of an initial payment of four thousand pounds, Jean le Bel closes his account on the Weardale adventure by telling us that they set sail from Dover, on 20 August 1327, pleased to turn their backs to: 'The threatening English and the discomforts of the campaign'. The Weardale campaign and its after effects gave Isabella and Mortimer no option but to agree terms for peace and the following year the treaty of Northampton finally recognised Robert Bruce as the King of an independent Scotland.

Of the participants in the Weardale adventure, our chronicler, Jean le Bel, left military service and devoted his life to the Church, eventually becoming a Canon of St Lambert de Liege. His: *True Chronicles* were published around 1356.

Robert Bruce died in 1329. He had requested Sir James Douglas to take his heart to the Holy Land and bury it in the Church of the Holy Sepulchre at Jerusalem. So it was that the embalmed heart was placed in a silver and enamel casket which Douglas kept around his neck. In 1330, Douglas, with six Knights and: 'Gentlemen of Name', set sail from Scotland to Seville. There they joined the forces of King Alfonso XI of Castille, fighting against the Moors of Granada. On 25 August battle was struck at Teba, on the frontier of Andalucia. The Moors feigned retreat and Douglas, fighting in the Vanguard of the King's army, followed. He was cut off and surrounded. The story tells that realising the hopelessness of his situation, Douglas cast the casket containing the heart of: 'The Bruce' among the enemy, exhorting: 'Now pass thou onward before us, as thou wert wont, and I will follow thee or die'. Sir James Douglas and those with him were cut down to a man, Douglas himself, pierced by five mortal wounds. Invoking the same right as had been by John Fitzmarmaduke at Perth, his flesh was boiled away, and his heart placed in a casket. His bones, the casket, and that containing the heart of: 'The Bruce', which had been retrieved from the battlefield were returned home by surviving companions. The heart of the: 'Black Douglas', Good Sir James, was laid to rest in his family vault in St Bride's Chapel. The heart of Robert Bruce was finally interred under the High Altar of Melrose Abbey.

Of Edward III of England, in October 1330, the now 17-year-old King, along with William Montague and a group of trusted allies, seized Roger Mortimer at Nottingham Castle. Charged with Treason, Mortimer was condemned to death and executed at Tyburn in London. Queen Isabella was exiled from court and imprisoned and Edward III would go on to rule England for a further 47 years. With his subsequent defeat of the Scots at Halidon Hill near Berwick and his victories over the French at Crecy and Poitiers, he would cement his reputation as the: 'The most feted warrior in Christendom, his court, the most glamorous in Europe'. The epitome of a chivalric, hero king, he would establish a new knightly order, the Order of the Round Table, and to house it, at Windsor Castle he would build a Round Table building with seats for 200 knights. Indeed he would become known as one of the greatest of England's kings, perhaps, as some suggest, the greatest of all mediaeval kings. The destiny foreseen for the teenage boy would be fulfilled; as the French chronicler, Jean Froissart tells us: 'His like had not been seen since the days of King Arthur'. A far cry from the wild Durham moors and the summer of 1327.

As for the unfortunate monks of Blanchland Abbey, their mortal remains were laid in a mass grave. And it is said that on certain days, perhaps the anniversary of their death day, or perhaps when the mists descend over Blanchland Moor; the mournful tolling of a bell can be heard and the shades of the slain monks can be seen once more walking the lost paths of their long ruined monastery.

Part Four

Chapter 12

The Apostle of the North

'I hate to see things done by halves. If it be right do it boldly, if it be wrong, leave it undone'

One Sunday during the reign of King Henry VIII, at the church in Kentmere, Cumbria, a travelling Friar had preached on and on, regaling his congregation about the evils of drink. A young boy had listened intently to the interminable hectoring, and then had turned to his mother and said: 'Mother, how dare he preach against drinking? He was drunk in our hall last night!'

But now the year was 1558, that same young boy had become a man and the man was now a prisoner with an escort. Heavy rain was falling on both. They would all be glad of a night's shelter, for their journey was a long one. From Durham to London they were bound, by order of Queen Mary Tudor, the prisoner no doubt reconciled to his fate; martyrdom at the Stake. An Inn for the night being reached, the horses are halted. But the prisoner's horse stumbles and throws its rider from the saddle. His leg is still twisted in the stirrup as the horse bolts. The leg is broken. He would now be cared for at the Inn, with ample time, before renewing his deadly journey, to reflect on how fate had brought him to this end. For this was a man: 'most holy and renowned among the northerne English'. He would become known as the: 'Apostle of the North'; his name, Bernard Gilpin, Rector of Houghton-le-Spring.

Born in 1517, the son of Edwin Gilpin of Kentmere Hall, Westmoreland, where the family had been settled since the time of King John; his uncle, who had been the head of the family, had fallen at the Battle of Bosworth, as a Captain of Horse under King Richard III. His father had then come into the estate and married Margaret Layton of Dalemain. Bernard was an intelligent child, one of six boys and: 'From early youth he was said to be a thoughtful turn'.

At 16 he was sent to Queen's College, Oxford, where he became an outstanding student of Theology, reading the Scriptures in their original Greek and Hebrew and was one of the first to be invited to attend Cardinal Wolsey's newly founded, Cardinal's College, which later became Christ Church. He was also invited to take part in public discussions about religious thinking of the day, and the movement away from Rome. Gilpin himself had been brought up a Roman Catholic but was also attracted by more liberal beliefs. He began to have doubts about Church doctrine and ritual and to question his own personal views; he also began to see in his mind a more direct connection between Christianity and the everyday lives of ordinary people. But his reputation grew and in 1552, he was invited to preach before the young King Edward VI. From then began his to rise in prominence. He had already, through his sermons, come to the attention, of William Cecil, later Lord Burghley and of Sir Robert Dudley and it was through Cecil that Gilpin would obtain a general licence for preaching. This was something that at the time was granted with great caution and then only to men of high character and ability; men who: 'fitted the bill'.

He remained as an Oxford academic until he was 35, when he was appointed by his mother's uncle, Cuthbert Tunstall, the Bishop of Durham; as Vicar of Norton. But Gilpin remained unsure of his faith, he continued in his outspoken and controversially liberal views on Catholic Doctrine but was still not fully convinced of the Doctrines of the Reformers. This gave him something of a crisis of conscience as he felt that because of the uncertainty of his own personal beliefs, he could not teach his new congregation well. If he himself was not convinced, how could he convince others? On the advice of Tunstall he decided to leave his Norton parish in the charge of a trusted deputy and leave for a time to travel abroad; and there he stayed for three years. But whist Gilpin was away, England changed. The young King Edward died, his Catholic half-sister, Mary Tudor became Queen; and the Reformation was halted. Those that had been persecuted now became the persecutors and Gilpin became sympathetic to the views of the English Protestant academics and theologians; fleeing their native country to avoid imprisonment or death at the Stake.

So it was that in 1556 Bernard Gilpin returned to England and, under the patronage of his great uncle, Cuthbert Tunstall; returned to his ministry. He was made Archdeacon of Durham and Rector of Easington. But Gilpin was appalled at what he saw in the: 'neglected state of the northern church'; greed and abuses among the incumbent clergy, the ignorance and corruption of priests not even resident in their own parishes and caring not for those for whom they should care. He began to preach openly about the: 'shameful negligence and manifest indifference' of the Church establishment. Of course, he soon made enemies. Some of them whispered: 'Heretic', they complained that: 'He preached repentance and salvation through Jesus Christ, rather than through the ceremonies of the Church'. At last a complaint against him was lodged with the Bishop of Durham, who judged the case himself and acquitted Gilpin, who then asked to resign either the Archdeaconry or the Rectory; when the Bishop would not consent to either, Gilpin resigned them both. Those that Gilpin had offended now decided to pursue their quarry. In all, 13 different charges of heresy were drawn up against him, and were dismissed, largely due to the influence of Tunstall. But the old Bishop could only protect him for so long.

It was at this time that Gilpin was installed at the place that he will always be most associated with; when, in 1557, he became Rector of Houghton-le-Spring. The Parish was large, covering an area of more that 24 square miles; and wealthy, it was then rated as the highest of any in England. No doubt Gilpin's enemies eyed it jealously and they did not rest in their quest to bring him down. Further accusations of Heresy followed, he was, they said, in his open criticism of it, an enemy of the clergy, a preacher of: 'damnable heresies', if allowed to continue, religion would be: 'totally unhinged by such doctrines as he was propagating'. More charges were made against him and in 1558, were laid before Edmund Bonner, Bishop of London, on whose behalf, an order was made for Gilpin's confinement.

Edmund Bonner: 'Bloody Bonner'; Mary Tudor's arch persecutor of heretics, had been at one time chaplain to Cardinal Wolsey and in 1532 had been sent to Rome as the agent of King Henry VIII, in the question of Henry's divorce. Of: 'overbearing and dictatorial manner' he had graduated in law, not theology. He soon gained a reputation, albeit spread by his enemies, for excessive cruelty in his treatment of heretics. He had lost his Bishopric and his liberty under the Protestant rule of the young King Edward VI but was released in 1553; on the accession of Queen Mary: 'and on Bonner fell the chief burden to stamp out religious dissent'. This would no doubt have given little comfort to Bernard Gilpin, as Bonner was represented by the Protestant reformers of the day as a monster, who: 'hounded men and women to death, with merciless vindictiveness'. But Gilpin had no choice but to answer the summons to appear before Bonner's Ecclesiastical Court and: 'he prepared his holy soul for martyrdom'. Before leaving Durham he asked Will Airy, his Steward, to select for him: 'a long garment, that he might go more comely to the Stake'. And so it was that Bernard Gilpin set out on his long road to trial and execution. And so it was also that Prisoner and Escort were caught in a rainstorm and looked for shelter in the night.

It was decided, that with Gilpin's leg broken, it would be impossible to carry on with the journey and deliver the prisoner to London and to Bishop Bonner, in a fit state for trial. He would remain where he was until he was able to resume the final, fateful part his journey. But this was never to happen, for, on 17 November 1558, Mary Tudor died. Elizabeth became queen, and Mary's prisoners were pardoned. So it was that because of Mary's death, Gilpin escaped his own; and he returned to County Durham where both his ministry and his reputation would grow. On the accession of Elizabeth I, several Bishops were deprived of their Sees, because they refused to take Elizabeth's Oath of Supremacy, acknowledging the Queen as the head of both Church and State. The vacant See of Carlisle was offered to Gilpin but he refused, alleging that he: 'had many acquaintances in that diocese, who he knew were not discharging their duty as they ought' and he would certainly, if he did: 'speedily be at variance with them'.

His parish of Houghton-le-Spring was very extensive, and the people, the chroniclers tell, were: 'sunk in ignorance and superstition', but Gilpin: 'condescended to the weak, complied with the unscrupulous, became all things to all men that he might by all means save some'. He provided well for his parishioners. Every Sunday between Michaelmas and Easter his Rectory was an open house where a free meal was provided. Three great tables were set with food; one for the gentry, one for the yeomen and one for the labourers. On Thursdays he gave out boiled meat to the hungry of his parish. It is also thought that, as part of the Michaelmas celebrations, Gilpin re-introduced the mediaeval custom of roasting an Ox or a Hog. A tradition continued as part of the annual: 'Houghton Feast' celebrations. Indeed, it was famously said of Gilpin's hospitality, that if a horse was turned loose in any part of the county, it would find its way to the Rectory of Houghton. Once, Lord Burghley, Queen Elizabeth's Secretary of State, who was on route from Scotland, visited Gilpin at Houghton and was both impressed and moved by Gilpin's hospitality and his way of life. On departing, he reached as far as Rainton Hill, where he turned back and exclaimed: 'Who can blame that man for refusing a Bishopric? What doth he want, that a Bishopric could more enrich him, besides that, he is free from the greater weight of cares'.

Along with John Heath of Kepier, Gilpin endowed a Grammar School, where he had students educated, procuring Masters from Oxford to guide them. The: 'Free Grammar School and Almshouses of Kepyer in Houghton-le-Spring' was confirmed by a Charter of Queen Elizabeth, in 1574, and Gilpin and Heath were appointed its first governors. Gilpin felt that hope was with the young and personally assisted with the cost of attendance of poorer boys. One of these students was Hugh Broughton, who would afterwards become an eminent Hebrew scholar and a Prebendary of Durham Cathedral. Broughton, however, was to prove: 'very ungrateful to his benefactor, and did all that he could to injure him'.

The year 1569, saw the: 'Rising of the North', when northern Catholic nobles rose in rebellion against Queen Elizabeth I, and sought to put the Catholic, Mary Queen of Scots on the throne of England. It is said that during the rebellion the insurgents came to Houghton-le-Spring and Gilpin being at the time away in Oxford, they: 'made great havoc'. Houghton was: 'full of corn and young cattell', the provisions intended for Gilpin's hospitality. All was taken, what could not be taken was destroyed; and it is said that foremost among the marauders was a man who, on Gilpin's intercession, had previously been saved from hanging: 'and this knave was the wickedest of all the rest in rioting away Master Gilpin's goods'. During the reign of Queen Elizabeth, Gilpin maintained his independence from the different and competing religious factions of the day. Nevertheless, they continued to court the support of a man so well respected, and he: 'excited the hopes both of the Puritans and the Papists'. Both were to be disappointed, for: 'He was thankful for the change from Popery on the one hand, while on the other, he did not think the objects for which the Puritans contended were of such a nature as to make it desirable to unsettle the established order of things'.

His parishioners loved him and he attended assiduously to the needs of all of them, regardless of their station, and visited not only the sick but also those in prison. He was well known for his acts of charity. If a poor man of the Parish lost a beast, Gilpin would send him one of his own. If a farmer had a bad crop, Gilpin would send him back his portion of the Tithe. A story is told that once Gilpin saw a farmer's horse drop dead at the plough. He gave the man his own horse as a replacement and when the poor farmer told him that: 'My pocket will not reach such a beast as that', Gilpin replied: 'Take him, and when I demand my money, then you shall pay me', of course the money was never demanded. But Gilpin was by no means merely parochial in his outlook. He saw with great regret the ignorance, superstition and lawlessness, that prevailed outside his own Parish and he began to take advantage of his general licence to preach; to wander across the North Country. He frequented the lands around Tynedale and Redesdale in Northumberland and these became Gilpin's most common destinations, where, it was said: 'Every Dale had its battle, every river its song. A rude species of chivalry was in constant use and single combats were practiced as the amusement in the few intervals of truce which suspended the exercise of war'.

It appears that these wild lands, described by Jean Le Bel, early in the 14th century, had changed but little; two and a half centuries later. Indeed, the Bishop of Carlisle decreed that: 'There is more theft, more extortion here by English thieves, than by all the Scots in Scotland'. But it was here that Gilpin set out to evangelise Northumberland, travelling on a mission to enlighten the ignorant inhabitants, seeing even these people as deserving of his ministry; and being entitled to salvation through the word of God. According to him, there was: 'No place too small to occupy, no people too low to elevate'. Where there was no church, he preached in barns and fields and on his travels the chroniclers tell that if he came across a beggar by the roadside he would give the unfortunate creature his cloak. But the age of the Mosstrooper had dawned and this was their land. The Border Reivers, who spent their lives in banditry, feuding and murder: 'The people were immersed in the deepest ignorance, and their manners were rude and barbarous in the last degree...It was in truth a country which few would choose of their free will to visit at all, but moved with the love of God and of souls, Mr Gilpin hesitated not to enter it'.

There are a number of well known stories surrounding Gilpin's travels in these parts, some perhaps are apocryphal, some may be true, but they do illustrate nicely the remoteness and lawlessness of the area at that time. He visited at all times of the year, preferring winter, around Christmas time, because at times of Holy celebrations, it was easier to gather the people together. He had no use for comforts on his journeys. One particularly cold night he was stuck in the snow. Anticipating a night spent in freezing conditions, he gave his horses to his faithful Will Airy and told him to keep himself and the horses in motion to keep warm, while Gilpin simply: 'ran about to keep the heat of his body'. He preached and gave alms, and by many of these people, he was regarded: 'as a prophet who had come among them'. Another story is related of a thief that stole his horses during the night. Eventually it came to thief's knowledge that the horses he had taken belonged to Bernard Gilpin, when at once he returned them; and craved forgiveness from the Rector of Houghton-le-Spring. The thief was said to confess that it was not the stealing of the horses that troubled his conscience, but the fact that, once he found out to whom they belonged: 'He was afraid of going down quick to Hell'.

One day in Rothbury Church, when Gilpin was in attendance, members of two feuding families began a quarrel. Gilpin berated them for their behaviour in church. For a short while tempers calmed but soon insults flew again, swords were drawn: 'and their weapons made a clashing sound, and the one side drew nearer to the other, so that they were in danger to fall to blowes in the middest of the church'. Gilpin jumped down from the pulpit and stood between the raised blades, insisting they stand down in the house of God. Even he could not get the warring factions to settle their differences; but he made them promise that: 'they would abstain from hostilities, at least in that sacred place'. On arriving at another church to preach, he saw a gauntlet had been hung from the rafters. This, he was informed was a traditional challenge to combat. He asked the Sexton to take it down, but he would not, for any that did was accepting the challenge. Gilpin himself took down the gauntlet and during his sermon waved it at the congregation; rebuking those that had set the challenge and preaching of the sin of such un-Christian conduct. It was said that after these events: 'Any one who was in terror of his enemies kept close in attendance on Mr Gilpin, believing his presence to be the best protection'.

Hugh Broughton, mentioned earlier, had been brought as a boy to Houghton-le-Spring. Gilpin had come across him, penniless while on a visit to Wales and with the permission of the boys parents, had brought him north. Broughton was fed, clothed and educated at Gilpin's expense and eventually Gilpin had provided for him to attend Queen's College, Cambridge to complete his education, there proving to be one of the foremost Hebrew scholars of the day and of great ability: 'but very inconstant'. As Gilpin got older, ruffling more and more feathers by continuing to rail about the corruption and shortcomings of the County Durham clergy; it is said that Broughton began to eye Houghton-le-Spring for himself, and do what he could to prejudice the Bishop of Durham, Richard Barnes, against the Rector. Richard Barnes himself, we are told by Hutchinson, was appointed to the See of Durham: 'In order to be a watch on the messengers from Scotland to the unfortunate Queen Mary'. He was on good terms with neither the people of his Bishopric, nor the clergy of his own Cathedral. Acting along with Broughton, was John Barnes, Rector of Houghton-le-

Skerne, the Bishop's spiritual Chancellor and his brother who was, according to the chronicler:

'A most untrustworthy man, immoral and covetous, and both oppressive and profligate in the administration of his office, which he exercised without restraint from the Bishop, in a most tyrannical manner. The Chancellor cherished a most especial enmity against Bernard Gilpin'.

A long standing feud would be played out between Barnes and Gilpin, with Gilpin: 'doing all he could to counteract the Chancellor's nefarious designs', and in turn, Barnes: 'pursuing Gilpin with undisguised enmity'. The Bishop was eventually persuaded to direct Gilpin to preach at a visitation he was shortly to make. Gilpin, however, was about to leave on one of his northern journeys and wrote to the Bishop, begging to be excused. When he received no reply, he took this as consent and went on his way. On his return Gilpin found himself suspended. He was summoned before Barnes at Chester-le-Street; and without notice, was asked by the Bishop to preach. He pleaded that he was not prepared, besides, he was under suspension. This was rejected by the Bishop who immediately revoked the suspension and commanded Gilpin, under obedience to his Bishop, to preach.

Gilpin said: 'Well sir, seeing it can be no otherwise, your Lordship's will be done', he paused, gathered his thoughts together, rose to his feet and began; noticing some of those present making notes of what he said. But he cared little for that and he proceeded to thunder to the Bishop and all present, against: 'the abuses and iniquities which were perpetrated in his name throughout the Diocese'. Gilpin laid the responsibility for the sad state of affairs squarely at the feet the Bishop and warned him that: 'he was responsible for all and could now no longer plead ignorance'. Afterwards, his friends told him that with his words, he had sealed his own fate: 'You have put a sword into your enemy's hands to slay you with'. But Gilpin replied: 'God's will be done concerning me'. Discussions took place. Gilpin was summoned to the Bishop and his supporters feared the worst. However, to everyone's surprise, Barnes came out with his famous declaration:

'Father Gilpin, I own you are fitter to be Bishop of Durham than I am to be Parson of Houghton; I ask forgiveness for errors past; I know you have hatched some chickens that now seek to pick out your eyes; but as long as I live Bishop of Durham, be secure, no man shall injure you'.

It has since been suggested that the Bishop's declaration was perhaps based more upon political realities than spiritual enlightenment, knowing, as he did, that because of his reputation, Gilpin himself had some powerful supporters. However, the Bishop was true to his word and Gilpin continued to practice his ministry, in peace, for the rest of his life. However, the hopes and plans of the ungrateful Hugh Broughton were dashed and, as the chronicler tells: 'it may be collected from his style, that his judgement by no means equaled his learning'. He died, we are told, in 1612, in obscurity and distress.

Eventually all those long years of travelling in the North Country began to take their toll. Gilpin's health grew worse. In a letter to a friend he bemoaned his weakened state: 'My greatest grief is that my memory is almost gone, my sight and also my hearing, fast failing me'. And in the end, it was not in the wild northern lands among the: 'rude and barbarous people of the borders' that he would eventually meet his fate; but on a visit to Durham City, where, crossing the Market Place, perhaps with a degree of irony, he was gored and grievously wounded by a panicked Ox. Gilpin survived the incident but would succumb to his wounds, and: 'Having bid farewell to his scholars, servants and friends, he

Durham City Market Place, where Bernard Gilpin was fatally gored by an Ox.

gave himself up to prayer, and breathed his last on the 4th March, 1583, in the 66th year of his age'. Gilpin was interred in the Church of St Michael and All Angels, Houghton-le-Spring, where his altar tomb was raised in the South Transept. In life, he was described as: 'tall and lean in person, with a hawk like nose and of charming and tactful manners'. He was known to be short tempered but for the most part he kept it under control. Temperate in diet and indifferent to dress: 'His clothes were ever such as cost not very deare; he could never away with gay apparel'

Several biographies would follow; most of those would echo the original. It was written by George Carleton, a former pupil and one of the first scholars of Gilpin's Kepyer School, who eventually became Bishop of Chichester. He dedicated his work to his former mentor. A man who was: 'By mere sincerity and straightforwardness, the one most powerful for good, throughout the turbulent Northern Lands in that troubled age'. A man that showed mercy in an age that showed none and: 'whose boundless charities and meritorious actions to enlighten his fellow creatures, obtained him the pre-eminent appellation of: 'The Northern Apostle'.

The Gilpin Window, Durham Cathedral.

Chapter 13

The Tale Anne Walker Told

'Hush a Ba! Babby, be! ; for Sharp and Walker kill't thou and me'

They say: 'Murder will out'; a fact of which Judge Davenport was chillingly aware, presiding as he was at the Durham Assizes, on Palace Green, under the very shadow of the Cathedral, in the year 1631. It was a case, the like of which he had never heard before. A case, the strange nature of which would eventually be drawn to the attention of no less a learned body than the Royal Society. But for Judge Davenport it was a case which disturbed him greatly and brought down upon him some intangible feeling of gloom and foreboding. During the trial he was a man, as noted by observers: 'who was very troubled'.

There are today stories of serious crimes, usually murders, being solved after conventional criminal investigation, with the assistance of all the resources of modern Police forces, have come to nothing; and the agents of law and order have resorted to consulting psychics for help. Numerous times, we are told, the gifts of such people have led the Police to the successful conclusion of a case; a body found, a suspect arrested, a crime solved. So help with solving mysteries has been, and still is, it seems, available from the realms of the paranormal. But in the case over which Judge Davenport presided in 1631, the crime, the brutal murder of a young woman, was solved not through the sight of a Psychic or the contact of a Medium, but through the direct intervention of the victim herself.

William Lumley, described in the chronicles as: 'an ancient gentlemen', had long had his suspicions about the fate of Anne Walker. He lived at Great Lumley, next door to John Walker, a man originally from Chester-le-Street, a: 'Yeoman of good Estate', and Anne Walker's uncle. Walker was indeed: 'a man in good circumstance', but he was not liked, not quite respected. It was said that the people of the village: 'all felt a constraint in his company, and had a feeling that he was not quite right at the core'. Anne: 'a pleasing young woman of about 25', had lived with Walker for some time, acting as his housekeeper. Of late, however, she had not been seen. Walker had put it about that Anne had been unwell and

'The Bloody Tree?' Old Mill Lane, Great Lumley.

120

The site of Lumley Mill and location of the appearance of the ghost of Anne Walker.

had gone to spend some time with an aunt at Chester-le-Street. But rumours about her sudden departure had spread rapidly through the village. It was said that she was with child, the father being her uncle, the very same man who had taken her in and promised her protection. The ancient William Lumley was convinced in his own mind what had happened to Anne, and who was responsible. He would later give evidence to that effect before Judge Davenport at the Durham Assizes. In the meantime however, time passed. Nothing was seen or heard of Anne Walker. The longer she was missing, the deeper and darker the rumours became: 'the neighbours were very wroth with Walker, whom they suspected'.

James Graham was a Miller. The mill he owned and worked was situated on the River Wear near Great Lumley, not far from where John Walker lived. It was a busy time of year for him. Autumn had turned into winter and: 'frosty dark December' had descended. Alone in the Mill during the dark days and the long nights, the flickering shadows brought to life by the candlelight and the mournful wail of the winter winds through the timbers could unsettle the mind, seize the imagination and persuade with a whisper that dread things lurked behind every sack, every shadowy beam. But James Graham, so the: *Monthly Chronicle* tells us, was of a character unsuited to fall prey to such superstitious fancies. He: 'would not court even an ignorant fear of the supernatural and he laughingly ridiculed all who thought differently from himself'.

So it was then, that one evening, Graham was in his Mill, working late. The Midnight Hour was ageing toward the first hour of the morning, yet nothing distracted the practical, no-nonsense Graham from the reality and necessity of completing his workload. That is, until he looked up and saw a sight that froze his heart and fixed his feet to the spot. His mouth dried as his racing pulse pounded in his temples and a film of perspiration began to coat his brow. His brain tried to make sense of what his eyes were seeing, for from out of the shadows a figure had appeared and was moving, slowly, towards him. Graham watched, transfixed, as the figure was gradually revealed in the flickering candlelight and the full horror of the vision smote him: 'Much affrighted and amaz'd he began to bless himself'.

The shape was that of a young woman, but such a cruel and ghastly mockery of womanhood as this he could not countenance. But there the shape stood in the candlelight, hair disheveled and sodden with the blood that streamed from five terrible wounds to her head. The phantom spoke to the Miller, and the sadness reflecting in her

Ruined, overgrown masonry is all that is now left.

eyes was echoed in the desperate appeal of her voice: 'I am the spirit of Anne Walker, who, while in the flesh, lived with your neighbour, John Walker; I was betrayed by Walker!' The spectre went on to tell Graham of the terrible events that had befallen her. How Walker, her uncle, had seduced her and made her pregnant; promising faithfully to treat her well and send her to her Aunt, where she would receive all necessary care. How she was taken away one evening by a collier named Mark Sharp. How Sharp had taken her to a lonely spot and under her Uncle's instructions: 'Slew me with a pick, such as men dig coals withal, and gave me these five wounds'. Her body Sharp had then thrown into a pit. The murder weapon and his blood soaked clothes, he had hidden under a nearby bank. The ghost of Anne Walker then fixed James Graham with a stare, and uttered a terrifying oath: 'And now Master Graham, you must be the man to reveal this base and cruel deed, else my spirit shall haunt you for ever'. With this, the grisly vision vanished. The terrified Graham ran from the darkness of the Mill, back to the safety of his home, and sat silently, in shock and disbelief. He told nobody of his experience.

Not surprisingly perhaps, Graham became a changed man. A circumstance noted by his family and friends. He became insular; the normally avuncular miller said few words. They noticed also his sudden aversion to being without a lantern during the dark, winter days, and to working at the Mill at all after night had fallen. For his part, Graham avoided even being alone in the Mill, for fear of the apparition returning.

Some little time past, Graham collected his wits and began to wonder whether tiredness, overwork and some dark winter mood had combined together in his brain to somehow bring about an encounter that had simply been imagined. Indeed, these were the thoughts he was thinking to himself early one evening, while walking, lantern in hand, when his path was blocked by the ghost of Anne Walker. This time the sense of terror was greater. The eyes and voice, no longer had the air of appeal, but of command: 'stern and vindictive', as Graham observed. Her request, however, was the same. Still Graham feared to go to the

Authorities. Surely they would think him mad. He had his good reputation to consider, a reputation which helped provide him with a good living. Once again Graham resolved to say nothing. On 21 December the Winter Solstice, when the spirits of the dead begin to walk the earth, the miller was walking in his garden. Again, and for the last time, the apparition appeared. This time, with an aspect: 'very fierce and cruel', the ghost of Anne Walker approached James Graham: 'And then so threatened him, and affrighted him, that he faithfully promised to reveal it next morning'.

What curse she had threatened, Graham would never disclose, but the next morning he went with his story, to the authorities. Both the Miller and his upstanding reputation were known to the Magistrate, which no doubt helped bring about an investigation into the alarming story. A search was duly made of the places Anne Walker had described and her mortal remains were indeed discovered, dumped where she had said, in the pit; with five terrible wounds to her head. The search was continued and the murder weapon and Mark Sharpe's bloodstained clothes were also found: 'The pick and shoes and stockings, still bloody in every circumstance as the apparition had related'. John Walker and Mark Sharp were duly arrested and sent for trial at Durham. There is no record of a confession from either, but there was some local gossip that Sharp had indeed admitted his part, saying that Walker had paid him £10 to carry out the crime.

Of course the arrest of Sharp and Walker and the explanation of how their crime was discovered caused a sensation among the local people; who nevertheless still considered that justice had been served. Evidence further damming Walker was given by William Lumley, the: 'ancient gentleman', who lived next door. He told the Court that, despite his great age, he very well remembered that Ann had been servant to her uncle and that it had been said that she was with child. Of course: 'Everyone knew' that Walker was the father, but Anne would never confide that this was indeed the case. She had been sent away, as everyone had been told, to her Aunt's house in Chester-le-Street to be taken care of throughout her: 'illness'. After some time, Mark Sharp had been noticed around the neighbourhood. He was, after all, something of a curiosity, originating as he did, not from the village nor even from the district, but from Blackburn in Lancashire; and he was known to be on friendly terms with Walker.

The prosecution went on to allege that one night, Sharp, on Walker's instruction, went to the house of Anne's aunt. Walker had already assured Anne that he would look after both her and the child and Sharp had now come to escort her back to: 'a private place, where she would be well looked to, till she was brought to bed, and made well again; and then she should come again and keep his house'. Instead, he took her to a lonely place and murdered her with a coal pick.

It appears from the chronicles that, as the trial progressed, the strangeness of the case and the whole eerie atmosphere under which the proceedings were taking place, began to pervade even into the courtroom. Judge Davenport was ill at ease throughout, as he later confessed in a letter: 'a very full and punctual narrative of the whole business'. An even more bizarre occurrence seems to have set the seal on this most supernatural of trials, and no doubt, given the nature of the other evidence, finally dammed Walker. A later, sworn statement by a Mr James Smart of Durham City, tells of how a Mr Fairhair, a Gentleman of Ford near Lanchester, and Foreman of the Jury, gave evidence under oath, that as the proceedings were taking place, to his horror, he witnessed: 'The likeness of a child, stand upon Walker's shoulders'.

Judge Davenport's Courtroom on Palace Green where Sharpe and Walker were found guilty of murder.

Indeed, so terrified everyone in court seems to have been, that Judge Davenport gave sentence on the first night of the trial: 'Which was a thing never used in Durham, before nor after'.

Perhaps the Judge feared that he himself might witness the vengeful ghost of Anne Walker. Perhaps, as was later commented upon, he considered that the apparition of the child: 'Was very fit and apposite, placed on Walker's shoulders, as one who was justly loaded or charged with that crime of getting his kinswoman with child, as well as complotting with Sharp to murder her'. Walker and Sharp were both duly found guilty, sentenced and hung at Durham. Although it is said that screams were long heard from the Old Mill Wood, Anne Walker's ghost was never seen again, and James Graham, the Miller, was freed from her terrible curse.

Nineteenth-century chroniclers placed the scene of the actual murder in a ravine in the Old Mill Wood, Great Lumley; known as Sharp and Walker's Gyhll and local people would for years baulk at the thought of walking by there. More recent tales tell that the spot where Anne Walker was killed is marked by the: 'Bloody Tree', an ancient oak, in Old Mill Lane. The whole event seems to have been accepted as authentic by a wide cross section of people. Naturally the local people believed it without question, but claims as to its authenticity also spread to minds a great deal more: 'enlightened'.

Joseph Glanvil: 'Chaplain in Ordinary to His Majesty, and Fellow of the Royal Society', had his book: 'Witches and Apparitions', published in London in the year 1681. The book contained a letter to Glanvil from a Dr Henry More, calling the Author's attention to a story. A story which he urged: 'You will do well, Master Glanvil, to put among your additions, it being so well attested'. The story was that of the trial of Sharp and Walker, which had previously been included in a narrative written by one, Master John Webster: 'A practitioner of Physic'. In his narrative, Webster stated that he had seen and read the letter that had been sent by Judge Davenport. Webster went on and said of the nature of the trial that: 'This I confess to be one of the most convincing stories, being of undoubted verity, that I have ever read, heard, or knew of and carrieth with it the most evident force to make the most incredulous spirit to be satisfied that there are really sometimes such things as apparitions'. Of course it must be remembered that this apparently supernatural episode, did take place during a time in our history when belief in the practice and power of Witchcraft and the Supernatural was commonly accepted, and not just among the: 'rustic folk'. Indeed, its inclusion in Joseph Glanvil's book suggests that: 'The belief in the supernatural agencies was then as rife among the learned as it was long afterwards among the ignorant'.

What then is the modern day reader to make of the facts in the case of Anne Walker? If James Graham himself, or someone known to him, had committed the murder; then perhaps the combination of his remarkable story, local dislike and suspicion of Walker and an eager acceptance by the people of supernatural agencies; would have made it relatively easy to: 'frame' Walker and Sharpe. However, there does not seem to have been the slightest suspicion that Graham had been party in any way to the murder. Had he perhaps, or someone known to him, been a witness to the dreadful deed? If so, why not report it immediately? Why fabricate such a fantastic story? A story which would no doubt, throw into question his sanity and be likely to jeapordise his reputation and thus his livelihood. Conversely, if Graham did not have such first hand or direct knowledge of the crime, how could he possibly have known the whereabouts of Anne Walker's body, the murder weapon and the blood stained clothes; if not from the very tale that Anne Walker told him; and therefore, if this is indeed the case, then the whole incredible story, as the court accepted, is to be regarded as fact.

By the more sober and outwardly respectable years of the late 19th century, attitudes toward the story had become more cautious, and chroniclers of that time suggested: 'That the whole legend is stamped with the superstitions of the time, and should be read rather as an illustration of how people then thought, than as a narration of verity'. Indeed, it is no doubt difficult for today's sophisticated generations to accept as fact, the supernatural circumstances leading to the arrest of Walker and Sharp and the subsequent events at their trial; but as a famous, if fictional, consulting detective once said: 'If you eliminate the impossible, whatever remains, no matter how improbable; must be the truth'

Chapter 14

Free-Born John Lilburne

'It is the men who stick in the stream, who make the times froth around them, or who dam it up for a future flood and rush – these are the history makers'
- The Monthly Chronicle

The English Civil War was still in its infancy. The young Captain of the Parliamentary Army looked around at the surviving men, at what was left of a 700 strong rag-tag band of rebels, dismissed by the King's Cavaliers as: 'All Butchers and Dyers'. Tired and bloodied, their resolve beginning to ebb away. Survival was now all of their thoughts; desertion was being whispered.

But the young Parliamentarian Captain had no thought of surrender. He would fight on, for that was his nature. He would fight on until his capture, imprisonment or death. Captured and imprisoned indeed he would be; but this day's young Captain would continue to fight all his life, for the rights of the ordinary man against what he saw as tyranny and oppression. He would be arrested and hounded; branded Agitator by the establishment, a troublemaker hell bent on Sedition and Anarchy. And he would eventually become, for some: 'The best loved man in England'. For he was: 'Free-born John'; John Lilburne, a one man campaigning army, fighting for religious freedom, equality before the law and a Parliament chosen directly by the people; ideas almost 200 years ahead of their time, in a revolutionary England still far from ready for such radical change.

The initial clash of arms of the Civil War had been at Edgehill, in Warwickshire. The battle had been bloody but indecisive. Both sides, of course, had claimed victory. The King's advance guard, 4,000 foot and 800 cavalry now moved on London. In their way was a force of Parliamentarians defending Brentford and the road into the Capital. The: 'Butchers and Dyers' had fought furiously for five hours but now all was almost over. Superior Royalist numbers had won this battle but their subsequent excesses in the sack of the town, in the midst of peace negotiations, would blacken their reputation and steel the supporters of Parliament against the King's cause. Parliament would eventually win the war: 'Free-born John' would live on to fight battles of a different kind.

John Lilburne was born in County Durham in 1615. The family home and estate was at Thickley-Punchardon, East Thickley: 'in the Parish of St Andrew's Auckland', not far from Bishop Auckland but the Lilburnes owned property across the County, including a fine Town House in Sunderland, where his uncle, George Lilburne, was Mayor. The Lilburnes had been merchants and landowners in north-east England since Bishop Hatfield's time and John's ancestry was littered with Royal Attendants and Courtiers. His paternal great grandfather, Bartholomew Lilburne, had been an attendant to Henry VIII at the Field of Cloth of Gold. His maternal grandfather, Thomas Hixon, had been a Keeper of the Standing Wardrobe at Greenwich Palace, his mother, Margaret Hixon, being brought up in the splendour of the Court.

It was at Greenwich, in 1598, that John's father, Richard, as an adolescent in the service of the Earl of Northumberland had met Margaret. A year later on, 29 October 1599, when

Richard was 16 years old, they were married. That same year Oliver Cromwell was born. Only six years later, Richard's father died and he, along with his bride, returned to the family home in County Durham. There they were to have three children, Elizabeth, Robert and John and both Robert and John would see their lives and their destinies played out against the backdrop of civil war and bloodshed, political radicalism and the execution of a King. Robert would rise to be a Major General in Cromwell's army and his would be the 47th signature on the Death Warrant of King Charles I. After the Restoration of the Monarchy he would die in prison. John was given as good an education as it was possible for his father to give him: 'I was brought up well nigh ten years together in the best schools in the North, namely, Auckland and Newcastle, in both which places I was not one of the dronessest schoolboys there'. He studied Latin and Greek and developed, from an early age, both a sharp mind and a ready tongue. Then, as an adolescent and encouraged by his father, he sought out an apprenticeship and moved to London to begin work for Thomas Hewson, Cloth Trader. So it was that the young son of a County Durham squire set out to make his mark in the changing world of 17th-century England. An England, it seems, quite ready for the momentous upheavals of revolution and war; but not, however, ready for John Lilburne.

In London John soon began to move among radicals and revolutionaries within the Puritan community. William Prynne, an Oxford Scholar and Lawyer and Dr John Bastwick, a physician and former soldier were both militant Puritans who had been fined, pilloried, mutilated and imprisoned by the Court of Star Chamber; guilty, it was claimed, of Libel and Sedition, of publishing pamphlets opposing Bishops and the Church establishment and the arbitary justice of the Star Chamber itself. Dangerous sentiments but sentiments shared by a growing number of the population. There was a mood for change and anger over the savage punishments meted out to dissenters. But these were days, as the *Monthly Chronicle* tells us, when: 'The Cobbler had to stick to his lapstone, or be counted a foe to the State'.

Lilburne began to share these sentiments and in him grew a hatred of the injustice he saw and a growing desire for a fundamental change in the way England was governed. He had read widely from the works of Martin Luther and John Calvin and he came to regard Bastwick as his: 'Pastor and Teacher'. Bastwick in turn considering John as: 'honest and religious, yet a mere Country Courtier and very rough hewn'. The anti-establishment pamphlets being produced were unlicensed and therefore illegal. John Lilburne, now it seems fired up with revolutionary zeal, volunteered to go to Holland, where publication of such works was legal, to have more of Bastwick's works produced and smuggled back into England. Thousands of illegal publications flooded in; condemning the Bishops, the establishment, the Church, the Court of Star Chamber and therefore, by implication, the King. But the traffickers were discovered and brought to answer.

John Lilburne, his mission accomplished, returned to England; and was also promptly arrested. Accused of publishing and dispersing seditious pamphlets he was incarcerated in Gatehouse Prison. There he lay for three months, without any trial, until he was moved to Fleet Prison where he was examined by the King's Attorney General, Sir John Bankes. He continued to deny any wrongdoing and was arraigned to be brought before the hated Court of Star Chamber. The Star Chamber had its origins in mediaeval England and had developed from judicial sittings of the King's Royal Council. By the time of the Stuart kings its power had grown to such an extent that, to the subjects of Charles I, it was simply a byword for the misuse of power by the King, his Ministers and his Bishops. Specialising in cases of Sedition, it was seen as a vehicle to suppress all opposition to the established order. No jury sat in the Court of Star Chamber and there was no right of appeal from it.

But John Lilburne had read widely, not only on religious matters, but on Politics, the Common Law and the rights of individuals. His time had come to make a stand, as he saw it, for Liberty against the oppression of the State. He protested against the manner and the injustice of his arrest and his detention without trial; he refused to offer his own defence; he refused to pay the usual fee to the Clerk of the Court, pleading: 'I am but a young man and a prisoner and money not too plentiful"; finally, and most importantly, he refused under Oath to say anything during interrogation; which might lead him to incriminate himself. For the first time the actual legality of the Oath had been questioned. He would not, as Fordyce relates: 'violate the maxims of the Common Law, by becoming his own accuser', and claimed his right under the law as: 'a free-born Englishman' not to do so. So it was that John Lilburne's soubriquet was coined and being found guilty of the charge of illegal pamphleteering, he was also declared guilty of: 'insufferable disobedience and contempt', and of setting an evil example. He was sentenced to be fined and to be whipped from Fleet Prison to Westminster, there to stand in the Pillory.

So the day of punishment arrived. It was 18 April 1638. The day dawned hot. The *Monthly Chronicle* tells us that John: 'Took his sufferings without relenting'. Stripped to the waist and dragged: 'at a cart's arse', he was lashed: 'above five hundred times from cords tied full of knots'; lashed so brutally that his shoulders swelled: 'as big as a penny loaf', the terrible wounds from the three strap whip made worse by the burning sun. Yet all the time he exhorted the cheering crowd to hear him. To hear of the injustice of the system that had brought him to this; to hear of the tyranny of those in power, and to hear of the freedoms which were the natural birthright of all Englishmen. At the Pillory he again denied any wrongdoing and addressed the crowd, he protested against the treatment of: 'A Gentleman and the son of a Gentleman in the north of England, two hundred miles from here, descended of an ancient and worshipful family, according to the estimation of the world'. He was weak and in great pain but as Mackenzie and Ross tell us: 'amidst all this Lilburne remained undaunted and unsubdued'. The *Monthly Chronicle* relates: 'He made mighty speeches against his persecutors and flung away pamphlets from the very Pillory, like the seeds of dandelions'. The Warden of Fleet Prison finally gave the order to gag him and even as he was locked into the Pillory, gagged so tightly that his mouth bled, he began, to the cheers of the crowd, to stamp his feet as a final act of defiance, like some wayward child of a revolution yet to come.

But this had been a Landmark Trial. Lilburne's refusal to take the Oath before the Star Chamber reverberated throughout the establishment and would have severe ramifications for that establishment. The Star Chamber, in desiring to make such a public example of yet another seditious pamphleteer, troublesome but of little consequence, had created Free-born John Lilburne. The people had a new Champion. But their Champion was taken from them. After a two hour ordeal, pinned in the Pillory, his untreated scourge wounds blistering in the sun, John was returned to Fleet Prison, there to be manacled in irons and held indefinitely. But Lilburne's public punishment had turned into a display of public sympathy, anger and support for the ideas he championed. An early gust of the anti-establishment wind that would end in the storm of the English Civil War.

Back in County Durham, John's father, Richard, imbued it seems with the same belligerent spirit, was involved in a legal dispute over the freehold of some land at Thickley.

Lilburne's argument was with a neighbour, Ralph Claxton, and the case was brought before Judge Berkley at the Durham Assizes on 6 August 1638. Lilburne demanded the satisfaction of settling the case by the ancient right of: 'waging battle'. Claxton, equally keen it seems on this form of rough justice, duly turned up with his Champion, George Cheney: 'in full array', who dutifully threw down his gauntlet. Lilburne appeared with his Champion, William Peverell, who responded to the challenge. Battle, it had been decided, was to be with Battons and Sandbags. The bemused judge tried to establish whether the ancient right was still proper or even still legal but as Hutchinson comments: 'Such were the barbarous customs, even of so late an era, that the decision of a title to lands was left to heaven, under the bastings of a Quarter Staff'.

The Judge ordered the Champions into custody until the next morning while the legality of the remedy was looked at. He also ordered them to appear at the Court of Pleas on 15 September where the case was further adjourned until the 22 December. The matter was even brought to the attention of the King, who, bouncing it straight back: 'desired the Judges of the Northern Circuit to consider how the dispute could be settled in another way'. They could not agree that personal combat should decide the day, but there was general consensus that, as the law stood, Richard Lilburne was entitled to his trial by battle; if he persisted. Lilburne did persist but the lawyers succeeded, by: 'discovering' a succession of legal technicalities, to defer the trial from year to year, until eventually trial by battle was finally abolished. John Lilburne's father it would seem would be the last man in England to demand the resolution of a legal argument by armed combat.

For two years John was kept in prison. Recovering his strength he began to write new pamphlets, recording in: *A Christian Man's Trial* and: *A Worke of the Beast*, his trial and punishment at the hands of the Star Chamber. Then, in 1640, the Long Parliament sat. During the proceedings, Oliver Cromwell spoke out against Lilburne's imprisonment. Parliament ordered his release, declaring that his arrest and punishment had been: 'Illegal, bloody, wicked, cruel, barbarous and tyrannical'. Almost as soon as he was freed he spoke out against the delay in punishment for the King's principle advisor, Thomas Wentworth, Earl of Strafford. Strafford: 'Black Tom Tyrant', was known for his harshness. Along with William Laud, Archbishop of Canterbury, he had been chief advisor to the King for 11 years and had urged the King to strengthen his position against Parliament; wishing, so he said, that prominent Parliamentarian John Hampden and his followers: 'were well whipped into their right senses'. He was disliked intensely and with his high handedness, cruelty and disregard for the ordinary people, he had for many come to symbolise the reign of King Charles. By order of Parliament he had been arrested for High Treason but the King prevaricated over signing the order for his execution. John Lilburne claimed that if this delay was due to the King, then the King should be removed. For this, he was arrested again. He was charged this time with the capital offence of High Treason and brought to trial before the House of Lords. However, their Lordships could not agree and the case was dismissed. John was released, the King signed Strafford's death warrant on 10 May and two days later: 'Black Tom Tyrant' was beheaded. That same year, the Court of Star Chamber was abolished by Act of Parliament.

Lilburne appeared to take a step towards: 'settling down'. He married Elizabeth Dewell, the daughter of a wealthy London merchant. Prominent in Baptist circles Elizabeth was also a political activist, herself being arrested in September 1641. Bess would remain with him for the rest of his stormy life and would always be: 'An object of my deare affections'.

But the storm that had been gathering now broke. In a move that polarised opinion and support against him, the King, with a detachment of his: 'Cavaliers', forced his way into the House of Commons in a vain attempt to arrest Parliamentarian ringleaders. Disaffection became rebellion. The division lines were drawn. The King raised his standard at Nottingham on August 22nd, 1642 and the English Civil War began. John Lilburne, naturally enough, supported the cause of Parliament and enlisted into the Army. So it was that Free-born John had already seen action at Edgehill before the retreat that had left him besieged at Brentford where his actions delayed the Royalist advance long enough to make safe both soldiers and artillery vital to the Parliamentarian cause. But inevitably, along with around 400 other men, Lilburne was captured.

Imprisoned in Oxford Castle and charged with High Treason for: 'taking up arms against the King' he expected death. Again he stood before his accusers: 'I am a gentleman and of a family of gentlemen, who have continued so ever since William the Conqueror, in the County of Durham'. A letter from him, smuggled out by Bess, was delivered to the House of Commons. The House declared that if the execution took place their response would be to invoke: 'Lex Talionis', the Law of Retaliation, by executing captive Royalist prisoners, like, for like. Bess, who was three months pregnant, then rode from London to Oxford to deliver to the King the letter from the Speaker of the House of Commons; setting out Parliament's decision. The sentence was lifted and five months later, in a prisoner exchange, he was freed. Free-born John, the hero of the people, was back. His father, however, was not faring well. In the earlier days of the war, the rural North was held for the King. Richard Lilburne wrote to John from County Durham: 'I have lost all that the enemy could finger of mine, all my stock, my corn and household goods and the rents of my lands'. John returned to the Army and rose through the ranks, first as a Major in Cromwell's Eastern Association, then as a Lieutenant Colonel of Dragoons. He fought in the Parliamentary victory at the Battle of Marston Moor but eventually began to grow suspicious of the characters who were now taking centre stage in the Army and in Parliament and mistrustful of the direction in which they were taking the revolution. Soldiers were being made to sign the: 'Solemn Oath and Covenant' which was seen by John, as a requirement dictated by the Scottish Presbyterian Church. Lilburne was not one to sign any oath; he refused, and left the Army. Six weeks later, the King was finally defeated at the Battle of Naseby.

John, becoming disillusioned with the lack of real change for ordinary people following the Parliamentarian victory, again became involved in pamphleteering; calling for a new system of government by maintaining: 'the right of the people to form a constitution for themselves', and gaining widespread support from soldiers and the general populous. Because of his continuing radical stance, he would be arrested and imprisoned, again and again, in and out of gaol for much of the next four years. In 1645, Bess, heavily pregnant, joined him in the Tower of London, where their daughter Elizabeth was born. Indeed two of his first three children would be born while he was in prison, one of them they even named; Tower. A pamphlet condemning his continued imprisonment, entitled: *A Pearle in a Dounghill*, was circulated by his growing number of supporters.

From prison he quickly became the most vocal and high profile critic of the new regime. Almost 40 pamphlets followed between 1646 and 1649 and in such works as: *England's Birthright Justified* and: *The Just Man's Justification* he criticised the supporters both of the King and of the Government. Claiming that reforms had not gone far enough, or had gone in the wrong direction, he proposed an entirely new system of democratic representation of the people, with representatives in Parliament being chosen by the people; making the popular point that soldiers who had fought and spilled their blood for Parliament, still had no right to decide who sat in it. This was very dangerous ground and Lilburne was marked as a major political threat, especially when he opposed the execution of the King, for by doing so he opposed the army: 'Grandees'. Cromwell agreed with some of the proposed new policies; the abolition of the Monarchy and the House of Lords was not questioned but although he championed the Sovereignty of Parliament, Cromwell was no social democrat. Government, he thought, was to be by the virtuous and the righteous, selected by those of standing and property; he feared that Lilburne and his supporters could de-stabilise his new order but he also knew that Free-born John: 'had the ear of thousands'.

While imprisoned in the Tower of London, John, along with the Leveller prisoners, William Walwyn, Thomas Prince and Richard Overton, began to write: *An Agreement for the People*, the final version of which would not be published until May 1649. Signed by Lilburne, Walwyn, Prince and Overton, it was hoped by its authors and by the popular movement, that it would be accepted by Parliament as the basis of a new Constitution for England and during October and November 1645, it was the subject of a series of debates at St Mary's Church, Putney, to consider the future Government of England. On the one side, the Army Grandees, including Cromwell and his son-in-law, Thomas Ireton; and on the other, the army agitators and Levellers, lead by Colonel Thomas Rainsborough. At what came to be known as the Putney Debates, the Levellers demanded a new type of Government, in which men had equality before the law, freedom of speech and association, a Government elected regularly by the people's consent and religious liberty. But their critics claimed they simply wished to: 'level' all social distinctions and to do away with private property. The demands were not met. Rainsborough was killed by a band of Royalists in 1648 and at his funeral his men cut into ribbons his sea-green regimental banner. Both the sea-green ribbons and John Lilburne, though never claiming to be one, would now forever be associated with the Leveller movement.

On leaving prison in late 1648, John returned to Durham on family business. A Smallpox epidemic in London had claimed his two sons; his wife and daughter had been severely ill. While in Durham he was offered a seat at the trial of the King, but he refused it, making no secret of his opinion that to execute King Charles was a mistake. A high profile state trial, he argued, would only bring sympathy for the King. The law existed equally for everyone. Charles Stuart should be tried in the ordinary courts as any common felon. So it was that Free-born John was not in London during the trial and execution of the King, however, he did return shortly after.

Lilburne now published, against a backdrop of widespread Leveller uprisings, another pamphlet: *England's New Chains Discovered*, highly critical of the new Government which he described as: 'Tyrannical, Usurped and Unlawful': 'What freedom is there left, …If this be not a new way of breaking the spirits of the English, which Strafford and Canterbury never dreamt of, we know no difference of things!'

- *England's New Chains Discovered*, 1649.

The fledgling Republic could not and would not allow his criticisms to continue. He was a threat to the Government, to the army and therefore to the State itself.

So it was that on 28 March 1649, over 100 horse with supporting foot soldiers came to arrest John Lilburne at his home. Once again he was thrown into the Tower, accused of

High Treason. Once again he was to stand trial for his life. But Lilburne had massive popular support and a number of petitions were raised for his release. One had been signed by 10,000 women, a thousand of whom, wearing the sea-green ribbons of the Levellers, handed it in to Parliament. But the: 'bonny Besses in their sea-green dresses', together with their petitions, were waved away.

The trial began on 24 October with Lilburne being brought before a Special Commission at the Guildhall. He stood before 40 dignitaries, including the Lord Mayor of London; his supporters packing the rest of the Courtroom. Free-born John refused to kneel at the Bar, he refused Counsel; he would defend himself and insisted that it was the Jury who were judges of both fact and law. Proceedings became riotous when, as the Prosecution read out the: 'Seditious' extracts from his writings, Lilburne's supporters cheered and applauded. He raised the rights of free-born Englishmen under Magna Carta, he argued from the Abolition of the Star Chamber, from the Petition of Right and from several laws from the reigns of Edward I and Edward III. At the end he turned to the Judge and said, not without a sense of the theatrical: 'Sir, my life is before you, you may murder me and take away my blood if you please!' The Jury refused to convict him and he was acquitted: 'amidst the joyous acclamations of the people'. It is said that in response to his acquittal, church bells were rung all across London, bonfires were lit and there was widespread feasting. He was eventually released from the Tower on 8 November along with Walwyn, Prince and Overton. So significant did this: 'people's victory' seem, that a special commemorative medal was struck, with John's portrait on one side and the names of all the Jurors on the reverse.

Once again Lilburne appeared to settle down, pursuing careers, first as a Brewer and then as a Lawyer. Two years later he represented his uncle, George Lilburne and others, who were claiming a lease of property in Harraton, County Durham. The owner had recently defaulted and become bankrupt and Sir Arthur Haslerigg had seized it for the Government, claiming it was public property. The case was heard by a Government Committee in Haberdasher's Hall, London. Of course the Committee found for the Government. Of course John Lilburne reacted at once, and in a new pamphlet: *A Just Reproof to Haberdasher's Hall*, he made accusations which Parliament considered treasonous. Of course this played right into the hands of his enemies and he was arrested and committed again to the Tower. The case was heard by the Council of State and John was banished from England: 'on pain of death'. So he sailed away and settled, for a short time, in Amsterdam.

Returning illegally in 1653 he was promptly re-arrested and charged once again with Treason. Further imprisonment and another show trial would follow. The scene this time was the Old Bailey; the date, 13 July 1653. Again the trial turned into a show of support for Free-born John; the Courtroom filled with over 600 of his supporters, cheering on their returning hero. Again he refused to kneel before the Court. Again he would act as his own Counsel and after a string of legal arguments and a two hour speech in his own defence, again; against the direction of the Judge, the Jury acquitted him: 'Not Guilty, of any crime worthy of death'. His supporters cheered so loudly that: 'The shout was heard an English mile'.

Cromwell, however, had considered the situation so potentially volatile that he had stationed nearby, and at arms, three regiments of foot and one of horse, fuelling a widespread belief that the Government still wanted to ensure Lilburne's execution. Anger spread throughout the massed ranks of John's supporters. Already, during the trial, thousands of leaflets had been circulated, bearing the slogan: 'And what, shall then Honest John Lilburne die! Three score thousand will know the reason why'. So John Lilburne was acquitted; but not released. It was off to Newgate, then into the protection of the Lieutenant of the Tower of London, who was required to detain him in safe custody: 'For the Peace of this Nation', as Cromwell and his Grandees: 'Enraged and Perplexed', wondered: 'What further will be done with him?'. A Royalist prisoner pointedly said at the time:

'The King raised a Parliament he could not rule,
The Parliament raised an army it could not rule,
The army made agitators it could not rule'.

They chose banishment, again, and a year later he was sent to Jersey and imprisonment in Mont Orgueil; Gorey Castle: 'There to evaporate his turbulent humours; whereof he is full'. And from where the Governor of the Island complained that his prisoner gave him more trouble than 10 Cavaliers.

Elizabeth, together with John's father, Richard, eventually petitioned Cromwell for his release; his brother Robert offered to stand security for his: 'peaceable demeanour', and in 1655, he was allowed to leave Jersey and was returned to Dover Castle; there to serve out his punishment. It was here that he was converted to Quaker beliefs and for the next two years he would actively preach at Quaker meetings. Although technically a prisoner, he had a reasonable amount of freedom; as long as he behaved himself. He was allowed to rent and regularly visit a house in Eltham, Kent, into which Elizabeth and their remaining children moved and where she gave birth to their 10th child. But a combination of illness and years of captivity had finally broken the spirit of John Lilburne. Suffering from: 'Gaol Fever', a disease spread by rats; he saw his family for the last time in the summer of 1657. His condition suddenly worsening, he died on 29 August. He was only 42 years old. For Elizabeth it was the end of a tempestuous marriage, her: 'Seventeen years of Sorrows'; of their 10 children, only three survived to adulthood. A simple Quaker funeral followed a public procession by John's sympathizers; many wearing the sea-green ribbons of the Levellers.

In just over a year, Cromwell was dead. In three years the English Republic, such as it was, would end, a Stuart Monarch would again sit on the throne of England; and the reforms of John Lilburne and the Levellers would be lost to future generations. Aloof, unbending, duplicitous Charles Stuart, firm believer in the Divine Right of Kings, had lost his head on the scaffold in Whitehall. Oliver Cromwell, the power behind the rise of Parliament and the Army and chief of the: 'Righteous Men', expired as a storm raged in the skies above him. Tempestuous, belligerent, argumentative John Lilburne died meekly, as a Quaker.

Described as: 'A great trouble world in all variety of Governments', historians have since been divided over the historical significance of John Lilburne. Was he a visionary, a reforming democrat 200 years before his time? A people's champion, fighting for the rights and liberties of the common man; or was he merely a quarrelsome, seditious and ultimately ineffective troublemaker, raging on the fringes of the great events of his time? Indeed, some would have it so.

Shortly after his death, an epitaph was released:

'Is John departed, and is Lilburne gone?
Farewell to both, to Lilburne and to John!
Yet being gone, take this advice from me,

Let them not both in one grave buried be;
Here lay ye John, lay Lilburne thereabout,
For if they both should meet, they surely will fall out'
And the Royalist Judge, David Jenkins famously said of him that: 'If there was none living but he, John would be against Lilburne, and Lilburne against John'.

However, the 18th century Durham historian William Hutchinson, commends Lilburne, for: 'He opposed the illegal exertions of Prerogative, as well as the unjust exercise of Parliamentary power; but in both was consistent in opposing tyranny, in whatever form it appeared'. In Hume's: *History of England*, Lilburne is described as: 'The most turbulent, but the most upright and courageous of human kind'; and his memory, according to Hutchinson: 'Is sweet to the lovers of liberty and their country'. In the end, Lilburne himself, in his work: *Legal and Fundamental Liberties of the People of England*, simply described himself thus: 'An honest and true-bred free Englishman, that never in his life feared a tyrant, nor loved an oppressor'.

The stance taken by Free-born John Lilburne in 1639, refusing to take the Oath before the Court of Star Chamber, reverberated through England. It has also been referred to in modern day American Courts of Law. In 1966 it was cited by the US Supreme Court, with reference to the Fifth Amendment in (Miranda vs. Arizona). Indeed if anything, Lilburne's legacy is today revered more in the United States than in his own country. Many of his supporters, and many of the descendants of the Levellers, took ship and moved to the New World. Some became Quakers themselves. So it was that over a century after their time, the ideas championed in the writings of John Lilburne and the Levellers found their way into the guiding principles of the American Declaration of Independence and subsequently into the basic freedoms enshrined in the American Constitution.

A statue of King Charles I now stands in Whitehall, close to the site of his execution; or martyrdom. Oliver Cromwell stands, Bible in one hand, sword in the other, outside the Parliament that he tyrannized; or freed from the tyranny of the Crown. But no great monument exists today, at least not to the knowledge of this author, either in the Capital or in his native County, to John Lilburne; a man who sought to elevate People over Parliament and Jury over Judge. Students of Parliamentary history or of Seventeenth Century England may well be familiar with the exploits of John Lilburne, but he remains largely unknown in his native County Durham; where today there is little remembrance of perhaps the most turbulent of her sons: 'Quarrelsome John', 'Honest John'; Free-born John Lilburne.

Part Five

Chapter 15

Mad, Bad and Dangerous

It is as well to hang for a hog, as a ha'penny'

Over the centuries, County Durham has been well served with an abundance of: 'Characters'. Singularly odd individuals, whose harmless ways and gentle, if eccentric, preoccupations have given amusement, usually unintentionally, to all who knew them. However, not all eccentrics were gentle and not all their preoccupations were harmless.

In 1820, the: 'Historian of Durham', Robert Surtees, published volume two of his great work: *The History and Antiquities of the County Palatine of Durham*. In it he described the Derwent Valley, thus: 'The surrounding scenery is wild and romantic, and the Darwent, fringed with the native wood, wanders through rich haugh grounds finely contrasted with the heathy hills which hem in the vale on the north and south'.

The River Derwent flowing, west to east, forms part of the border between County Durham and Northumberland. The Valley through which it passes is surely well suited to be a land of myth and legend; scenic and remote, from high open moorland to fertile green fields and deep wooded valleys. But the beauty and tranquility of today's Derwentdale belies the fact that in centuries past, it was a land of secrets, shadows and superstition; of Mosstroopers, murder and mayhem. Deep within wooded glades lurked Witches, and on the wind that wailed over bleak moorland were carried echoes of the hoof beats of wild horses and the cries of wilder men.

'A gloomy presence saddens the scene,
Shades every flower and darkens every green,
Deepens the murmur of the falling floods,
And breathes a browner horror of the woods'.
Richardson: *Stray Leaves of Northern History and Tradition*.

The notoriety of the Derwent Valley perhaps reached its peak during the 17th century. The chronicles tell that Witches practiced their secret art; Mosstroopers were elevated in the imagination of the populous, far beyond the status of the cattle thieves and murderers that they were; and the Devil himself was a visitor on more than one occasion.

In 1641, the year before the outbreak of the English Civil War, a pamphlet published in London described in sensational detail, the: 'Most fearful and strange newes', of the Devil, in the bizarre form of a headless bear, terrifying the family of Thomas Hooper of: 'Edenbyres, nere the River Darwent, in the Bishoprick of Durham'. Thirteen years later, on the 19 August 1654, at Benfieldside, he appeared again; this time taking possession of a Quaker meeting, and causing those present to: 'shriek, yell and roar'. A curse was even laid upon the unfortunate Preacher; one of his congregation wishing: 'that all the plagues of

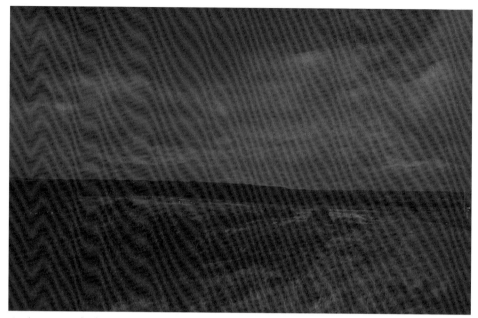

A view towards the Derwent Reservior from Muggleswick Common. A landscape as wild as the people and the tales that it gave birth to.

God might fall upon him'. An eyewitness reported: 'such a representation of Hell, I have never heard of; nothing but horror and confusion'.

Where the: 'Prince of Lies' walked, there his acolytes followed; and Witches danced with the: 'Divil', cast their spells, were reported and were arrested by the authorities. In 1673: 'Ann Armstrong of Buksnuke, Mary Hunter of Birkenside, Dorothy Green of Edmundbyers, Elizabeth Pickering of Whittingslaw, Annie Whitfield of Edmundbyers, Alice Dixon of Muggleswick Park, Catherine Elliott and Elizabeth Atchison of Ebchester and Isabell Andrew of Crooked Oak'; were all arraigned to stand before the Assizes. And so the people of the lands around Muggleswick, Ebchester and Allensford, where: 'Divers Witches confess to the Divill', breathed a collective sigh of relief; being freed from that shadowy, malign influence. But for a further century others would continued to practice their art until, we are told, Elizabeth Lee of Edmundbyers, the last of their kind, died in 1792.

Contemporary with the Witches were the Mosstroopers, some of whom achieved almost legendary status in the popular imagination. The fierce, swashbuckling figures who rode off on daring moonlit raids and epic wild rides across dark, windswept, lonely moors, seeking their quarry in the distant valleys of Weardale and Teesdale:

'And, toiling through the scenes surrounding, saw
The coming plunder, or the searching law'.
Barrass: *The Derwent Valley.*

Two of the most notorious of their kind were Rowley Harrison, who rode from near Muggleswick; and Thomas Raw of Allansford. Both were active at the same time, both managed to evade the law, and, after both being publicly excommunicated by the Church for their wicked ways, they died within two years of each other.

This then, was the Derwent Valley in the 17th century:
'For in these woods, and in that wilder day,
When lawless minds essayed no beaten track,
But loved adventure, as they loved the prey'.
Barrass: *The Derwent Valley*

And it was in this remote and lawless corner of the County Palatine, that another: 'Character' made his mark, his name; Ralph Maddison. His was a notorious career of infamy, which began in the ale houses of Shotley Bridge, and ended on the gallows at Durham. It seems that the wildness of his native land found a match in the wildness of his spirit; and he came to be known to all in those parts, only by the name of: 'Mad Maddison': 'Because of its fitness to give some idea of his insane and immoral conduct'.

Maddison it seems had spent his childhood living in somewhat privileged circumstances, his family owning considerable estates in the neighbourhood and the young Ralph being brought up in a: 'plain good house' on the banks of the river, immediately opposite Shotley Bridge; which Surtees describes as then being a small village on the south side of the River Derwent. As a child he had no formal education, he grew up: 'sudden and quick in a quarrel'. The mischievous pranks of his boyhood amused his father who had no interest in trying to: 'mould the coinage of his fevered brain', and continued to indulge the young Ralph, who, it was said, was habitually disobedient to his mother, insolent towards the servants and a bully towards other: 'less robust' youths. His father it seems, did all he could to encourage the youngsters waywardness.

Early in his career, his antics seem to today's reader to be no more than those of an overgrown schoolboy, irritations as opposed to downright roguery. A favourite pastime of his was to plague the local landowners by prowling the countryside at night and overturning their stacks of hay and corn. A story is told that one old man, who had often been annoyed this way, foiled Maddison by building his stack around the stump of an old ash tree. Maddison, obligingly, came in the dead of night to: 'cowp ower' the stack, but it resisted his utmost efforts and Maddison, convinced that witchcraft was at work: 'ran away in great fear'. When he reached manhood, the chronicles tell that Maddison was made a Warden of the locality. Rustling and banditry were common and Maddison, being a member of the local landed establishment, was given some sort of responsibility to bring the outlaws to justice. However, as was said: 'In his excursions against the Mosstroopers he must have acquired their predatory dispositions, and learnt to practice their dextrous villanies'. And as he grew older in years, so his acts of nuisance grew in malevolence. It was said that: 'in him every inch that was not a fool, was a rogue'.

At the time in which the story is set there were several fords across the River Derwent at Shotley Bridge. One of these was the scene of an infamous incident concerning Maddison. Recent rains had put the river in spate and the ford was flooded. An old dame wished to cross but was unable to as the floodwater was too deep and too fast. She told that she had accepted an offer from: 'a canny man', of a ride across the river on the back of his horse. The: 'canny man' was Maddison, who spurred his horse out into the middle of the river, and promptly pushed the old dame off, and into the flood. She had often heard of: 'Mad' Maddison, unfortunately for her she had never before seen him. As she crawled, half drowned from the river, some way down stream; she knew she would not forget him: 'laughing heartily, like a genuine water kelpy'.

His exploits began to bear the signs of an increasing malevolence, and contempt for both society and authority. One day while out walking, he passed a woman laying out two squares of linen, to bleach. Maddison lifted one up and walked off with it. The poor woman had the temerity to complain about the theft and suggested that one day Maddison would have to pay dearly for his wrong doings and excesses. Maddison turned on his heels, stole the other square of linen and said to the woman: 'Then I will have both, for it is as well to hang for a hog as a ha'penny'. They were to prove prophetic words.

For the local land owning classes during the reign of Charles II, leisure time, of which there was much was spent largely in the ale houses of the district. Many of these land owners it is said, developing more than a passing taste for the bottle. Historians record that: 'Joviality, degenerating into senseless brawling, rude hectoring and outright homicide occasionally, was a prominent feature of country life under the Merrie Monarch'. Ralph Maddison was no exception to this state of affairs. He grew in gracelessness. His tyranny often fuelled by the quantities of drink he consumed. True to his reputation, 'Mad' Maddison became: 'one of the foremost among the Derwentdale Royster-Doysters', and the constant terror of all who had occasion to go near his house, or any place he was accustomed to frequent. Eventually, even his own family began to suffer because of his excesses.

One night, after a momentous drinking session, the Chronicles tell at: 'The Bridge End' public house, his son-in-law had become so drunk that he was unable to walk unaided. Maddison made the selfless offer that his son-in-law should ride home on Maddison's own horse, while he, the more sober of the two, would trust to his feet. The senseless son-in-law was duly hoisted on to the horse; back to front. However, unknown to him, Maddison had placed a bunch of thorns under the saddle. The animal reared in pain and with the young man's head still facing the horse's tail, it darted off across the River Derwent in a state of wild agitation. The unfortunate rider managed somehow to cling on until the horse had galloped as far as Black Hedley, where he could do so no longer. He was thrown off and killed. It seems Maddison was not content with this. When his daughter, said to have been a beautiful woman of great talent, married for a second time; Maddison approved not of her choice. However, the man she chose for a second husband, John Elrington, had wealth and property, and therefore was indeed of some use to: 'Mad' Maddison.

The two men did not get on. Indeed a protracted, bitter and eventually violent feud developed between them. In time Elrington presented a petition against his father-in-law, to the Justices of Assize at Newcastle. In it he stated that: 'I, being a gentleman of good extraction, and endowed of a large estate, hath had the bad fortune to match myself to the daughter of one Ralph Maddison; who being a person of very bad life and conversation, hath persuaded me to convey my estate to the said Maddison and his heires'.

Elrington, it appears had effectively made Maddison a tenant for life; an action which he had quickly come to regret, as Maddison had then begun to put pressure on his son-in-law to sell off parts of his estate. It is unclear exactly why, but Elrington suggests that Maddison needed the money to keep himself out of prison, or worse. The petition states: 'for the saveing of his life at the last assizes; and this year, falling into the same danger againe'. Elrington went on to allege that Maddison had tried to extort money from him with threats, and had enlisted the help of one Captain Featherstone and a Mr Thomas Hunter, to assist in the intimidation: 'not getting it, he threatens violence'. Eventually Maddison even stole: 'deeds and writings' from Elrington's home. In the petition submitted to the assizes, Elrington begged: 'protection against Maddison and his son Joseph'.

George Neasham, in his: *History and Biography of West Durham*, published in 1881, tells us that a manuscript, in his day housed at York Castle, included a diary entry for 30 May 1681. The entry recorded that on this day, Elrington was prosecuting his father-in-law, for theft and arson. Elrington claimed that: 'Maddison, his son Joseph, Thomas Pattyson of Unthanke, and Robert Thompson, did carry away from his estate, four oxen; six cowes, young beasts; and five score and tenn of yewes and hogges'.

Elrington further claimed that Maddison had confessed to him that in March 1678, he had: 'burnt Joseph Rawe's houses at Benfieldside and Nun's House Stable, with match, gunpowder, and tow'. Maddison, found guilty, was ordered to be burned in the hand as a punishment. His son Joseph was acquitted. 'Mad' Maddison had had his fill of Elrington, and the feud was eventually brought to a head when he took a gun and tried to shoot his second son-in-law. Elrington survived the attempt, but the die was now cast. It would only be a matter of time before Maddison eventually did kill someone, and that inevitable tragedy came about, equally inevitably it seems, through a drunken argument.

The scene of the murder was said, appropriately enough, to be an ale house in Shotley Bridge, again, the: *Monthly Chronicle* suggests the: 'Bridge End'. Little is known of the victim, Laird Atkinson, except that from his title it is probable that he was another local landowner, of a similar station to Maddison. Little more is known of the circumstances leading up to his death, other than that a quarrel had begun between the two and Laird Atkinson: 'fell dead under the madman's hand'. Apparently feeling no remorse, Maddison swore a loud oath that he would shoot any man that ventured to come near with any magisterial warrant to take him. Nobody dared approach the madman, whether because of who he was or what he was. Therefore, it being impossible to apprehend him in the normal way, the militia was sent for and Maddison was reluctantly forced to flee. He made his way to a tenant's house where his horse was stabled. He mounted the beast: 'his own wild horse, a gallant dapple grey, the swiftest ever known in the country round, and of particular high temper', and rode off to freedom into the wild lands of Derwentdale.

Unfortunately for him, however, his horse had no appetite for the flight and on reaching Muggleswick Park, refused to go any further. This would later, by the local folk: 'be construed as a providential interposition, and a proof that the abhored shears were opening to cut short the thread of life'. Maddison was forced to go on foot and seek refuge in a nearby wood. The chronicles tell that he was eventually found, hiding inside a large hollow yew tree. He was unceremoniously dragged out and carried, bound, to Durham and to his trial.

Sykes: *Local Records*, quoting directly no doubt from the original entry in the diary of Durham diarist, Jacob Bee, gives the following brief report for 16 September 1694: 'Laird Atkinson of Cannyside Wood was killed by Ralph Maddison of Shotley Bridge. He was afterwards hanged for the murther'. Neasham even suggested that Bee may have been a spectator at the execution. If he was, the Durham diarist would have witnessed the final act of a singularly wild and violent life, even by the standards of the day.

And so it was that: 'Mad' Maddison's career of villainy, his adventures, from the amusing to the hateful, ended that day on the gallows at Durham. Described in the: *Monthly Chronicle*, as: 'one of those turbulent characters to whom the unsettled condition of the north had given birth', for ages after, all along the Derwent Valley, his name would be used to frighten forward children.

'Mad Maddison will catch you,
Mad Maddison, come and take this naughty bairn!'

Chapter 16

Poland Was My Cradle

'Mysterious nature who thy works shall scan
Behold in size a child, in sense a man'

If you go to Durham Cathedral and enter with your fellow visitors, through the great North Door, passing the glowering eyeless mask of the Sanctuary Knocker; turn right through the modern porch, go straight forward for a few paces and you will come to the Remembrance Window. Cast your eyes downward to the floor and in front of the poppy wreaths you will see a small square slab, upon which are carved the letters J.B. Beneath it lies a man, not of Durham, nor even of England. No great benefactor to the City or player on the national stage. A curiosity perhaps? So why include him in this book? Well, possibly succumbing to pressure from my daughters. That said, however, it is surely worth this short piece to sketch an outline of his remarkable, and remarkably long life.

There is an old saying which describes Durham City as being famous for, among other things: 'Wood, Water and Pleasant Walks'. Indeed the City is still: 'sold' today, partly on its scenic riverside vistas. Surely, however, one of the oddest sights ever to be seen there was the gentle perambulations of two seemingly mismatched friends early in the 19th century. One, a man of considerable size, was Stephen Kemble, one time Shakespearean Actor, Impresario and manager of a theatre in Saddler Street. Kemble had been an actor of some merit, born in Herefordshire in 1758, into a theatrical family. His elder sister, Sarah, as Sarah Siddons was one of the most famous actresses of her generation, renowned for her portrayal of Lady Macbeth. Both Sarah and Stephen's elder brother, John, were headline acts at the Drury Lane Theatre in London.

Kemble was originally sent off to train in the medical profession: 'But the reminiscences of the fascinations attending the profession of his parents, proved too powerful'. So he returned to the stage and became a touring provincial actor, in 1783, appearing as Othello at Covent Garden at the same time as Sarah and John were staring at Drury Lane. He then became a manager, and managed theatres in Edinburgh, Newcastle and Durham; but he continued to act and though, at five feet nine inches tall and weighing 18 stones, he made an awkward Hamlet; he was famous for playing Sir John Falstaff: 'without any padding'. Eventually exiting the stage for good, he retired: 'in elegant ease', to Durham, where he read: 'with the sons of the principal gentlemen of the district'; and where his wife Elizabeth, also an excellent actress, was a favourite with the Durham audiences.

Mr Kemble's walking companion, however, was little over three feet high. This was the: 'Little Polish Count', Jozef Boruwlaski; and how he came to stroll the green and pleasant riverbanks of Durham was one of the most unusual stories in the old city's history. His life is well documented, not least through his Autobiography, which he had published between 1788 and 1820 and although he may have been prone to embellishment; most of it is probably true.

Born in Halicz, Poland in November 1739, measuring only eight inches long, he was one of a family of six children born to a minor landowner. Both his parents were of normal size, as were three of his siblings, an elder brother being over six feet tall.

Durham River Banks, beloved of Jozef Boruwlaski.

His father died when Jozef was only nine years old and times became hard for his mother. A family acquaintance, the Lady Caorliz, a wealthy widow, offered to adopt Jozef and attend to his education. After a while, however, the widow remarried and became pregnant and Jozef fell out of favour. At 15, he was taken under the wing of Countess Humiecka, a local aristocrat, went to live with her, and under her patronage his basic education was completed and he began to tour the courts of the high and mighty of European society.

During an early visit to Vienna he was presented to the Queen, Maria Theresa, who was at the time, at war with the King of Prussia. She asked him his opinion of the Prussian Monarch: 'Madam, I have not the honour of knowing him, but were I in his place, instead of waging a useless war against you, I would come to Vienna and pay my respects to you, deeming it a thousand times more gracious to gain your esteemed friendship than to obtain the most complete victories over your troops'.

Clearly, from an early age, in a world in which charm, flattery and a sharp tongue were prized, both as tools and as weapons, the young Jozef had already become skilled in their use. So impressed was the Queen that, on noticing Jozef admiring a diamond ring that she was wearing, she removed it and gave it to him. However, the Queen's gift was too large for his tiny finger so she called over a young princess and asked her to give Jozef a ring of hers. Jozef remained in Vienna for six months and there he was taught to dance by Angelini; the Ballet Master to the Royal Court.

From Vienna his tour, and his worldly education continued, to Germany and then to France; to Versailles, and to Paris where the Countess Humiecka was a frequent visitor and where all the Royal Courts and houses of the Nobility were opened to him. He was introduced at the Court of Count Oginski, the Grand General of Lithuania, who was a friend of Humiecka. He was taught music and, under the instruction of the celebrated Pierre Gavinies, he developed into an accomplished violinist; a skill which would partly ensure his future: 'living'. So now he could dance and he could play the violin, his Courtly manners were impeccable and he was the darling of every Court he attended; but even so, there was a darker side to the patronage of his like. Having a Dwarf as a Court attendant was: 'fashionable'. The motives of those who patronised them could be mixed. However, if it was: 'fashionable' to keep Dwarfs at Court, as an amusement and an entertainment, the patronage of these singular people by the rich and powerful of society, meant for them, no doubt, the difference between a luxurious and pampered lifestyle; and abject poverty. Distraction, amusement, diversion, and novelty perhaps; and of course this was before the time of the callous: 'Freak Shows' of the 19th century, but even in these early days there were signs of the future fate of people like Jozef. The story is told that one evening, the Count put on a: 'Grand Entertainment'. As part of the evening he had Jozef put inside a serving platter, which was then placed in the middle of the dining table. Saying to his guests that he would now treat them to an: 'extraordinary dish', out popped Jozef: 'To the no small astonishment and diversion of the ladies'.

When he was 25 he returned, via Holland, and Germany, to Poland and the Royal Court, where he became a frequent visitor, by now acquiring the familiar name of: 'Joujou'. The King kept at his Court, a Dwarf named Nicholas Ferry; familiarly called: 'Bebe'. The growing attention given to Boruwlaski suggested to Ferry that he had a rival for his privileged position and with growing dislike and animosity Ferry attacked Joseph, while both were at Court. A fight ensued during which: 'Bebe' tried to throw: 'Joujou' into the fire. They were finally separated by the King himself; who later had Ferry whipped.

Perhaps it was a case of out of the fire and into the frying pan, when Jozef first fell in love; with a French Actress who was appearing in Warsaw. Unfortunately his feelings were not reciprocated; Josef was crushed and he: 'Withdrew into himself, like the injured snail into its shell'. Indeed he was to be 40 years of age before he eventually found someone to love him. The beautiful, Mademoiselle Isallina Barbourton was in the service of Countess Humiecka. Isallina was of normal size and of French parentage; her family had been settled in Warsaw for some time. Romance blossomed between the two but Humiecka disapproved. She forbade them to see each other but they continued, infuriating the Countess, who, for so many years Jozef's Patron, Guide and Mentor, now: 'Sent him adrift into the wide world and dispatched Isallina to her parents'. Jozef had been dependant on the Countess for his living, however, in light of the affection and goodwill he had acquired at the Polish Court, the King granted Jozef an annual income and bestowed upon him the title; 'Count'.

In 1780, Jozef and Isallina were married; but how now to make a living? Friends suggested he tour and make concert appearances playing the violin, others suggested making money by exhibiting himself as a curiosity, giving private audiences to the rich and well connected of Europe. So it was that with Royal Letters of Introduction, Jozef and Isallina began to tour. The following year they were back in Vienna where the first of their three children was born, all to be of normal size. Here, Jozef was introduced to an English Diplomat with whose support he began another tour, taking Isallina to Frankfurt, Mannheim, Strasbourg, Brussels and Ostend. They toured Scandinavia and even reached the Middle East and the Turkish Empire. Jozef, 'Count' Boruwlaski, had become a: 'Celebrated Dwarf' and as such a continuing curiosity.

In 1782 they came to England and fell under the patronage of the Duke of Devonshire. Jozef was presented at the Court of the Prince Regent, later King George IV, who encouraged him to relate his singular life in a memoir. He had his likeness painted by Sir Edwin Landseer and began a tour of English cities; however, in Britain his musical talents were less in demand than his curiosity value and for three years he: 'exhibited himself for a livelihood'. Undeterred, he toured Ireland, which he loved and where he: 'appeared' with the: 'Irish Giant', Patrick Cotter. After spending two years there, he returned to England, via Whitehaven in Cumbria and then to Newcastle. He visited Edinburgh and together with the exceptionally tall lawyer, Neil Ferguson, excited the curiosity of the public. The artist John Kay produced an etching of Ferguson and Jozef together and they held joint Concerts and Public Lunches for paying customers. There were even times when Jozef simply held court to paying visitors in his own rooms.

A further tour followed, to Liverpool, Manchester, Birmingham and Oxford. Under the patronage of the Duke of Malborough, he spent time in the splendour of Blenheim Palace. And eventually he came to Durham, as the friend and guest of Mr Thomas Ebdon, a Minor Canon and celebrated singer in the Cathedral. Here he stayed for some time before setting out again on his travels. By now, the beautiful Isallina had deserted him, and after a time he resolved to emigrate to America. But after appeals from his friends he decided to return to Durham and stay with Mr Ebden and his sisters. So Jozef Boruwlaski, musician, socialite, darling of the Royal Courts of Europe was a strange adopted son of St Cuthbert's City. He spoke fluent French; English: 'with a tolerable freedom' and he quickly became at once a curiosity and a familiar sight to Durham residents. Fordyce tells us that: 'The Prebendaries of the Cathedral generously allowed the Little Count a handsome income' and he settled

'Durham is my quiet place, where my weary bones shall rest' – J.B.

down to live the rest of his life in his: 'Quiet Place', where, Fordyce goes on: ' The polite and easy manners of Count Joseph Boruwlaski, and his general intelligence, gained him a large circle of friends;' though in the early days he would often suffer the indignity of being plagued by young boys, who would pull at his pigtails, and for which he would: 'cane their backs for them'. In 1821 Jozef was again presented to George IV, who was preparing for his Coronation. Jozef gave to the King a copy of the memoirs which George had encouraged him to write. For which, in return, the King presented Jozef with a gold watch.

Stephen Kemble died on 6 June 1822, and left Count Jozef to walk the riverbanks in solitude. After a time Mr Ebden also died but Jozef was prevailed upon to remain in Durham and reside with the Ebden household. He became a well known and well respected figure, both in polite Durham society and around the streets of the City. He enjoyed reading the literature of his adopted country and was an admirer of the works of Sir Walter Scott; whose lines are carved into Prebends Bridge, across the river from the small cottage into which Jozef finally moved. He was supplied with miniature knives, forks and spoons. He observed all the minutiae of etiquette and at Durham: 'His circle of friendship comprised all the best and highest of all the great folks attached to the Cathedral'. A letter in: 'The Times' told that once Jozef was asked if his wife was still alive, to which he replied: 'No, she is dead, and I am not very sorry, for when I affronted her, she put me on the mantelshelf for punishment'. By now a well known figure in the City, there was never a sideways glance at his diminutive frame; and everyone had a kind word for the: 'Canny A'ad Man'.

When Jozef settled in Durham, local memory was still fresh of the defeat of Napoleon, when Bonaparte had been burned in effigy in the Market Place. During his life he had seen many places and many things. Revolution in France had done away with the old order and much of the world he had known. But times, even in Durham, were changing. In the relatively short time he would live in the City, he would bear witness to many of the great changes and advances of the age. The old was beginning to make way for the new: 'Progress' was all around. He had seen George IV crowned King and had seen the great North Gate of Durham Castle, which, for hundreds of years had spanned the top of Saddler Street, pulled down; to allow easier access for carriages. The year 1823 saw the first Gas Works built in Durham, below Framwellgate Bridge; the Victoria County History proclaiming rather grandly that: 'The Lighting of the streets constituting a new epoch in the history of the City'.

In 1825 an event occurred, probably of even greater importance than gas lights in Durham City, with the official opening of the Stockton and Darlington passenger railway; the first of its kind in the world. In this quest for progress and change, even the great Saints in the Cathedral were not spared. In 1827 James Raine opened, for the first time since the Reformation, the grave of St Cuthbert. Three years later the resting place of Bede suffered the same enquiry and when the investigation was concluded and the grave covered for the last time, the inscription so familiar to us all today was added. In 1828, the old world again gave way to the new when the approach to Flambard's: 'Old Bridge' was improved and all the old battlements taken down; and Lord Londonderry laid the foundation stone of his own coal port at Seaham Harbour. In 1831 William IV was crowned King, the second Monarch Jozef had seen ascend the British throne.

Also, in a foretaste of an industrialised Durham yet to fully develop, a Miner's Union was established for the region. Indeed such was the pace of the increase in coal mining at

The: 'Count's House', near Prebends Bridge.

this time, that a group of Teresian Nuns, who had, some years before, fled the advance of the Revolutionary Guard during the French Revolution and had eventually settled in the peace of Cocken Hall at Leamside; had now to flee their tranquil retreat: 'because of the advance of coal mining activities'. Two years later, in 1832, Jozef saw Durham embroiled in political agitation over the progress of the Great Reform Bill. After the House of Lords had rejected the Bill a protest meeting was held in Old Elvet; eight thousand people attended. The following year, he witnessed the abolition of Slavery in Britain.

If Jozef was witnessing the beginning of the new age he was also witnessing the end of the old. The death of William Van Mildert, in 1836, closed the last chapter of the epic story of the Prince Bishops of Durham. But the closing of that chapter was followed by the opening of another, when the Dean and Chapter approved the foundation of a new University; and the prosaically named Municipal Corporations Act ushered in a modern way of government for Durham. The year of Jozef's death, 1837, would see a new queen and the Victorian Age would begin.

Through all this, Count Jozef Boruwlaski strolled and charmed; played his music and moved effortlessly among Durham Society, spending his last days in comparative seclusion. He was only ever known to drink water, no wine or spirits; his attitude to alcohol: 'I do not need him, I leave him alone'. He eventually died on 5 September 1837. A cultured little man of impeccable manners, who stood only three feet three inches high and lived to his 98th year. The Durham Historians have related their descriptions of him. William Fordyce tells that: 'His figure was graceful and symmetrical, and when in his prime, his countenance was noble and manly'. Richardson tells: 'The extraordinary small stature, great age, and lively genius of this amiable person entitled him to be ranked as one of the most singular products of nature'. He had left three children and three editions of his Autobiography, in which, Fordyce rather punningly relates: 'the interesting details of his life are minutely described'.

He had seen the excesses of the French Revolution and the streets of Durham lit by gaslight. He had moved among crowned heads of Europe. He had seen the accession of three English Monarchs, the founding of a Miners Union and the Saints that lay in Durham having their rest disturbed in the name of progress. His one time combatant and fellow: 'Celebrated Dwarf' Nicholas Ferry, had not the longevity of Boruwlaski and died before his twentieth birthday. Pierre Gavinies, the violin teacher who had given Jozef the means to live the life of an accomplished musician, was to become Professor of Violin at the Paris Conservatory; and the little Princess in the Austrian Court of Queen Maria Theresa who, so long ago, had given Jozef her diamond ring, was Marie Antoinette, who as the future Queen of France, would meet her fate at the Guillotine during the French Revolution.

A Folly, originally built in the garden of the Ebdon's property in South Bailey, became known as the: 'Count's House'. It is still known as that and popular tradition continues the myth; its location, still known as Count's Corner, close by Prebends Bridge.

In 1951, a wax profile portrait of Jozef Boruwlaski was acquired by the Metropolitan Museum of Art in New York. Nearer home, in Durham's Town Hall, a life size statue of him stands underneath his portrait. A glass cabinet, close by, houses some of his clothes and possessions. So you will find him now in the Cathedral, the small slab simply engraved with his initials marks the spot, an unusual companion indeed for the Saints and Prince Bishops of his adopted home.

Chapter 17

Of Sermons and of Songs

This is a tale of two clerics. Two devout but very different men, both of whom kept faithful accounts of their lives and of the times in which they lived; It is from their diaries that a unique record has been handed down to today's reader and from which this short piece has been compiled.

John Wesley

'If you desire to know who I am, my name is John Wesley'

It was 28 May 1742, when a 39-year-old John Wesley first set foot in Newcastle. He had come north to carry on the successful work he had previously carried out, spreading the Gospel to the Colliers of Kingswood near Bristol. The mining communities of the North-East, he thought, would be receptive to his message of a new kind of worship.

At Newcastle, he made his way to Sandgate, one of the poorest areas of the town, and was appalled by the: 'drunkenness, cursing, and swearing, even from the mouths of little children'. So, preaching his first sermon and singing the hundredth Psalm, he soon attracted a large crowd of curious onlookers, who gawped and stared at him: 'with the most profound astonishment'. John Wesley's work in the North East had begun. By the end of the year he had laid in Northumberland Street, the foundation stone of the: 'Orphan House', his first Methodist base in Newcastle. He would become a frequent visitor, sometimes staying for weeks at a time and Newcastle, along with London and Bristol would be one of his: 'missionary bases'.

In 1745, however, his work in Newcastle was interrupted by the threat of Bonnie Prince Charlie's Jacobite army. Edinburgh had fallen, government forces had been defeated at Preston Pans; Wesley found Newcastle under arms and the inhabitants: 'in a state of utmost consternation'. But the Jacobites were eventually defeated on Culloden Moor near Inverness and John Wesley began to journey in safety across the North East. He travelled, always on horseback, to the western dales where he found a ready audience with the people of the Lead Mining Communities. Indeed, from the ruins of Blanchland Abbey he preached to a congregation of Lead Miners from Allendale. In Weardale, Methodism had already arrived; brought by Christopher Hopper, a Gateshead schoolmaster whom, it was said, had journeyed there over: 'quagmires and enormous mountains', to spread the word.

When Wesley eventually reached Ireshopeburn he preached for the first time under a thorn tree; but only eight years later, High House Chapel, the first Methodist Chapel, and spiritual home to Methodism in Weardale; was built by Lead Miners. Wesley would make 13 visits to Weardale and would continue to preach under the Thorn Tree at Ireshopeburn; when his congregation was too big to be accommodated in the Chapel.

From Weardale he rode over the moors into Teesdale, where a Chapel was founded at Newbiggin which would be frequented regularly by Wesley and where his original pulpit is still in use today. His early visits to Barnard Castle, however, did not go smoothly.

John Wesley's Thorn Tree, Ireshopeburn, Weardale.

William Fordyce reports that during one early open air Wesley sermon, the townsfolk: 'staunch resistors of innovation in religion', brought out the town Water Engine and: 'Showered down their blessings upon his head'. Wesley had to beat a hasty retreat with the men of Barnard Castle, their Water Engine in tow, in full pursuit.

Nonetheless, his visits continued and his movement gathered momentum. In response to his restless, tireless energy and his unshakeable belief in the power of the Word and the power of prayer, Methodist Societies sprung up in remote townships and villages all across the Durham Dales. They grew and they prospered, until, at their peak in the late 19th century, there were 22 Chapels in Weardale alone. Wesley's flock, however, were occasionally prone to: 'lapses' and the enthusiasm that they showed without fail during his visits, waned somewhat in his absence. On one occasion he tells: 'I came just in time to prevent them all turning Dissenters, which they were on the point of doing, being quite disgusted at the Curate, whose life was no better than his doctrine'. Fordyce, however, even questioned how deeply Wesley's teachings had, in reality, been felt by his followers: 'So frequently does it happen that they fall away, that it is to be feared the imagination is more affected than the heart'.

The: *Victoria County History* tells us that Wesley was also a frequent visitor to Hartlepool, where he was always well received, but where he sometimes believed that his efforts were having little effect, later writing that: 'Surely the seed will spring up at last even here, where we seemed so long to be ploughing on sand'.

September 1757, saw Wesley in Durham City, where he preached: 'in a pleasant meadow near the riverside'. The congregation was large and a little wild but he tells that: 'in a short time they were deeply attentive......... Towards the close, I was constrained to mention the gross ignorance in the rich and powerful people throughout the nation. On this they drew near and showed serious attention'.

In May 1780, he was again in Durham and travelled out to Shincliffe, where he stopped to preach at the house of a Mr Parker. However, the resulting congregation became too large for Mr Parker's house and Wesley had to stand by a nearby Willow Tree, from where to him, it: 'seemed as if the whole village was ready to receive the truth'. It is thought that Willow Tree Avenue was named after the site of Wesley's sermon.

At the age of 81 he was still travelling on horseback between Weardale and Teesdale, sometimes in appalling weather. However, gradually and inevitably, age caught up with him and writing from Darlington to a friend in Weardale in 1790, he bemoaned the fact that he was unable now to continue his horseback journeys: 'That time is past. All I can do now is visit the chief Societies. I hope to see our friends in Weardale and Barnard Castle, and I believe

Stanhope Market Cross, where Wesley preached; the original Cross is now in the Churchyard.

that will be as much as I must attempt'. In March 1791, almost a year after seeing his: 'blessed people' of the Durham Dales for the last time; John Wesley passed away. He had criss-crossed the County of Durham, preaching and singing and spreading his message to Lead Miners and to Colliers; to Keelmen, Labourers and Farmers. His pulpit had been the Street and the Market Square; the Meadow, and of course, the Thorn Tree.

Throughout his Ministry, Wesley never actively sought separation from the Church of England; or the setting up of an independent Ministry among his own followers. He and his Ministers continued to attend Anglican Services and the times of Methodist preaching was arranged so that it did not interfere with: 'Church Hours'. But his work was not that of abbey or church. His message was a world away from the refined, scholarly questioning of cloistered Durham, whose occupants were at that time, as recorded by J.L. Low, in the *Durham Diocesan History*: 'A cultivated class, but mostly above rough parochial work'. With Wesley they had: 'No placid Christian gentleman, but a thunderbolt of God'.

A poem was written by an anonymous author, to commemorate the centenary of Wesley's death:

'One hundred years have passed away
since Wesley preached, since Wesley died;
The Tree still stands, without decay.
It's beauty by the highway side.
It seems that long that tree may stand,
John Wesley's monument to be.
Saved from the Woodman's ruthless hand
For Weardale's prayer is ' Spare that Tree"

John Bacchus Dykes

'He is remembered here as a faithful priest, and known throughout the world as a composer of hymn tunes'

On a dank, grey, January morning in 1876, the mournful tolling of a single bell rang out across St Oswald's churchyard in Durham City. It announced the laying to rest of a remarkable man. John Bacchus Dykes, Vicar of St Oswald's and Honorary Canon of Durham Cathedral. A man who embodied, it was said, a: 'singular musical talent, in alliance with genuine piety'. A prodigious composer of hymn tunes, his work is still often to be heard today. The sailor's hymn: *Eternal Father, Strong to Save*, beseeching the Almighty's protection: 'For those in peril on the sea', was the favourite of US President, Franklyn D. Roosevelt and was sung at his funeral in 1945. It was also played as John F. Kennedy's body was carried up the steps of the Capitol building, to lie in state, following his assassination in 1963. The tune was written by Dykes. And tradition has it that, on a freezing Atlantic night in 1912, survivors of the sinking of the: *Titanic*, reported that the last piece the orchestra played before the great ship slipped beneath the waves, was the hymn: *Nearer My God to Thee*, for which Dykes had written the tune: *Horbury*.

A mild mannered, scholarly man; possibly the greatest hymn tune composer of his or any other generation, his final years were darkened by his involvement in an unprecedented legal dispute; when Dykes took an action at the Court of Queens Bench, against the Bishop of Durham himself.

John Bacchus Dykes was born into an Evangelical family, in Hull, on 10 March 1823. The third son and fifth child of 14, he was baptised by his own grandfather, the Reverend

Thomas Dykes, a friend of the MP and slavery abolitionist, William Wilberforce. Small, pale, described as never looking: 'tall or robust' and painfully shy, he received his early education at Kingston College, Hull. His musical talent soon became apparent, playing by ear the violin and piano and by the time he was 10 years old, he was playing the organ in his grandfather's church. However, his health would never be strong, and on Christmas Eve, 1840, aged 17, he contracted Scarlet Fever. He survived but was left with: 'a delicacy in this throat and a weakness of voice', which would remain with him the rest of his life. Eventually leaving the family home, he attended St Catherine's Hall, Cambridge, where he was co-founder and President of the Cambridge University Musical Society and it was at the outset of his University career that he began his prolific and lifelong passion for writing.

He was 26 years old when, after being appointed Minor Canon of the Cathedral, he arrived in Durham City, initially taking up lodgings in South Street. Very soon after, he began writing to his family, telling them of his new home: 'I like Durham exceedingly. The view from my window is hardly to be equalled in England. It exactly faces the glorious west end of the Cathedral and I am separated from it only by the river. I wish you could see the view from my window this moment! It is glorious, lit up so splendidly with the sun'.

Later that same year, to his great excitement, Dykes was appointed Precentor of the Cathedral, his new duties included the management of the choir, and the superintendence of the religious instruction of the boys. He wrote enthusiastically to his sister about his appointment, mentioning his new salary of £340 a year, which enabled him to take a small cottage in Hollingside Lane: 'a very pretty little cottage, about a mile out of Durham, with a nice bit of garden and a very fine prospect'.

Dykes now began to write in earnest. As well as theological papers and music for the Cathedral Choir, he wrote a succession of hymn tunes, which, when played in the Cathedral, he found to be well received. His name began to be noticed, and when the Revd John Grey, Rector of Houghton-le-Spring, published his: *Hymnal*, 13 of Dykes' tunes were published in it. Eight more appeared in the second edition. He began to record in his diary, details of his compositions. On 1 June 1859, he describes writing down his tune: *Horbury*, to the words of: *Nearer my God to Thee*. However, for such a prolific composer he was a man unconvinced of his own worth: 'I write so slowly and think so slowly. I have no fluency in thought or direction. Never mind, God knows my deficiencies, if he has work for me, he will enable me to do it'.

The following year Dykes first heard of the projected publication of a new hymn book to be called: *Hymns Ancient and Modern*. On 12 October 1860, he wrote off to the musical editor, offering seven of his tunes for publication and saying that: 'some of them are sung in the Galilee Chapel of Durham Cathedral, and are very popular'.

The seven, including: *Holy, Holy, Holy, Lord God Almighty*, *Jesu Lover of My Soul*, to the tune of: *Hollingside, Nearer my God to Thee*, and: *Eternal Father, Strong to Save*, were accepted. He subsequently wrote 12 more for the appendix to the first edition, and 29 for the second edition. Eventually, 55 of Dykes' works would be published in: *Hymns Ancient and Modern*.

On 18 September 1862, Dykes became Vicar of St Oswald's Church in Durham City. However, even the hard work and new demands of a large Parish did not curtail his musical composition. Twenty eight of his tunes were published in Chope's: *Congregational Hymn and Prayer Book*. Chope had previously offered prizes for the best tunes for: *Rock of*

The Western Towers of Durham Cathedral, the view from Dykes' lodgings.

Ages, Cleft for Me, and: *Jerusalem the Golden;* Prizes Dykes had won. He directed an amateur choral society in Durham and in 1863 conducted the first choral festival to be held in Durham Cathedral. Recording the occasion in his diary, he tells of: 'Two thousand voices, the whole of the Cathedral a dense, surging mass of living beings'. In August 1864, he declined the offer of Precentorship of Westminster Abbey and described writing down the tune for: *Lead, Kindly Light,* after it came to him while walking along The Strand, in London.

Charles Baring, Bishop of Durham, began his episcopate in 1861. Bishop Baring was, as contemporary chronicles record: 'a resolute low churchman'. He regarded himself as guardian of the values of solid Anglicanism and feared, in his own words: 'those who are striving to effect the disestablishment of the Church of England'. The earlier part of the century had seen a popular church revival, influenced by the so called: 'Oxford Movement', an affiliation of High Church Anglicans, that encouraged Church of England Ministers to take it upon themselves to introduce changes in Liturgical Practise and to promote more vigorous use of ritual and spectacle; endeavoring to bring more: 'colour' to their services, in an attempt to reverse the trend of falling church attendances. They felt, as Dykes himself put it: 'that an ugly church and a dull service would never bring them back'. Gradually Dykes began to introduce his own small: 'improvements' into the Church ritual at St Oswald's. His curate, Mr Kempe, was enthusiastic in his support, and early in 1866, he presented the Church with violet stoles. Dykes, however, remained cautious about major change, although he was enthusiastic about one small addition to his church services; that of a 14th-century crucifix, dug up in a Durham garden. However, the first clouds of the coming storm had already settled upon the horizon. The Bishop, suspicious of what he saw as Anglo-Catholicism, had refused to licence a Curate at Houghton-le-Spring: 'unless the Rector abandons the use of the invocation', before the sermon. Dykes, however: 'maintaining a certain independence of judgement', continued with his innovations and on Christmas Day, 1867, vestments were worn at St Oswald's Church.

More and more demands were now being made on Dykes' time. As well as writing academic theological papers, he was by now assisting with editorial work on: *Hymns Ancient and Modern,* and was involved in the publication of a collection of 20 childrens hymns, 13 being his own compositions. But the pressure began to take its toll. His diary records: 'I have so many things to think of, what must I do? What leave undone? Lord teach me'. He wrote tunes for Welsh and American hymn books, even tunes for Swahili words; though these he considered difficult: 'The Swahili language does not lend itself well to musical rythm'. The: *Pall Mall Gazette,* some years later, reported that during the tour of *Buffalo Bill's British Wild West Show,* about 40: 'Indians', with an interpreter, were taken to the morning service at the Congregational Chapel, West Kensington where: 'They were accommodated with seats in the transept and during the service they sang the hymn *Nearer my God to Thee,* in their own tongue... These remarkable looking men in their picturesque costumes, bedecked with paint and feathers, presented the most striking picture'.

Dykes also wrote music for the Nonconformists, for which he attracted some criticism from within his own church; even though it was said that his hymn tunes: 'were valued and used as much in any nonconformist congregation, as in his own church'. J.L. Lowe's *Diocesan History of Durham,* published in 1881, records that: 'a recent notice in a local paper tells of a rough and miscellaneous congregation on shipboard, at the Antipodes, presided over by a dissenting Minister, being moved to tears by the sweet, plaintive tones of *Eternal Father, Strong to Save,* set to Dr Dykes music'.

St Oswald's Church, Durham City, where Dykes was Vicar.

Dykes' parochial work increased. He was suspected by the Bishop of being an Anglo-Catholic, after all, his eldest brother, Thomas had become a Jesuit Priest; but, paradoxically, he had a special pew reserved in St Oswald's Church, for Nonconformist Ministers, on their regular visits to his Sunday evening services. After losing his Curate, his already large Parish was enlarged to include another nearby pit village; however, good news arrived in April 1873, in the form of a letter from the Church Commissioners, undertaking to pay two Curates stipends of £120. The fist Curate was appointed and Dykes was busily seeking a second, when, on 4 July a letter arrived from Auckland Castle.

The Bishop required, before licensing the Curate at St Oswald's that Dyke's cease his: 'innovations' and give a written pledge that he would not require the Curate to wear coloured stoles, turn his back on the congregation, or take part in the burning of incense; even though he knew that incense was not used in any church in the Diocese. Dykes despaired. It seemed to him that the Bishop, in his mistrust of innovation and ritual, was prepared to halt the progress that had been made in the church revival. Dykes himself was from an Evangelical background; Indeed, it has later been said of his services, that the style of the Celebration of the Eucharist: 'would not have been disapproved of, even by Wesley'. He felt that the Bishop's action and his demands exceeded his authority, and were possibly even illegal and he refused to sign any document that the Bishop wished him to sign, considering: 'that the Church had made a grand mistake in the neglect of the externalities of worship'. Being a man well known and well liked, he was encouraged to resist. The situation became entrenched. He wrote in his diary: 'Lord teach me what to do, Lord forgive me if I am acting wrongly…What is to be the upshot of it, only God knows'?

A man of: 'never failing placidity of temper', Dykes hated disputes of any kind. Now he was involved in a bitter one against the Bishop of Durham, who: 'as a man, he sincerely respected and liked'. Nevertheless he refused to back down. He was advised by his lawyers that the Bishop was indeed acting illegally in his demands, and that Dykes should further pursue the issue. The English Church Union shared the legal expenses and there was even a: 'Dykes Defence Fund' raised for the cause. A case was stated for the opinion of Counsel and in consequence of Counsel's opinion; application was made to the Court of Queen's Bench, calling for the Bishop to show just cause. Dykes, however, did not relish an appearance before the Court: 'Oh! That I had more readiness of utterance and self possession. I feel like a perfect fool when I have to make a speech'. On 19 January 1874, the case came before Judges Blackburn, Archibald and Quain, sitting at the Court of Queen's Bench. Without even hearing Dykes' main arguments, the Judges ruled in favour of the Bishop. It was a devastating blow to Dykes. The case was lost. He was left with an enlarged Parish, no Curates to help with the workload; and the enmity of his Bishop.

As one sad year passed, another began. Anxiety and overwork soon took their toll and his health deteriorated dramatically. He tells us: 'Could not think what to write about. Despondent about my unreadiness, could get no ideas... Tried to make a tune, but could not, God's will be done'. His diary entry for 4 March 1875 records: 'Tried to pray, could not. Walked to Croxdale, prayed all the way back'.

Sunday 7 March 1875, was to be the last Sunday that the Revd John Bacchus Dykes preached at St Oswald's Church; and on that day the diary that he had kept faithfully for so many years, was ended. He wrote no more. Almost another year had passed, when, on 22 January 1876, as Susan, his wife of over 25 years was reading to him a prayer from the Service for the Visitation of the Sick; he peacefully passed away. He was not quite 53 years old. St Oswald's Church was full on the morning of Friday 28 January 1876. The congregation inside joined by large numbers more from the streets. After the funeral service, which began with Dykes' own: *The King of Love My Shepherd is*, he was laid to rest in the Churchyard; and there he lies today.

In such esteem had Dykes been held, that when it became known that his family had been poorly provided for, the money he had received for his tunes having mainly been given to charitable causes; a fund was raised for their benefit. It quickly reached £10,000, when it was stopped. His biography, compiled by Dr J.T. Fowler, was published in 1897. In it Dr Fowler said that: 'To all who had the advantage of knowing him as a friend or Pastor, his singularly engaging personality remains, after 20 years, as a vivid and cherished memory'.

Indeed, he was remembered by the Parishioners of St Oswald's, simply as a Parish Priest and years later parishioners still recalled him with fondness; one old lady claiming that: 'When he was here it was more like our Parish Church. Nowadays, people seem to come from other parts of Durham. Sometimes I see University lads there...Oh! he was very fond of music. They say that some of the tunes we sang were his and that he had a room in the vicarage where he made them up'. Dykes' lasting legacy was indeed his collection of hymn tunes. In all, about 300 were published. Many are still known and sung today. Some, such as: *For All the Saints*, existed only in manuscript form at his death. Others, it was said, remained unpublished, in the choir books of Durham Cathedral. Rarely writing a tune unless the words were sent or suggested to him, later critics maintained that some of his work was too: 'songlike and sentimental' to be sacred. However, Dr Fowler tells us that Dykes composed: 'as the spirit moved him, without conscious plan'.

On 23 December 1915, the Archdeacon of Durham dedicated a new organ at St Oswald's Church. Built by the renowned Durham organ builders, Messrs. Harrison and Harrison, it was designed to represent continuity of worship at the old church. This was symbolised by the incorporation of several hundred pipes from the previous organ, the same one played by Dr Dykes for his own services. The Archdeacon dedicated the new instrument: 'To the glory of God, and in memory of his servant, John Bacchus Dykes'.

A friend of Dykes once recalled an incident outside St Oswald's vicarage, when, in conversation with a workman, he asked the man if he knew who was to be the next vicar? The man did not know; but he did say: 'They'll never get another gentleman like Dr Dykes'.

Part Six

Chapter 18

Radical Jack; and the Mainsforth Historian

Mr Robert Surtees Esq

'I shall not see the Peach Blossom, 'twas thus they heard him say'

'Some months ago, I happened to read somewhere, that it is the bounden duty of someone in every locality to write the History of that locality, so that those who come after may learn to be loyal to the community into which they are born'. So wrote James J. Dodd, in the preface to his book, published in 1897: *The History of the Urban District of Spennymoor*.

And so indeed he did, in the best traditions of previous Victorian: 'Antiquarians'. Indeed, judging by the wealth of subsequent books on County Durham's long history, ranging from learned academic works, to collections of old photographs, so have many others, unto this day. None, however, have compiled a more comprehensive, detailed and scholarly work, than Robert Surtees of Mainsforth; antiquarian and author, friend and correspondent of the great romantic novelist, Sir Walter Scott.

The first general *History of the County Palatine of Durham*, written by William Hutchinson, was published in 1785. The first volume of Surtees work appeared about 30 years later, a far more elaborate and expensive work. In 1834, Mackenzie and Ross published their *History of Durham* and this was followed by others, first by William Fordyce and then by J.R. Boyle. So who was Robert Surtees and why has he, more than any other, come to be known as the Historian of Durham.

The only child of Robert and Dorothy Surtees, Robert was born in the 18th year of their marriage, on 1 April 1779, in South Bailey, Durham City, and baptised the next day in St Mary-le-Bow Church. He spent his early years in relative isolation at Mainsforth Hall with his father, an excellent agriculturalist with natural talents for drawing and painting and his mother, who had a talent for poetry. Robert followed in these interests and also developed an early and lasting interest in everything ancient, beginning with his collections of Roman Coins and other items from antiquity. As a youngster he had a delicate constitution and would always suffer from poor health but at Mainsforth he found solace in nature and his native countryside. His early education was provided by the Bishop Middleham schoolmaster, Edward Smith, his introduction to Latin, it was said, mixed in equal parts with learning to fish in Cornforth Beck.

Later he was sent to Kepier Grammar School, at Houghton-le-Spring, the establishment founded around 200 years earlier by Bernard Gilpin and John Heath; where under the instruction of the Headmaster, the Reverend William Fleming, Robert became a good Latin Scholar and where his love of all things antiquarian thrived. On school holidays he journeyed to Durham and Sunderland to seek out old coins to buy, identify and add to his collections. Indeed, it was later said that it was during his time at Houghton that he first hinted of his idea of writing a History of Durham. In 1796 he entered Christ Church, Oxford, where as a diligent and hardworking student he developed a talent for composing Latin Verse. His habits were, according to William Fordyce: 'Social though prudent; and he possessed some humour and much conversational talent.'

In spring of 1797, on the death of his mother, he came home to Mainsforth but returned to Oxford and three years later, received his BA. From Oxford he entered the Inner Temple to study Property Law. But Robert would never practice as a lawyer, as in 1802, his father died and he was required to return to Mainsforth: 'An island site in an implacable waste of coalfields', to take up his inheritance. Five years later he married Anne Robinson of Middle Herrington, a sister of one of his old Kepier School companions. They would remain devoted to each other, though childless, and Surtees, without a close family of his own, developed a close and lasting friendship with that of his wife.

Now Robert Surtees began in earnest to collect the huge amount of material for his History. The darkness of wintertime was spent indoors, poring over deeds, documents and family pedigrees but his joy was to be outdoors. Following a downturn in his health, he employed an assistant to transcribe his documents and a Groom to take him travelling the County Durham countryside. Indeed most of the summer months were spent wandering the woods and green lanes around Mainsforth, or in his horse and trap, off in pursuit of his county's history and he wrote that: 'God has placed me in Paradise'. Shiels, his Groom, complained, however, that it was: 'Weary work, for the Master always stopped the Gig; we could never get past an old building'. Surtees copied inscriptions in churches and minutely examined every place he thought may offer some possible delight of antiquity: 'clearing away the dust which ages had spread over their ruins'. Slowly and painstakingly, the raw materials for his: 'Magnum Opus' were gathered together.

He read quickly and had an almost retentive memory. He was able therefore to gather a vast array of disparate information and gradually piece it together for his text. His social standing allowed him ready access to the records of Durham Cathedral and permission was easily obtained to examine the pedigrees, deeds and documents of notable County Durham houses. He also employed agents in London to search records there and gradually: 'the fragments that time had scattered, found their place of reassembly in his mind'. His method of composition, however, was eccentric. He would wander his terraced garden piecing together in his head, obscure inscriptions, scattered documents or rediscovered pedigrees of old County Durham families. Returning to his library he then made his jottings, and thus, as Fordyce relates: 'The History was really printed rather from rough notes than a regularly written manuscript'.

Among his: 'Sporting' neighbours, Surtees must have been a bit of an oddity. When journeying around his estate he would scatter flower seeds in the dykes and hedgerows. When friends accompanied him on summer walks he would stop them from eating the wild strawberry's which grew in the lanes around Mainsforth, telling them that they were for: 'those who had no gardens'. He was also in the habit of leaving purses of money, where his estate workers would find them, thus providing for them some anonymous but welcome financial assistance. He took part neither in fox hunting nor in the other traditional country pursuits expected of someone of his social standing. Once, when a neighbour asked him why he spent so much time and money in searching out old records, he replied: 'I wonder why you spend so much time and money in following a pack of hounds after a poor hare'. He, as his father had done, enjoyed gardening and had a love for the natural world around him. He loved dogs and his home was often home to many. Working horses from his estate, weary with age and at the end of their useful working lives were turned out into his paddocks, to live out the rest of their natural lives in peace, instead of going to the slaughterer. A social, cheerful individual, with those who shared his interests, Surtees struck up a lasting friendship with his fellow Antiquary and Historian, the Revd James Raine, who assisted him in the preparation of his material.

Apart from a short trip to France and Belgium, he would live most of his life at Mainsforth. He was offered, as was the system of the day, a seat in Parliament, which he declined; a Prebend's Stall in Durham Cathedral was his, if he agreed to take Holy Orders; he did not. His passion remained the compilation of the huge amount of genealogical and antiquarian information needed for the completion of his great History of Durham, the first three volumes of which would appear in 1816, 1820 and 1823, and as Fordyce notes: 'Between the compilation and composition of his book, and writing and corresponding with his literary friends, the remainder of the years of this excellent man now passed'.

Surtees was always attracted to any links with a romantic or tragic past; he was practiced in developing rhymes and had a gift for composing new: 'old ballads' and improvising fantastical stories for the local children about: 'Monsters and Hydras and Chymeras Dire'. He began a long standing correspondence with Sir Walter Scott, who was at the time gathering material for what would eventually become his: *Minstrelsey of the Scottish Border*. Surtees sent to Scott a series of papers containing: 'newly discovered' old ballads of the northern counties, which had, Surtees declared, been collected from a variety of: 'original scources'.

The: *Death of Featherstonehaugh*, he wrote, had apparently come from an 80-year-old woman from Alston Moor; *Bartram's Dirge*, Surtees had taken down from: 'The imperfect recitation of a withered crone, Ann Douglas, who weeded my garden'; *Lord Derwentwater's Goodnight*, from a child who had been taught it by a servant. All were from the pen of the squire of Mainsforth and all made their way into Scott's classic works, Scott being convinced as to their authenticity. In gratitude to Surtees, there appeared in the first edition of Scott's work, an acknowledgement to his friend: 'Richard' Surtees, Scott's mistake was not corrected by Surtees, so in future correspondence, Richard, it would remain. A firm friendship blossomed between the two men with Scott visiting Mainsforth in 1809 and he later wrote to the Lakes Poet, Robert Southey, advising him: 'If you wish to make any stay at Durham, let me know, as I wish you to know my friend Surtees of Mainsforth. He is an excellent Antiquary, some of the rust of which study has clung to his manners; but he is good hearted, and you would make the summer eve short between you'.

It has never been known why Surtees should seek to mislead Scott about his: 'ancient ballads'. Indeed, it seems strange that someone who did not have the heart to correct Scott about a misquoted Christian name would set out deliberately to mislead. It has been said that there was: 'a quite enchanting and solemn waggishness about Surtees'. Perhaps then it was simply a prank that got out of hand. It has been suggested that once the material had

The Church of St Michael, Bishop Middleham, where Robert Surtees, the Historian of Durham, is buried.

been published, Surtees simply did not dare to disclose his secret. Perhaps it was merely a small spark of mischief in the: 'Simplicity and Guilelessness' of Surtees' personality; or perhaps it was just that he could. In Robert Chambers': *Book of Days; a miscellany of popular Antiquities*, the Scottish author severely criticised Surtees for misleading Sir Walter Scott, suggesting that once his first deception had been successful, Surtees should not have hoodwinked his trusted friend again. To further compound the deception, or so it would seem, Surtees had even added a number of so called: 'historical' notes to support his fictions: 'The better to blind the editor to the general falsehood…thus we see the deceptions of the learned historian of Durham, were carefully planned, and very coolly carried out'. Sir Walter Scott died on 21 September 1832, never knowing, some say, of Surtees' deception.

From 1830, his own health began to deteriorate and in January 1834, he became ill after visiting his Mother-in-Law, at Hendon. He travelled back from Durham City to Ferryhill on the outside of a crowded Coach, in freezing winter weather. On his return to Mainsforth he complained to Anne about feeling unwell with a cold. It soon developed into pleurisy. Surtees quickly weakened. On his deathbed, he lamented to his: 'Dearest Annie': 'I shall never see the peach blossoms or the flowers of spring' but reassured her that: 'I have left for your life every sixpence I possess and I hope the sun will go down brightly on your latter days'. On 11 February he died, in the 55th year of his age; leaving the fourth and final volume of his monumental *History of the County Palatine of Durham* still to be published. From all the long bright summers of his searchings: 'It was his fate to die at the close of a long dark winter'. Surtees' coffin was borne by men from his own estate to his final resting place in the graveyard of St Michael's Church in Bishop Middleham. Robert Southey, then Poet Laureate, a position which Sir Walter Scott had refused, attended and spoke at the funeral.

Unfortunately for poor Anne, because of unsuccessful land and property dealings and the substantial expense involved in the preparation and publication of his work, at his death Surtees' debts exceeded his resources and Anne was required to convert personal property into money in order to offset them. So it was that at Mainsforth, in December 1836 and January 1837, Surtees' library, papers and collections were sold off at auction. Of the manuscripts prepared for his History, some were purchased by James Raine: 'The person of all others, the most competent to render them available for the credit of Mr Surtees' memory and for the benefit of the public'. Anne Surtees lived on for another 30 years at Mainsforth Hall: 'A good specimen of those peculiarly English mansions in which comfort and elegance are happily united'. Situated: 'on a very quiet road, with a fringe of ancient trees and a Rookery', the Hall stood at the west end of Mainsforth Village until it was pulled down in 1926.

Politically, Surtees was described as: 'moderate, though inclined to the liberal side'. In person, William Fordyce tells us that from his early days he was: 'plain in the extreme, both in manners and dress. Fashionable bronze and effrontery he despised; and coxcombry was no part of his mind…he hated all artificial manners and had a thorough contempt for dancing and the etiquette taught by dancing masters, which he deemed ridiculous. Hence, to many his manners seemed rude and unpolished'.

In conversation or argument, he was known to easily use both wit and, where he thought necessary, sarcasm. What was said of Dr Johnson, was also said of Surtees: 'If his pistol misfired, he would knock you down with the butt-end of it'.

Of Surtees' literary indulgences, or idiosyncracies, or deceptions, in his dealings with Scott; it was suggested by the: *Monthly Chronicle* that: 'in the department of literary mystification, few men were ever more successful adepts than Robert Surtees'. Robert Chambers went further. He found it difficult to understand how Surtees, to all others an honourable and upright gentleman could have so deceived Sir Walter Scott, and to Chambers, Surtees would remain: 'The perpetrator of one of the most dexterous literary impostures of modern times'. It has also been suggested by later commentators that Surtees' own *History of Durham* concentrated too much on the minutiae of Antiquity and Genealogy and passed over the tremendous social and political changes that were taking place around him as his History was being written. But the: *Monthly Chronicle* goes on to say that: 'The example which he gave of a North Country gentleman turning aside from races and fox-hunting, and from the squabbles of Parish Vestries and Petty Sessions, to the more dignified pursuits of literature and antiquarianism, was a service to society which ought never to be forgotten'. And William Fordyce praised the sheer scale, breadth, and detail of Surtees' monumental: *History of the County Palatine of Durham*: 'which must long remain a monument of his research, learning and industry'.

On 27 April 1834, a meeting was held at the Queen's Head Inn, in Durham City and the Surtees Society was formed in honour of the author, his friend James Raine being appointed its first Secretary. The Society, the oldest of its kind in England, was established for the furtherance of Surtees' work and it continues to do so to this day.

John George Lambton, Earl of Durham

'I would say that I feel; no fear of your opposition and little need of your support'.

It is a strange and yet familiar sight, a Greek Temple atop a Durham Hill. A folly perhaps? If so, a grandiose one indeed.

Hephaestus was the Greek God of the Furnace and of Fire; of Craftsmen and of Artisans. He was especially worshipped in the forges of Athens, where instruments of beauty and of war were crafted in the flames of industry. A god of Ancient Greece far more appropriate perhaps for 19th century County Durham than those other citizens of Olympus; Apollo, the God of Light and Learning; or Dionysus, the God of Wine and Merriment. And so it was that County Durham's Greek Temple was designed as a replica of Hephaestus' own in ancient Athens.

It was built to commemorate John George Lambton, Earl of Durham; Privy Councillor and Lord Privy Seal from 1830 to 1833. Ambassador to the Court of St Petersburgh, Lord High Commissioner of Canada and a Knight of numerous overseas Orders of Chivalry; of St Andrew and St Alexander Nevsky; of St Anne; of the White Eagle of Russia and of Leopold of Belgium; and High Saviour of Greece. He had also been High Steward of Hull. But he was widely known to his contemporaries, as Radical Jack. When the foundation stone of his monument was laid, on the top of Penshaw Hill, on Wednesday 28 August 1844, by Thomas Dundas, Earl of Zetland, Grand Master of the Free and Accepted Masons of England, William Fordyce tells us that 10,000 spectators, including 400 Members of the Provincial Grand Lodges of Freemasons looked on. The: *Monthly Chronicle* is even more generous, estimating 30,000.

The Lambtons had been resident in County Durham for over 800 years. Indeed, so the legend tells, it had been a crusading ancestor of that same family who, in mediaeval times had slain the monstrous beast, the terror of all the lands: 'On byeth sides o' the Wear': the: 'Famous Lambton Worm'.

However, the subject of this short piece, John George Lambton, was born in 1792; the same year as popular revolution had brought an end to the French Monarchy and King Louis XVI, was sent for trial for crimes against his own people. John's father, William Lambton, was Member of Parliament for Durham, a radical Whig and dedicated to parliamentary reform. But when William died, aged 33, his wife remarried, and young John aged only five, was left in the care of guardians, who attended to his education and the considerable Lambton business interests, during his minority. Educated for three years at Eton, his guardians, naturally enough hoped and expected that he would go on to university. But Lambton saw his future in the army; his grandfather had been a Major-General in the Durham Light Infantry, and young John was granted a commission in the Tenth Dragoons, at the height of the wars against Napoleon Bonaparte. His career, it seemed, was set.

But Lambton was never one to follow a lead laid down by others and two years later he suddenly announced that he had eloped to Gretna Green where, on 1 January 1812, he'd married Henrietta Cholmondley, over the Blacksmith's Anvil. The marriage was later blessed by a church service but tragically it was not to last. After bearing John three daughters, Henrietta would die of Consumption in 1815. It also seems that the disease was passed on to the children, all of whom would die before reaching the age of 20; indeed Lambton's own health was never strong. But in 1813, this particular: 'Young Lambton', came of age and inherited the large Lambton estates, including the hugely profitable coal mines; thus becoming: 'King of the Coal Country' and in an instant, one of the richest men in England. With an annual income of around £80,000 a year, he once famously declared that an income of half that was: 'The sort of income that a man could jog along on' and: 'King Jog', as was his first soubriquet, was born.

He entered Parliament as an MP for Durham and quickly established a reputation as an effective speaker and excellent debater. He became one of the most active of the Whig members of Parliament and a leading light in the ranks of their reforming leader, the Northumbrian, Charles, 2nd Earl Grey. Later marrying Grey's daughter, Louisa, it looked as if Lambton had a glittering political future, but he made a number of enemies, even among his Whig colleagues. Lambton, of: 'imperious manners and somewhat dictatorial bearing', was headstrong with a fiery reputation that would dog his political career. Once, when accused of being a liar, the insult was settled by dueling pistols on Bamburgh beach. Fortunately for both protagonists their aim was no cooler than their tempers; neither was hurt but honour was settled. To his political enemies Lambton was too unpredictable and reform minded for the Party's own good, they disliked what they considered his: 'overweening sense of his greatness and rank'. But he was zealous in the matter of reform. He wrote to Earl Grey telling him that: 'Everything depends upon that greatest of all virtues in a politician, activity'. Of course in the words of Antony Jay and Jonathan Lynn, that fictional Permanent Secretary to a contemporary Cabinet, Sir Humphrey Appleby, later commented that it was indeed true that all politicians liked lots of activity; it was their substitute for achievement.

Throughout his own coal fields, unlike other Coal Owners of the day, he gained the respect of the miners who worked for him. Though strongly opposing the burgeoning Miners Union, he introduced his own practical improvements to the working lives of the men. He supported Humphrey Davy in his development of the Miners Safety Lamp, which was tested in Lambton's collieries; and with the establishment of the Lambton Collieries Association, provided benefits for those incapacitated by accidents, illness or old age. He also developed an intense business and political rivalry with the staunch Tory, Charles Stewart, Marquess of Londonderry, whose equestrian statue now stands in Durham Market Place.

But unrest was sweeping the country; there were riots in major cities across England. The year 1819 had seen the Peterloo Massacre, when reform protestors in Manchester had been charged by the cavalry and 11 innocent people had died, almost 500 being injured. Social Reform was being demanded by the masses, as was Parliamentary Reform. Those in power refused to countenance any such thing. Others, including Lambton and his Whig allies, pursued reform; for reform, they thought, was better than Revolution. The system of Representation in Parliament was corrupted by the notorious: 'Rotten Boroughs' that bore no relation to representation of the people. Many parliamentary constituencies were owned by Peers of the Realm, who were invariably the Member for their own constituency. The franchise was limited, there was no secret ballot; open votes would expose rural workers to the keen gaze of their employers. After an election in Newark, which went against the wishes of the campaigning landowner, he simply evicted all his tenants. Seats in the House of Commons could be bought, sometimes with a lump sum, sometimes with an annual payment. The infamous parliamentary constituency of: 'Old Sarum', which consisted, so it was said, of: 'Three fields and a Thorn Bush', returned two Members of Parliament. The County of Cornwall returned 42 Members and Yorkshire, 26. However, the industrialised cities of Manchester and Leeds, with a joint population then around 148,000 people, had no Members of Parliament at all. Once in Parliament, various sinecures were available to Members; insubstantial official positions with little, if any responsibility, but which nonetheless paid substantial financial benefits.

The system was unsustainable, popular unrest grew to dangerous proportions and eventually the Tory Government collapsed. The Whigs took power, Earl Grey became Prime Minister, Radical Jack was in the Cabinet and to him and a: 'Committee of Four', Grey gave the task of drafting the Great Reform Bill. Much of the Bill was drafted at Lambton's own London home and at length it was presented to Parliament. Delayed by a Tory majority in the House of Lords, led by the Duke of Wellington, it took the threat of mass popular revolt, with slogans like: 'The Bill, the whole Bill and nothing but the Bill'; 'The voice of the people is the voice of God' and 'May the sun always shine on the Reformers', eventually to persuade a reluctant King to create 50 new Whig Peers in order to get the legislation through the House of Lords. On 7 June 1832, The Great Reform Bill received Royal Assent. There had been whispers that had the Bill not gone through; Lambton would have been the focus and figurehead of mass rebellion. To his enemies these whispers further dammed him, but for the general populace the name of Radical Jack Lambton would remain synonymous with Reform.

But by now Lambton was personally at odds with his political colleagues on a number of issues so, in 1833, he resigned from the government and after lobbying by Earl Grey, was created Earl of Durham and Viscount Lambton. A prestigious foreign posting was to follow, when he was made Ambassador to the Court of Tsar Nicholas I of Russia. Sent to ease the sometimes strained relations between the two countries, Lambton, so often at odds with his fellows in domestic politics, formed a good relationship with the Russian

Court and was granted privileged personal access to the Tsar. From the day he arrived in Cronstadt, where Tsar Nicholas was inspecting his fleet, until the day, in 1837, when he finally returned to England; his mission was deemed by all to have been a success.

However, once back home, relations, which had been bad before his departure, became worse. He had personal tragedy, losing a son and a daughter, within two years. Suffering badly from Rheumatic Fever and chronic Migraines, he became virtually impossible to work with as his illnesses induced bad tempers, impatience and outspokenness, which sometimes led him to insulting even his allies. He quarrelled with most of his colleagues, even with Earl Grey. The nobility considered Lambton to be vulgar, flamboyant and irascible and disliked him intensely. His allies in the Whig Party, however, still lobbied for his return to mainstream politics. There were even whispers of him as a possible future Prime Minister. But in the present, with reform legislation now in place, William Lamb, Lord Melbourne had succeeded Earl Grey as Prime Minister and Lambton no longer enjoyed the top level support that once he had. Melbourne wrote that: 'Everybody, after the experience we have had, must doubt whether there can be peace and harmony in a Cabinet of which Lord Durham is a member'.

In 1837, there was insurrection in Canada. The British Colony was at the time two separate Provinces, each with its own legislature and both subordinate to the British Crown. Upper Canada was essentially British, Lower Canada, incorporating Quebec and Montreal, culturally under French influence. Trouble had arisen between British traders and French settlers. There was unrest and a feeling that both Provinces had been neglected by the British Government and there was general resentment about how the Colony was being governed. Unrest had escalated into violence. If Canada was not to go the same way as America had gone before it, something had to be done; because if such significant history was allowed to repeat itself, then the British Government would undoubtedly fall.

Perhaps unsurprisingly, Lambton it was who was offered the job of resolving the issue. Clearly it would take him away from the centre of British Government, possibly for years, and if he was to fail in his mission, his enemies at home would be handed the ammunition with which to finish him off politically. Reluctantly, following a personal request from the young Queen Victoria, who had been advised by the Prime Minister, Lambton agreed to go; Lord Melbourne granting him virtually unlimited powers, the title of: 'Special Commissioner and Governor General' and the British Government's promise of: 'The fullest and most unflinching support'. So, in April 1838, he set off in style, fitting out his expedition to the personal cost of £10,000. Together with his wife and family, he took a large staff, consisting mostly of fellow radicals hand picked by him, crates of Champagne, chests full of silver, carriages and the horses to pull them, two regimental orchestras and a French chef. They all arrived in Quebec at the end of May. Lambton decided on a grand entrance into the City. Attired in a military uniform decorated with silver lace, he rode on a white horse at the head of a long procession of state with bands playing and canons firing. But after the pomp, he quickly set about the real business.

He declared a general amnesty for the prisoners taken during the insurrection. Only eight men were retained, accused of murder of the Queen's Officers. He travelled across the Colony, talking to both the British and the French settlers. He was popular, he quickly gained the trust of all sides and he succeeded in calming the troubled waters. But an ocean away, his enemies were making their move.

There had been murmurings of discontent about his choice of staff and therefore, implicitly, about his judgment. Particular criticism was leveled at two of his closest associates who had been involved in personal scandals. He was bluntly warned by the Government: 'Steer clear of low company', to which came the equally blunt reply: 'Do not interfere with me at work; impeach me afterward if you will'. He began to suggest to the Government that if Canada was to remain as a possession of the British Crown, then the long term solution to the constitutional problems being experienced, was to give the Colonial citizens as much freedom to govern themselves under a single, central legislature, as the citizens of Britain. They then, he argued, would become more, rather than less loyal. But to some, the suggestion of giving Colonials more freedom for self-government, smacked of disloyalty to the Crown, and it was not well received in London. The: *Times* newspaper called Lambton: 'The Lord High Seditioner' and one of the few to support him was the renowned philosopher and political theorist, John Stuart Mill. His enemies began to line up.

But Lambton's fatal mistake was in relation to the eight prisoners accused of murder. Instead of putting them on trial and hanging them, he decided to banish them for life to Bermuda; with a warning that if they ever returned to Canada, it would be deemed to be an act of treason and they would be executed. This time the haughty Lord Durham had overstepped his mark. He had no legal jurisdiction in Bermuda; also, he was incorrect in law, as there was no law that allowed a threat of a death sentence for a crime not yet committed. His enemies, once again wrung their hands, in particular, Lord Brougham, his former ally in reform and now a bitter enemy. A Bill was introduced into the House of Lords to limit Lambton's powers and bring his: 'failed' mission to an end. A political battle ensued between his supporters and his enemies. Lord Melbourne, who had promised him: 'The fullest and most unflinching support', feebly opposed the Bill and his enemies were triumphant. His mission to Canada was ended and he was recalled, though Lambton first learned of his fate, not through official government channels, but from an American newspaper which carried the news. Admitting defeat he tendered his resignation but stayed on in Canada for a while to tie up loose ends. He was held in high regard and there were demonstrations of support; effigies of Melbourne and Brougham were burned in the street and when the time did come for his departure: 'spectators filled every window and every house top and though every hat was raised as we passed, a deep silence marked the general grief for Lord Durham's departure'. Canada bid Lambton a sombre farewell and he sailed at last for England.

But he returned, once again, to massive popular acclaim. Radical Jack was back and Radical Jack meant reform. Perhaps now was to be his time. With guaranteed support there was surely plenty of time for him to become Prime Minister, he was after all, still only 47 years old. But his physical strength was failing. He continued to work on his: 'Durham Bill', setting out his recommendations on the future governance of Canada. That Canada must be at liberty to determine her own future, as a federation with allegiance to the British Crown. His report was presented to Parliament in January 1840. In July of the same year he died of Tuberculosis; Lady Durham and Earl Grey were at his side. However, his: 'Durham Bill' would be adopted and a Canadian Act of Union would become effective in 1841. Lambton's recommendations would become the basis for the model of British Colonial Government for the next hundred years. But he remains a figure who divides opinions.

In a modern exhibition commemorating the 150th anniversary of Ottawa's selection as the Canadian Capital, Lambton's was one of about a dozen portraits of figures, prominent in Canada's history. After six months it was removed, it was claimed, after a Montreal

Penshaw Monument, built in memory of: 'Radical Jack' Lambton.

newspaper alleged that they were honouring a British Aristocrat who had tried to subsume French language and culture into British: 'Rule'. Academics rallied round to criticise its removal, with phrases like: 'political correctness run amok'; for it was recognised that Lambton was a man of his time and that: 'He had a profound and very useful impact on Canada'.

Physically, he is said to have been: 'A man of medium height and elegant bearing', socially, again, he divided opinions; being apparently both: 'Able, intelligent, liberal, imaginative, energetic and a shrewd political analyst'; and also: 'Haughty, obstinate, tactless and unpopular with a number of political contemporaries'. Perhaps he was just simply all of these. Following his death, a Committee was formed, Public Meetings were held in Newcastle and Sunderland and a Subscription Fund was set up in order to establish a suitable memorial to Radical Jack Lambton. Architectural designs were then commissioned for a lasting monument in recognition of: 'The distinguished services he rendered to his country, as an honest, able and patriotic Statesman and enlightened and liberal friend to the improvement of the people in morals, education and acquirements'.

The design chosen, based upon the Thesion; the Temple of Hephaestus, in Athens, was by John and Benjamin Green of Newcastle and it was built by Thomas Pratt of Sunderland. The Subscription Fund reached around £6,000, which paid for most of the construction work, but funds ran out before its completion, so the roof and the planned interior were never added. Penshaw Hill, the site chosen for the Monument, was owned, like other great swathes of County Durham, by the Marquess of Londonderry and was donated by him, in recognition of the Lambton family's historic, and no doubt legendary, associations with the site. Fordyce tells us that the Monument was built there primarily for the prominence of the location and the imposing effect it would have on the surrounding landscape; it was intrinsically rather plain with: 'nothing in the shape of ornament or meretricious decoration being introduced'. It was, it seems, 'intended to be viewed principally from a distance'.

Interestingly, Benjamin Green also designed the column in Newcastle City Centre upon which stands the monument to Earl Grey, the companion in Reform and father-in-law of Radical Jack.

Lambton's funeral was held on 10 August 1840 and on that day, in Chester-le-Street, Durham City and South Shields, shops were closed and draped with black flags. Ships on the Tyne and the Wear had their colours hoisted Half-Mast and the bells of Newcastle and Gateshead tolled from 11 o'clock in the morning until three in the afternoon. At Lambton Castle, mourners began to assemble from the early morning. The Earl lay in great state in his coffin in the Great Dining Room, mourners making their way there to pay their last respects and seeing that: 'The outer coffin was of the richest description, being formed of the finest Genoa crimson velvet, relieved with gold ornaments'. At half past two in the afternoon, the funeral procession formed up. One hundred and seventy-five carriages and other vehicles and over a thousand people, stretched in a column over a mile long, and made their way to Chester-le-Street, where his body was interred in the Church of St Mary and St Cuthbert. In all that day, so Richardson tells us, not less than 20,000 people, either followed the procession, lined the route or attended the church. He willed the whole of his estate to his wife. His only surviving son, now Earl of Durham, had been born on 5 September 1828: 'And was at the time of his accession to the Earldom, in the 12th year of his age'. Four years later, Radical Jack's lasting memorial on Penshaw Hill was unveiled.

It is perhaps ironic that recent discussions have centered around the: 'removal or not' from Durham Market Place of the statue of the Marquess of Londonderry, a Coal Owner noted neither for his liberality towards the Durham Miners, nor for his zeal for social and parliamentary reform; but whose statue we are told, has become an: 'Icon' of the City. Some may argue that in this place, a memorial to John George Lambton, Earl of Durham would be far more appropriate. Radical Jack may well have agreed.

Chapter 19

Rock, Water and Bad Air

'Come, me little washer lad, come let's away,
We're bound down to slavery, for four pence a day'

In the summer of 1919, a young poet wandered across the lonely, wild moors of Weardale. He rested for a while beside an old well shaft, picked up a pebble and dropped it into the black depths, hearing a low splash and ripples spreading in the darkness far below. This small event would be an inspiration throughout his life and would be a recurring theme in his works. The young man was Wystan H. Auden, who came to be regarded by some critics as possibly the greatest English poet of the twentieth century; and this was the beginning of his lifelong love of the rugged landscape of County Durham's: 'Lead Dales'; Teesdale, Weardale and Derwentdale.

The scene of this seminal event for Auden is thought to be a lonely spot between Rookhope and Blanchland, at the old Sikehead Chimneys, and he recalled it in his 1940 poem: *New Year Letter*. Auden was overwhelmed by the vastness of the moorland scenery, the bleak desolation and remote beauty of the landscape of Rookhope and of Alston Moor, of Derwentdale and of Blanchland Moor; and the crumbling skeletons of old winding sheds, wheels, chimneys and arches. Relics of an industry by then disappeared but which once had thrived in these parts.

'To those who are accustomed to cultivated plains, or the luxuriance of gently undulating lands of moderate height, the wild and solitary aspect of the moors and mountains of Teesdale and Weardale is impressive and sublime'

- A.B. Wright: *History of Hexham*

Lead has been mined in the County Durham Dales for centuries, perhaps even millennia. Tradition tells that the Romans extracted ore from the high hills and the 18th century Durham historian William Hutchinson tells that from antiquity, in the hills around Eggleston, were found: 'several ancient basins formed of stonework scattered over the moor, wherein lead ore was smelted, or run by force of fuel heaped upon it, assisted by the wind, before a mill or bellows was used'.

In the 12th century, lead was produced from Alston Moor for King Henry II's Windsor Palace. Fifteenth century documents, from the reign of King Edward IV, also refer to lead mines on Alston Moor. Records from the reign of Queen Elizabeth I refer to a lead mine previously demised by the young King Edward VI, to the Bowes family; and there was continued leasing and transfer of the Lead Mines of the Durham Dales down through the years. But it was not until the 18th and 19th centuries that ore extraction would reach its zenith. Britain was then the largest producer of lead in the world; and collectively the Durham Dales was the country's principal Lead Mining area. Out of more than 93,000 tons of lead ore mined in Britain in 1850, 21,000 tons came from Durham and Northumberland. The industry that grew up for its extraction would change the landscape of the Dales and would set, almost as a breed apart; the people who worked the mines and depended on them for their survival.

Lead ore had already been extracted from the northern Dales by the London Lead Company; the Company which had originally been granted assent from Queen Elizabeth

I: 'For smelting down lead with pit coal and sea coal' and which eventually received a Royal Charter in 1692. The rich mining area around Alston Moor had formerly been part of the estates of the Earl of Derwentwater, executed for his part in the 1715 Jacobite Rebellion. His mines were confiscated to the Crown and many were then leased on. In 1750 the London Lead Company took over a large number of these leases, beginning its major interest in Lead Mining in Northern England. In another 20 years it had made inroads into Teesdale, acquiring mines at Newbiggin and at Eggleston, where, in 1771, a smelting mill was opened. By 1781, Hutchinson tells us neighbouring mines were in full production. From then on, both Lead Mining and the London Lead Mining Company, also known as the: 'Quaker Company', were to figure prominently in the life of Upper Teesdale. The biggest employer of labour in the district it moulded both the working and the social lives of the people; and the mining, smelting and transportation of ore transformed the landscape in which they lived. Communities, scattered across sometimes bleak, inhospitable terrain, would see advances in communication and transportation and the populations of places like Newbiggin, Eggleston and Middleton were suddenly expanded by droves of lead miners, hoping to exploit the rich veins of: 'Argentiferous Galena'.

A 19th-century description of Frosterley paints a picture of neighbouring Weardale at the time: 'At Frosterley is a commanding eminence, with a crushing mill and washing places. The first indications of Lead Mines which appear. The rocky bed of the river, the precipitous face of Limestone Quarries, the diminished verdure of the hills and their abrupt formation, now indicate the geology of the Lead Mine measures, and gradually continue to form the characteristic features of a Lead Mining district'.

And so both the reader and the traveller are introduced to the Weardale Lead Mining industry and the landscape that it helped create.

The Weardale Mines were worked extensively by W.B. Beaumont. Most were leased from the Bishop of Durham, who owned the land, and it was estimated that the Blackett-Beaumont Mines in the Allendales and Weardale together, employed upward of two thousand men and boys. In the mid-19th century it was said that they produced a quarter of the total lead ore production of England and a 10th of all lead ore produced in Europe.

As demand for lead increased, so the industry grew and improvements to working practices and advances in

The Killhope Wheel, Killhope Lead Mining Centre, Park Level Mine, Weardale.

170

mechanisation were quick to follow. The early long trains of pack ponies carrying the precious ore across the fells along the: 'Galloway Trods', gave way to road transport by horse and cart. But, as it was for their Coal Mining counterparts to the east of the County, for the Lead Miners of County Durham, life remained hard and work remained dangerous.

For the sake of this short sketch of the life and times of the Lead Miners of County Durham, we are guided by a contemporary description, included in William Fordyce's: *History of the County Palatine of Durham*. The piece expands upon the fair treatment of the Miners by the Mine Owners; the author acknowledging the difficult conditions under which the Miners worked but enthusing that despite this, to their hard work: 'They cheerfully exerted themselves'.

Our contemporary chronicler records that the Miners themselves were, in general, a strong, healthy and active body of men; Noted by their spirit of independence, many evincing: 'considerable intellectual activity and acquirements'. We are told that in their spare time they pursued country and sporting pastimes. Hare Coursing was a favourite, no doubt adding protein to the cooking pot. Cricket was played and our chronicler tells us that wrestling was taken very seriously with annual contests at Newcastle and Carlisle. A musical band was formed which played: 'modern' Waltzes and Polkas: 'With a precision and effect which are highly creditable alike to their good taste and steady application'. The Band practiced in a hall at Newhouse near St John's Chapel, provided at the expense of the Beaumont Mining Company. There were well stocked libraries with magazines, newspapers: 'including the *Times*' and volumes of books, including: 'the amusing works of Charles Dickens'. In Teesdale, schools were managed by the London Lead Company and we are told were well supported and admirably constructed; a testament to Victorian patronage. All in all: 'The regulations of the London Lead Company' sought to encompass the religious, moral and intellectual education of: 'the great body of workmen employed in Teesdale'. As a group of men, our chronicler describes the Lead Miners as well behaved and enthuses that, in few other places can the inhabitants be: 'A more orderly, well conducted race of people'. We are told that the Miners did not work during Christmas, Easter and Innocent's Day. Apart from that, we are assured that they: 'Are not particular as to other holidays'.

The mining communities themselves even set up: 'Benefit Societies' to ensure financial security for their Members; however, our chronicler despairs that some were imprudently run, with little emphasis on retaining funds to offset future difficulties. He goes on to say, however, that they were: 'Revived, for a time, by the liberality of the owner of the mine'. These Societies were looked upon as the necessary bedrock for the moral development of the miners and their families, giving a sound sense of the value and interrelationship of time and money: 'Those vast two elements of all that is good or for evil to the labouring classes'.

So the overall picture that is painted is one of communities that were honest and independent of spirit, if somewhat rough and ready and lacking in the finer social graces. Of Miners who were hard working but fairly recompensed, who faced injury and possible death in the mines but with the hazards to their safety largely offset by the generosity of the Mine Owners. A stoic: 'race of people', of high moral fibre, self-sufficient and happy with their lot; who had turned away from drink and were rarely profane in their language; swearing was almost unknown, and who spent their leisure hours in intellectual, sporting and countryside pursuits. Their welfare was supported by the altruism of benevolent employers who oversaw their physical, moral and social well-being.

Perhaps not quite a Victorian rural idyll, but nonetheless a fine example of that age's ideal of the noble, honest worker and his community, with its own place in the world of 19th century County Durham. And generally speaking, the Lead Mine Owners of County Durham did indeed provide schools and promote education and welfare schemes for the men and their families, so in that respect, the Lead Miners were, by some way, more fortunate than their Coal Mining counterparts. However, in this instance, is has to be acknowledged that our guide, as printed in Fordyce, was in fact Thomas Sopwith FRS; Principal Agent to W.D. Beaumont, Esq. Member of Parliament; and Lead Mine Owner.

The reality was perhaps somewhat different. It is unlikely that the Miners were as hale and hearty as our chronicler would have it. As well as injury from explosion and rock fall, the build up of bad, oxygen deficient air in flooded and ill-ventilated tunnels, filled with the fumes of gunpowder; and in particular the inhalation of dust from crumbled lead ore or blasted rock, inevitably took their toll on the health of the Miners. Dust inhalation caused major respiratory problems, as it did in the Coal Mining industry, and in a lot of cases, from going underground at the age of 17 or 18, within two or three years, most men would have badly damaged lungs. Long term breathing problems and potential premature death were likely to follow. Unfortunately, in the earlier days, the Miners themselves knew nothing of the dangers of the dust, thinking that their poor health was simply down to the bad air. Their wooden clogs, worn so that their footwear would not rot in the constant wet, instead left their feet vulnerable. Many developed the same condition that was later suffered by soldiers in the Great War, and known to them as Trench Foot. A badly infected foot could quite possibly lead to blood poisoning and Gangrene.

The contemporary account in Fordyce tells us that the Lead Miner's food was plain and simple and the majority of men had turned away from the dangers of alcohol. Indeed: 'A great number of young men in Weardale pledged themselves to abstain from intoxicating liquors until thirty years of age'. But the men were generally thin, pale and undernourished. A poor diet, containing very little protein did not serve well, men carrying out hard physical labour over long hours underground. Porridge with honey, Rye Bread and boiled Potatoes were a staple of mealtimes.

Miners would organise themselves into: 'Partnerships' of anything up to a dozen men. The amount they were payed for their work was agreed by the Partnerships negotiating a contract, a: 'Bargain' with the Mine Owners or their representatives. In its negotiation the Miners would have the advantage of their experience in locating and working the richest veins, and in agreeing a Bargain: 'Their discernment is brought fully into play'. But the Bargains would be fixed according to the market price of lead at the time and of course the market price could rise; or fall and the vein of lead ore to be worked could be rich; or poor. It was often a gamble. Though acknowledging that some miners could be unfortunate, our guide goes on to say that others could make: 'Large earnings of wages'. They worked together, on piecework, being paid only for the ore that they produced. They would then divide their earnings equally between them. Perhaps to offset the possibility of a lucky Partnership striking it too rich, Bargains had to be re-negotiated every three months. The Miners were generally paid for their work, either half yearly or annually. In the meantime they were given a subsistence allowance by the Mine Owner, so called: 'Lent Money'. This would be deducted from their final pay, along with sundry expenses for their tools, powder and so on, and if their final pay was less than Lent Money received, then the debt to the Mine Owner would be carried over to the next pay day, when perhaps, with a little luck, more hard work and a richer vein of ore, they would make it into credit. However, it was possible for a miner never to escape his debt to the Mine Owner. For most of the 19th century, Lead Miners wages were lower than those of Coal Miners but they gradually increased to anything up to £55 a year by the 1870s.

Of all the institutions associated with Lead Mining it was perhaps the Lodging Shop, or Mine Shop that was the most notorious. Introduced around 1818, they enabled miners to remain on site at the mine and: 'relieved' them of their need to walk the sometimes considerable distance across the moors to and from their place of work.

Normally staying a week, the Miners would arrive on Monday morning and return home on Saturday, usually working 40 hours in eight hour shifts. The Mine Shop was where the Miners rested, ate and slept. Conditions were atrocious. Sometimes up to 50 men would occupy 16 bunks, sleeping three in a bed, with another at the foot. Evidence given to a Commission set up to look at these notorious conditions tells that the Mine Shops, especially in the early days: 'were such as not fit for a swine to live in'. Overcrowded and insanitary, the men slept on mattresses filled with straw. It was cramped, unhygienic and uncomfortable, with only a small fire for cooking, and not much fuel. There was no privacy, and nowhere for drying their wet clothes. The Commission was told that the shop floor was sometimes inches deep in filth, potato peelings and water. But worst of all it was said, was the unremitting stench of dirty bodies and wet clothes which permeated the air. One young boy giving evidence stated that: 'I lodged in one of the shops, 21 one of us slept in the same room; there were 12 beds; there was a bad smell'. Indeed it was generally accepted that: 'The breathing at night, when all were in bed was dreadful; the workmen received more harm from the sleeping places than from the work'. Outside were only the Mine and the miles of bleak moorland. During dark winter days, the men may not have seen any daylight and tiredness, isolation and boredom brought their own problems, with tensions often leading to fights. An unofficial leader was usually chosen and a Code of Conduct enforced, normally based on the teachings of the local Sunday School or Methodist Chapel, reinforced and encouraged by the Mining Company.

As well as the health hazards already described, the Lead Miners were also faced with potentially very dangerous working conditions. Flooding was a constant hazard. The use of volatile Gunpowder to blast away rock, also led to the danger of unwanted explosion and rock fall. Naked flames from candles were their only source of lighting, and lead poisoning was an obvious but unrecognised threat. However, unlike the potential for large scale disasters in Coal Mines, accidents in Lead Mining usually happened to individuals or small numbers of men. Injuries, tragic deaths and remarkable escapes from rock falls or explosions, were regularly recorded in the newspapers and local publications of the day; as well as for posterity in the works of contemporary chroniclers such as M.A. Richardson. There was no danger of gas escape in Lead Mines; unlike in the great coalfields to the east, where Methane, the dreaded Firedamp; and Afterdamp, the deadly mixture of Carbon Dioxide and Carbon Monoxide; claimed the lives of hundreds of miners. So there is not therefore, in the Lead Mining Industry of County Durham, the same legacy of large scale disasters, with great loss of life, which so often figured in the chronicles of the Durham coalfield communities. But both men and boys still died in the Lead Mines. Indeed, our chronicler acknowledges the hazards that were faced by the Lead Miners, but writes that accidents were extremely rare, giving credit for this to the expertise of the miners themselves but also to their employers, pointing out for example the safety benefits of: 'The abundant supply of timber, which is provided by Mine Owners' and stressing that, unlike the tools they needed to earn a living, this being: 'Altogether independent of the workmen's wages'.

In the 18th century, women had been employed and had struck their own: 'Bargains', working on the Washing Floors, where the lead ore was initially separated from the rock and washed. By the middle of the following century, however, although some women workers remained, young boys, most often the sons of the Miners, had largely taken over the duties of the Washing Floor, on a fixed daily rate of pay. In 1842, a Report was released which made public, evidence that had been given to the: *Royal Commission on the Employment of Children in Mines.*

The Report showed that, as in the neighbouring Coal Mining industry, boys of a very young age were used as labour in the Lead Mines. Some, again as in the Coal Mines, were employed underground as Trapper Boys, opening and closing trap doors to allow for access and ventilation. Most, however, were employed as Washer Boys, working outside on the washing floor, and being paid according to their age and the number of hours they worked. This cold, hard, wet job, working all day in constantly running cold water, served as both an income and an introduction for them to life in the Lead Mine, as underground work would usually only begin at around 17 or 18 years of age. In earlier years, boys as young as eight had been used but at the time of the Report, the Washer Boys would be anything from nine to 18 years old. Previously, a boy of nine might have earned four pence for 13 hours work and at the time of the Report, wages could be six or seven pence for a 12 hour shift.

It was a general condition of their employment that they learned to read and write, something which they were helped to do at the local Wesleyan Sunday Schools. Attendance proper at school, which began at six years of age, usually only happened over the bleak winter months, when hard frosts made washing the Lead Ore impossible. Their education usually finished at their 12th birthday. It would not be until 1872 that the rather grandly entitled: 'Metaliferous Mines Regulations Act', demanded that no boy aged less than 12 years, nor any women or girls be henceforth employed in Lead Mines.

Most men, as well as working in the mines, either also did paid work on farms or worked their own smallholdings to supplement their income and their diet. But there were still times when food for the mining communities was in short supply and to put a meal on the table for their families, miners took what was available from the land around them; a rabbit; perhaps a brace of pheasant or wood pigeon. They also took grouse from the surrounding moors. So long had they been doing this that they had come to regard it as a right; one of the few: 'perks', in an otherwise grindingly hard life. However, according to the law of the Dales, shooting and poaching were strictly forbidden: 'and would infallibly lead to loss of employment'. For the moors belonged to the Bishop of Durham and had done since the 12th century and the time of Hugh of Le Puiset.

In 1797, as a sign of things to come, a notice had been posted on behalf of the Bishop, setting out to the miners in the clearest terms that as the moors belonged to him, then all the game living on the moors was also his. Anyone taking that game was doing so illegally and therefore poaching and orders were given that all caught poaching would be prosecuted under the law. But the miners continued to seek out and take for the pot, their: 'Bonny Moor Hen' and things eventually came to a head early in the 19th century.

The Bishop at the time was Shute Barrington, who, in 1811, had dispatched troops to break up a strike of Coal Miners at one of the Dean and Chapter's mines at Chester-le-Street. On the advice of his Weardale stewards he ordered to the valley, two separate groups of armed constables and gamekeepers, to arrest eight individuals known to be poachers. The Bishop's men joined forces at Wolsingham and from there were led across Bollihope Common, bypassing Stanhope so as not to draw attention to their mission. Their destination was St John's Chapel, where they hoped to surprise their suspects. Once there, the house of two Lead Miners, two brothers, was surrounded and quickly enough the Bishop's men had their quarry arrested and clapped in irons. But news of the raid was out and spread like wildfire along the Wear Valley. By the time the houses of the other suspects had been reached, all the birds had flown. The people of the Dale began to close ranks; there were hurried discussions about what to do. It was decided that they must at last make a stand against the greed of a Bishop and fight for what they considered their right, to be able to take a bird for the pot. They would arm themselves against the agents of the: 'Fat Man of Auckland' and prepare to face the invading constabulary.

For its part, the constabulary had made no secret that the two captives were to be hauled off to Durham City, there to answer for their crimes. In readiness for the journey they were thrown into the cart that was to transport them there. But the Bishop's men had failed to capture their other suspects and in what seems to have been a deliberate move, on arriving back at Stanhope, they stopped for rest and refreshment at the Black Bull Inn, hard by the Church and the Market Cross. They had received intelligence that the miners were gathering and would make a move on them. The plan; to wait for their suspects to come to them. So while partaking of refreshments, they posted armed Officers as lookouts and awaited the onslaught of the vengeful miners. But, as the saying goes: 'Be careful what you wish for'.

The miners had their own intelligence, on reaching Eastgate they were met and told about the trap that had been set for them. They decided to send a group of the best armed men across the River Wear to approach Stanhope, undetected, from the south. The main body, as a diversion, would continue along: 'rioting' into the town. They were confident; after all there were many more of them than there were of the Bishop's men. Concentrating on the main group of miners approaching from the west, the constabulary was taken completely by surprise when the: 'advance guard' stormed the: 'Black Bull'. A fierce engagement ensued, hand-to-hand fighting following volleys from firearms: 'Oh they fired along till their powder was done, and then they laid on with the butt-ends of their guns'. The Bishop's men were routed. Mercifully nobody was killed, but in the melee, one constable lost an eye; another had his arm broken. When the landlady of the: 'Black Bull' complained about blood on her floor, she was told with contempt: 'Mix it with meal and make Black Pudding of it'. Almost as a symbolic gesture, the two arrested men were brought out into the market square, where they had their shackles publicly removed.

This violent incident, which occurred on 7 December 1818, was recorded in a ballad entitled: 'The Bonny Moor Hen', written, it is thought, by a local schoolmaster and two verses of which are recalled below:

'Now the times being hard and provisions being dear,
The miners were starving almost we do hear,
They had nought to depend on, so well you may ken,
But to make what they could of the Bonny Moor Hen.

Looking over the Rookhope Valley from the top of the Incline.

There's the Fat Man of Auckland and Durham the same,
Lays claim to the moors and likewise the game,
They sent word to the miners they'd have them to ken,
They would stop them from shooting the Bonny Moor Hen'.

In the end it seems that, given the strength of feeling apparent in the Weardale Lead Mining Community, about their: 'Bonny Moor Hen', that the Bishop relented and surprisingly, considering the level of violence involved in the affray; no charges were ever brought.

With the increasing importation into Britain of cheap lead ore, mainly from Spain, demand for Durham lead began to diminish towards the end of the 19th century. In Teesdale, the London Lead Company was wound up and Lead Mining finally ceased in 1905. With the demise of their industry some lead miners found new work in quarrying. Others took their skills and travelled east to the vast Durham coalfields; some left English shores altogether. And in today's Weardale, their descendants sometimes return and visit the excellent Weardale Museum at Ireshopeburn, where family history records can be made available for anyone wishing to trace their own personal Lead Mining heritage.

In a County where: 'Coal was King', the Miners of Durham's Lead Dales are perhaps less well remembered. There are today, many memorials to the Durham Coal Mining Industry; a Pit Wheel, or perhaps a replica; on a village green, beside a road, or on the site of an old colliery. An inevitably melancholic list of the dead, on a half forgotten cemetery memorial; victims of some disaster or other. But what of the County's Lead Miners? Today, the renowned Killhope Lead Mining Centre, at the old Park Level Mine in Upper Weardale, brings to life for new generations their work and hard times. But as far as the men

The lonely moors and old Lead Mining landscape, so beloved of W.H. Auden, looking towards Sikehead Chimneys.

themselves and their vanished industry are concerned, to misquote the epitaph of Sir Christopher Wren in St Paul's Cathedral; if you wish to see their memory, look around you.

Look around the open moorland of County Durham and you will see the now ruined traces of an industry, once as vibrant, as full of promise and disappointment, as the Gold Rushes of the American west; and where the Lead Miners of County Durham were as numerous as the rabbits that now make their home on Rookhope Incline. You will see perhaps an archway with a road going neither under nor over it. You will see what Auden saw, so many years ago; the remains of winding shops, of smelting operations and of lonely chimneys; standing like distant, ghostly sentinels. Where once there was noise, bustle, industry and grime, all is now calm and apart from the lonely cry of a Curlew carried across the moor on the wind's breath, or the low distant hum of a motor car engine, or the startled: 'kek,kek,kek!!' of a: 'Bonny Moor Hen'; all is now quiet.

A.B. Wright relates: 'We love the Lakes with all the affection any man can feel; but we would not forget the Dales that lie like honesty in a poor house, or like a pearl in an oyster'.

Chapter 20

A Sparrow's Flight

'Of toil stupendous, in a hallowed seat of learning,
where thou heard'st the billows beat on a wild coast'

Some time ago, I was enjoying a leisurely lunchtime amble around Durham Cathedral when an overheard remark made me smile. I was in the Galilee Chapel, the light and airy Moorish style Lady Chapel, built by Bishop Hugh of Le Puiset. The Galilee Chapel is often cool and quiet in comparison with the rest of the building, tourists and visitors seeming sometimes just to pass it by. Indeed there are times when you can linger alone there and slowly take in the atmosphere, the silence and the gentle light; as warm fingers of sunlight reach in through the windows and caress the 12th century floor. On this occasion, however, I was not alone. Following me was a small party of tourists, the nationality of which I will not reveal, though they all spoke excellent English.

'Hac Sunt Fossa BEDAE Venerabilis Ossa'; says the inscription, carved by an unknown mason, into the cover of a huge blue marble and stone tomb which stands at the southern end of the Chapel; telling us that this is the final resting place of the Venerable Bede. Though Bede's magnificent original shrine, which stood on the same spot, was destroyed in the 16th century, the surviving tomb is still a substantial memorial to the Saint and Scholar; an acknowledgement perhaps of the reputation of its occupant. You cannot really miss it. However, just in case you do, nearby, on the wall, is a simple sign which says: 'The Tomb of the Venerable Bede'. Also on the wall, and next to the sign, is a carved wooden door, about two feet square, presumably covering a small store cupboard, recessed into the stonework.

Bede's resting place in Hugh of Le Puiset's: 'Galilee Chapel'.

The Tomb of: 'The Venerable Bede'.

The: 'Father of English History'.

I was just about to continue my wanderings and leave Bede to the sunshine and the silence, when the tourists, who had been gazing around bewilderedly at the ancient delights of the Chapel, strolled heedlessly by the aforementioned huge, blue marble and stone tomb and stared at the wooden cupboard door. From the cupboard door the eyes of one lady flashed to the sign upon the wall and with eyebrows creased in contemplation, flashed back again to the cupboard door: 'Why did they put a man like that into such a small tomb', was the hazy, semi-rhetorical question: 'Yeah!', came the hazy, semi-rhetorical answer.

To complete this book, we travel back again to Anglo-Saxon England, to when the seventh century moved into the eighth; a time that some historians have called the Golden Age of ancient Northumbria. It was a time well before the existence of cosmopolitan centres of population, when, for the Anglo-Saxon people, travel by water was more important than travel overland, when learning and culture were centred in the monastery and the Royal Court and where the Northumbrian Church, previously influenced so heavily by the Celtic Missionaries was now looking outward to Europe and to Rome.

Benedict Biscop was an Anglo-Saxon noble, a: 'thegn', who had been in the service of King Oswy of Northumbria. Being of such social standing he would have known relative privilege, by the harsh and unforgiving standards of the time. But, we are told, at the age of 25, Benedict gave it all up and: 'renounced the secular life, despising the service of the world'. In the year AD665 he began a pilgrimage to Rome and it was a journey that would change both his own life and the direction of history for the Northumbrian Church. After reaching Rome, visiting the shrines of St Peter and St Paul, after whom he would later name his churches; and taking: 'deep draughts of sacred knowledge', he took holy orders and became a monk.

Later, he went again to Rome and acquired many sacred books before returning to his native Northumbria. Once back he discussed his: 'mission' with the new king,

Ecgfrid, who was so impressed with the vision and zeal of Benedict that he made him a grant of: '70 hides of land' on the north side of the River Wear. And there, at the river's mouth, he began the construction of a religious centre. Benedict became Abbot of his new monastery of Wearmouth, but his was a wandering spirit. He made further trips to the continent, indeed he was probably absent from his monastery more than he was present. He went again to Rome and to France. When he returned he did so with new ideas, and a vision of what the Northumbrian Church could be; inspired by what he had seen. But: 'zealous for the embellishment of his church' Benedict brought back more than just the vision, he brought back people with the abilities to bring that vision to fruition; masons, skilled in building after the: 'Roman fashion' in stone, craftsmen and artists in glass. He brought John the Arch-Chanter from the Vatican to instruct the monks in Plainsong. He brought many precious books, some of international importance, to found a library that would become one of the most important in England. He brought: 'paintings on sacred subjects for the decoration of the church' and precious vessels for the altar. Fordyce tells us that the ceiling of Benedict's church was covered from wall to wall with a picture of the Virgin Mary and the 12 Apostles, the south wall with illustrations of incidents from the Gospels and the north wall with subjects from the Apocalypse. And so, as Bede related, by the use of such colour and vibrancy: 'the humble disciple, whose ignorance of letters excluded learning at one inlet, might feel his faith confirmed, and his religious impressions strengthened, by surveying, whithersoever he turned, either the gracious countenance of the Saviour, the awful mystery of the incarnation, or the terrific scene of the last judgement'. Bede himself would later say that Biscop had wished to bring something new to the religious establishments of Northern England. What he brought was light and colour and song and a new monastic way life, in airy buildings made of stone; where before there had only been the smoke filled dampness of wooden churches.

As far as the Kings of Northumbria were concerned, it was in their interest to rule over a peaceful, controllable kingdom and if, through the introduction, establishment and development of one unified religion for its people, this could be guaranteed; then so much the better. Also, for the benefit of those beyond the boundaries of their land they were keen to show themselves as: 'Kingly'. They wished to demonstrate that they were no longer: 'Barbarians', petty rulers of some cultural backwater, remote on the fringes of Europe, with a people who still worshipped the spirits of wood and water. They wished to be seen as scholarly and pious; as patrons of religion, learning and culture. Their kingdom faced east across the sea to Europe and to Rome and they wanted to be recognised as shining examples of cultured, European Christian kingship. For even in simple, practical terms, acceptance and recognition in Europe meant increased trade; increased trade meant increased wealth; and increased wealth meant increased power.

And Biscop had brought back ideas from the: 'civilised' Roman world. Indeed, so impressed was the King that he granted Benedict a further 40 hides of land at the mouth of the Tyne, at Jarrow, and on the 23 April AD685, the second of the twin monasteries was born. The original dedication stone of St Paul's, which Bede may well have seen being laid, can still be seen today. At Jarrow, Benedict placed in charge Ceolfrid, a man also of noble birth, who had entered the monastic life at the age of 18 and who had accompanied Benedict on pilgrimage to Rome. He would eventually succeed Benedict as Abbot of the twin monasteries: 'adding largely to the plate and vestments of the church, and nearly doubling the library'. It is thought that the: *Codex Amiatinus*, the oldest complete Latin Bible in existence was commissioned by Ceolfrid, as a gift to the Pope in AD716. Perhaps Bede had a hand in its writing. Benedict would remain Abbot for 16 years, Ceolfrid, for a further 27 and between them they brought together a very diverse group of people with new skills and new ideas. And so it was, that with the patronage of the King, the vision of Benedict and the steady determination of Ceolfrid, that timber was exchanged for stone and the twin monasteries of Wearmouth and Jarrow, home to around 600 monks and workers, quickly developed into a major centre for learning, not just in Anglo-Saxon England, but also in Europe.

Around the year AD686 Benedict returned from a fourth journey to Rome to find his patron, King Ecgfrid, had been slain in battle, and plague had ravaged his beloved monasteries: 'All who could read, or preach, or recite the antiphons and responses were swept away', only Ceolfrid, the Abbot, and one: 'young lad', had survived to keep the holy services going. It is thought that this one young lad was: 'Beda the Presbyter'.

'At the age of seven, I was, by the charge of my family, given to the Reverend Abbot Benedict, and afterwards to Ceolfrid, to be educated'.

With these words the man we know today as the Venerable Bede described the beginning of his life at the monastery of Wearmouth; a life that would be lived within the confines of the twin monasteries of Wearmouth and Jarrow; a life that would never be lived further south than Whitby or York, or further north than Lindisfarne.

It is written that Bede was born on the: 'Sundur-Londe', possibly land on the north bank of the River Wear, sundered from the North Sea coast by the river, land which had been granted to Benedict by the King. There is a traditionally held view that the Monastic Communities of Bede's day deliberately sought out lonely, wild spots; a view probably reinforced by stories of savage Viking raids on remote and vulnerable Anglo-Saxon monasteries. The reality was probably that the area into which Bede was born would have been reasonably well populated, with Anglo-Saxon settlements scattered along coast and river bank; for theirs was not a life governed by roads and overland travel but by the routes of river and sea.

Little, if anything, is known of Bede's childhood, indeed much of his life remains obscure; but he was given up, it is said, to the care of Benedict and Ceolfrid, who were to prove: 'very able and very learned teachers'. Bede must have been an equally able student and he tells us that he was made a Deacon, in his 19th year and a Priest at 30. And under the encouragement and inspiration of Benedict and Ceolfrid, Bede flourished and the twin monasteries of Wearmouth and Jarrow would become one of the greatest centres of culture in the west.

And there Bede established his reputation as a historian and a scholar; a reputation that has endured into the present day. Of course Bede, as you would expect from his background, wrote many works on theological and biblical studies and translations of sacred texts. He gave us a written version of the life of his mentor and inspiration, Abbot Ceolfrid; and he also completed a life of St Cuthbert, without which our knowledge of the Patron Saint and of his life and times would be by far the poorer.

In his religious works Bede, while possibly not having an: 'agenda', certainly wrote as a man of his time. He was a traditionalist, who embraced Roman orthodoxy, and to a certain extent the major part that had been played by the Celtic Church in Christianising the North, was played down by Bede in his writings.

But Bede also wrote works on science and grammar; and on historical studies. Indeed, what most consider his Magnum Opus, his: *Ecclesiastical History of the English People* is a record of events chronicling the story of his own Anglo-Saxon people: 'as I have been able to ascertain them from ancient documents, from the tradition of our forebears, and from my own personal knowledge' Written, probably between AD725 and 731, it was in this work that Bede put forward the concept of the English People, the: 'Gens Anglorum' and the notion of England as a unified country. And it is surely no coincidence that around 150 years later, King Alfred the Great, following his victory over Danish invaders, and in his attempt to rebuild England as a single nation state, ordered Bede's: 'History' to be translated into the Anglo-Saxon language; because he considered it: 'Most necessary for all men to know'. Bede's: 'History' was a genuine attempt to faithfully record the story of the English, as it was known in his time. It was not an invented or an embellished history, unlike that of Geoffrey of Monmouth and others that would come after.

The foundation of Wearmouth and Jarrow as a centre of learning was the legacy of Benedict Biscop and Ceolfrid; and the Northumbrian church of the day became perhaps Europe's brightest star. But through Bede's scholarship and writing, it would be his name that would become known around the Christian world. His manuscripts would find their way across the sea to the Continent and works written in Wearmouth and Jarrow would eventually be found in St Petersburg and Florence. Fordyce tells us that Bede was even invited by Pope Sergius, to visit Rome itself, but he declined to go: 'Bede was not to be allured from his cell by the smile of potentates or the courtesy of princes'.

The last chapter of Bede's: 'History' was written in his 59th year. And towards the end of his time he looked back across his closeted, cloistered life of devotion and learning: 'From the age of seven I have spent my entire life within the monastery, devoting all my pains to the study of the Scriptures; and the observance of monastic discipline and the daily charge of singing in the Church. It has ever been my delight to learn, to teach or to write'. His last work, the translation of St John's Gospel, into the Anglo-Saxon language, he completed just before he died, on 26 May AD735; dictating the last few chapters to his faithful pupil Cuthbert.

Obviously Bede is often talked about in conjunction with the fathers of the Northern church, St Cuthbert and St Aidan; but Bede's life was very different to theirs. Aidan, remembered as the founder and first Bishop of the monastery and See of Lindisfarne was an appointment by Royal Commission. He came at the request of King Oswald of Northumbria to Christianise his people and he was the architect of the Celtic Christian Church in Anglo-Saxon Northumbria. Where others would follow, he was first; and from the beginning Aidan walked with the King and was an honoured guest at Oswald's table. Cuthbert, in his early days, had been a missionary among the: 'Barbarians' of the northern lands. He wandered the countryside, evangelising a people for whom the old gods were still as powerful as Cuthbert's one God. Later, Cuthbert turned away from worldly life and lived as a solitary, searching for his own personal God. In contrast, Bede's was a cloistered world, confined to the twin monasteries. He lived the humble life of a monk; orthodox in his beliefs and his way of life. But it was a cloistered world which was nonetheless at the centre of learning, the peak of culture; from where Bede's scholarship, his teachings and his words would radiate out to an emerging nation of all England, still waiting to be born.

Perhaps in some ways Bede has never received the recognition to which he is surely fully entitled. Indeed, even today, he seems to lie, to some degree, in the shadow of St Cuthbert.

After Bede's death, St Boniface described him as: 'He who shone lately among you as a candle of the Church'; and the: *Diocesan Histories* acknowledge, rather stiffly, that to Bede: 'We are indebted for all we know of the introduction of Christianity into Great Britain' Perhaps academics see it slightly differently, with the historian and broadcaster, Michael Wood, suggesting that: 'Bede is the first and greatest historian of the English'

So it was that: 'The most distinguished ornament of the Northumbrian Church…one of the most distinguished of the English Race', ended his earthly life and was buried at Jarrow. And it was not until the year 1022, during the reign of Cnut the Great, that Bede's bones found a final resting place in Durham. For in that year, the Sacrist of Durham, one Aelfred, a notorious collector of relics, removed them from his Jarrow grave and brought them to lie with the body of St Cuthbert. When Jarrow's loss was discovered, questions were asked about the whereabouts of the remains and Aelfred replied: 'No one can answer that question so well as I. You may be assured, my brethren, beyond all doubt that the same chest which holds the hallowed body of our Father Cuthbert also contains the bones of Bede, our revered teacher and brother'.

And there he remained, until Hugh of Le Puiset commissioned a great and sumptuous shrine for him, which was placed in his Galilee Chapel. The shrine is now gone, but unto this day, Bede lies in the same place.

So it is then, that two Anglo-Saxon Northumbrians, who lived around 1,300 years ago and died within a generation of each other, both now rest in Durham Cathedral. St Cuthbert, Patron Saint of the Northumbrians, lies in high honour at one end of the great building, built as his shrine. At the other end, high above the River Wear, the same river that he would have known as a child, lies Bede; perhaps understatedly, perhaps befitting his nature; in the cool quiet of Le Puiset's Galilee Chapel. A legend tells that the mason that had been instructed to carve an inscription into Bede's blue marble tomb cover could not think of a suitable phrase or soubriquet to describe its occupant, so he broke off from his labour for rest and perhaps, inspiration. When next he returned, he found to his great astonishment, that the inscription had been miraculously completed, simply with the word Venerable; perhaps a modest enough epitaph, and one which may well have put a smile on the face of the: 'Father of English History'.

But perhaps we will leave the last words on the The Venerable Bede and indeed, almost the last words in this book, to that other County Durham historian, Robert Surtees, who lamented, that after Bede's death: 'The lamp of learning, trimmed by the hand of a single monastic who never passed the limits of his Northumbrian province, irradiated, from the cell of Jarrow, the Saxon realm of England, with a clear and steady light; and when Bede died, history reversed her torch and quenched it in deep night'.

So we know from the legend that today, Bede's bones lie in the Galilee Chapel of Durham Cathedral, under the carved blue marble of his tomb; well at least they do not lie nearby, in a cupboard, in a wall, behind a carved wooden door.

THE END

Cumulative Index

Hackworth, locomotive pioneer
Rock, Water and Bad Air – The Durham Lead Miners
St Cuthbert and the Lost Bombers – The story of an alledgedly unsuccessful: 'Baedeker Raid' by the Luftwaffe
Lest We Forget – The Durham Coal Miners
A Sparrow's Flight – The Venerable Bede
Nine Hundred Years – Stories of Durham Cathedral

References

Standard References

Archaeologia Aeliana *The Journals of the Proceedings of the Society of Antiquaries of Newcastle upon Tyne:* From 1822
Boyle, J.R. *The History of the County of Durham:* 1892
Denham, M.A. *The Denham Tracts:* 1846–1859
Fordyce, W. *The History and Antiquities of the County Palatine of Durham:* 1855–1857
Hutchinson, W. *The History and Antiquities of the County Palatine of Durham:* 1785–1794
Lowe, J.L. *Diocesan Histories: Durham:* 1881
Mackenzie E. & Ross, M. *An Historical, Topographical and Descriptive View of the County of Durham:* 1834
The Monthly Chronicle of North Country Lore and Legend: 1887–1890
Richardson, M.A. *The Local Historian's Table Book of Remarkable Occurrences:* 1841–1846
Simeon of Durham *A History of the Church of Durham:* Llanerch Reprint 1987
Simeon of Durham *A History of the Kings of England:* Llanerch Reprint 1987
Surtees, R. *The History and Antiquities of the County Palatine of Durham:* 1816–1823; 1840
Sykes, J. *Local Records: Historical Register of Remarkable Events:* 1824–1833
The Victoria History of the Counties of England *A History of Durham:* 1928 Ed.

Further References

Aird, W. *St Cuthbert and the Normans:* 1998
Andrews, W. *Bygone Durham:* 1898
Armstrong, P. *Stirling Bridge and Falkirk 1297–98:* 2003
Ashby, M. *England in the Seventeenth Century:* 1958
Baker, D. (Ed.) *The Early Middle Ages 871–1216:* 1966
Bayfield Roberts, Rev. G. *The History of the English Church Union 1859–1894:* 1895
Boyle, D. *Blondeli's Song:* 2006
Brockie, W. *Legends and Superstitions of the County of Durham:* 1886
Bryant, A. *The Age of Chivalry:* 1963
Bygate, J.E. *Durham, the Cathedral and See:* 1899
Collingwood, W.G. *The Lake Counties:* 1939
Colville, Sir John. *Those Lambtons:* 1988
Cooper, L. *Great Men of Durham:* 1956
Fowler, J.T. *The Life and Letters of John Bacchus Dykes:* 1897
Eden, Sir T. *Durham:* 1952
Ellis, P.B. *The Ancient World of the Celts:* 1998
Fawcett, J.W. *Tales of Derwentdale:* 1902
Gillingham, J. *Yale English Monarchs: Richard I:* Yale University Press
Hindle, T. (Ed.) *The Domesday Book; England's Heritage, Then and Now:* 1985

Hodgkin, J.E. *Durham:* 1926

Gallop, A. *Buffalo Bill's British Wild West:* 2001

Gidlow, C. *The Reign of Arthur; From History to Legend:* 2004

Haines, R. *King Edward III*

Jerningham, H.E.H. *Norham Castle:* 1883

Kenyon, J.P. (Ed.), *Dictionary of British History:* 1986 Reprint

Lomas, R. *North-East England in the Middle Ages:* 1992

McLynn, F. *Lionheart and Lackland: King Richard, King John and the Wars of Conquest:* 2006

Morris, M. *A Great and Terrible King; Edward I and the Forging of Britain:* 2008

Mortimer, I. *The Perfect King: The life of Edward III, Father of the English Nation:* 2006

Neasham, G. *The History and Biography of West Durham:* 1881

Nicholson, R. *Edward III and the Scots: The formative years of a Military Career 1327–1335:* 1965

Nicolle, D. *Arthur and the Anglo-Saxon Wars:* 1984

Pease, H. *Northumbria's Decameron:* 1927

Poole, A.L. *Domesday Book to Magna Carta 1087–1216*

Pope-Hennessy, U. *Durham Company:* 1941

Ramsden, D.M. *Teesdale:* 1947

Rivet, A.L.F. & Smith, C. *The Place Names of Roman Britain:* 1979

Roffe, D. *Domesday; the Inquest and the Book:* 2000

Ross, D.R *James the Good: 'The Black Douglas'*

Sadler, J. *Border Fury: England and Scotland at War 1296–1568:* 2005

Selkirk, R. *On the Trail of the Legions*

Stenton, F. *Anglo-Saxon England:* 1989 Reprint

Traquair, P. *Freedom's Sword; Scotland's Wars of Independence:* 1998

Turnbull, L. *The History of Lead Mining in the North East of England:* 2006

Wacher, J. *Roman Britain:* 1978

Watson, F. *Under the Hammer: Edward I and Scotland 1286–1307:* 1998

Wedgewood, C.V. *The King's War; 1641–1647:* 1973

Wood, M. *In Search of the Dark Ages:* 1981

Wood, M. *Domesday: A Search for the Roots of England:* 1986

Wood, M. *In Search of England:* 1999

Journals, Articles and Other Publications

Craster, H.H.E. *A contemporary record of the Pontificate of Rannulf Flambard:* Archaeologia Aeliana: 1930

Dean and Chapter, Durham Cathedral. *The Treasures of Saint Cuthbert*

Forbes, I. Lead and Life at Killhope

Fowler, J.T. *An account of the excavations made on the site of the Chapter House of Durham Cathedral in 1874:* Archaeologia Aeliana 1880

Graham, F. *Roman Durham:* Northern History Booklet No. 85, 1979.

Heatherington, D., Backhouse, B. & Dawson, N. (Compiled by) An *Extract of the Rev. Mr. John Wesley's Journal: His Journey's through Weardale, May* 1752 *to June* 1790:

Heron, T.M. *The Little Count: Joseph Boruwlaski:* 1986

Hutchings, A.J.B. *In Praise of John Bacchus Dykes 1823-1876:* Durham University Journal: 1950

Offler, H.S. *William of St. Calais: First Norman Bishop of Durham:* Transactions of the Architectural and Archaeological Society of Durham and Northumberland: 1950.

Offler, H.S. *Rannulf Flambard as Bishop of Durham (1099–1128):* Durham University Journal

Offler, H.S. *Murder of Framwellgate Bridge:* Archaeologia Aeliana 1988

Richardson, I.A., Romans, Revd T. & Wright, R.P. *Old Durham:* Archaeologia Aeliana: Nov. 1943.

Yeats, C. (Ed.) *A Christian Heritage: a collection of addresses in honour of the 900th anniversary of Durham Cathedral:* 1993

Young, A. *William Cumin: Border Politics and the Bishopric of Durham 1141–1144:* Borthwick Paper 54, 1979

Internet Websites

In addition to the above, there is today a wealth of historical information available on the Internet. Much of it makes interesting reading; however, care should be taken and it is for the reader to satisfy themselves as to the accuracy of individual Websites.